Sweet Charity

The role and workings of voluntary organisations

Edited by Chris Hanvey and Terry Philpot

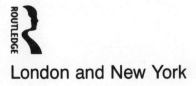

London and New York

First published 1996
by Routledge
11 New Fetter Lane, London EC4P 4EE

Simultaneously published in the USA and Canada
by Routledge
29 West 35th Street, New York, NY 10001

Phototypeset in Times by Intype London Ltd
Printed and bound in Great Britain by Mackays of Chatham PLC,
Chatham, Kent

British Library Cataloguing in Publication Data
A catalogue record for this book is available from the British Library

Library of Congress Cataloguing in Publication Data
A catalogue record for this book has been requested

ISBN 0–415–13800–0 (hbk)
ISBN 0–415–13801–9 (pbk)

To John Pierson
and
Linda Ward
in friendship

Contents

List of illustrations   ix
Notes on the contributors   x
Introduction   1
Chris Hanvey and Terry Philpot

1 To the millennium: the changing pattern of voluntary
  organisations   7
  Stuart Etherington

2 Map of the new country: what is the voluntary sector?   22
  Marilyn Taylor and Joan Langan

3 Swimming together: the tidal change for statutory
  agencies and the voluntary sector   39
  Ray Jones

4 A mixed blessing? How the contract culture works   58
  Norman Flynn

5 From those who know: the role of service users   69
  Clare Evans

6 Standing up to be counted: campaigning and voluntary
  agencies   82
  Francine Bates and Jill Pitkeathley

7 In trust: the changing role of trustees   93
  Kate Kirkland

8 Giving in trust: the role of the grant-making trust   111
  Nigel Siederer

 9 A lawful endeavour: charities and the law   128
   Roger Winfield

10 Balancing the books: charitable finance   144
   Pesh Framjee

11 At the top: the role of the chief executive   157
   Mike Whitlam

12 Beyond the rattling tin: funding and fundraising   173
   Jeremy Hughes

13 Marketing force: meeting true need   189
   Ian Bruce

14 Light at the end of the tunnel? A European perspective   207
   Quintin Oliver

   Name index   221

   Subject index   223

Illustrations

FIGURES

3.1 A typology of voluntary organisations   44
3.2 Organisational orientation to service users   45
11.1 Conceptual model for planning processes   162
12.1 Donor development pyramid   180
13.1 Voluntary organisation marketing   195

TABLES

2.1 Organisational forms   31
4.1 Sources of income for charities   61
8.1 Sizes of trusts   118
8.2 Subject interests of trusts   118
13.1 Not-for-profit/voluntary organisation customers   193

Contributors

Francine Bates has been assistant director, public affairs and training, Carers National Association, since 1991. She previously worked in housing.

Ian Bruce is director-general, Royal National Institute for the Blind, and a visiting professor at the City University Business School where he is honorary director of VOLPROF, the Centre for Voluntary Sector Not-For-Profit Management. He has previously held senior and managerial positions in the London Borough of Hammersmith and Fulham, Volunteer Centre UK, Age Concern and Unilever. He wrote *Meeting Need: Successful Charity Marketing* (ICSA/Prentice-Hall) in 1994.

Stuart Etherington is chief executive, National Council for Voluntary Organisations. He was previously chief executive, Royal National Institute for Deaf People. Before RNID, he was director of Good Practices in Mental Health, and policy officer, British Association of Social Workers. He is a qualified social worker. His publications include, most recently, *The Morality of Private Care* (Tavistock, 1989) and *The Essential Manager* (Pavilion Press, 1993).

Clare Evans is director, Wiltshire Users' Network, an independent user-controlled organisation. She is a qualified social worker and trainer with experience in the statutory and voluntary sectors. An increasing physical impairment led to the use of services to provide daily personal care, and in 1991 she was instrumental in setting up, with others, Wiltshire Users' Network, a county-wide user-controlled organisation which exists to promote user involvement and for which she now works. She is co-author, with M. Hughes, of *Tall Oaks from Little Acorns* (Wiltshire Community Care User Involvement Network/Wiltshire Social Services Department, 1993).

Norman Flynn is professor of public management, City University of Hong Kong. He was formerly a research fellow at the London School of Economics and Political Science. He has researched contracting in community care for the Department of Health and the Joseph Rowntree Foundation. He is author (with R. Common) of *Contracting for Care* (Community Care Joseph Rowntree Foundation, 1992) and (with D. Hurley) of *The Market for Care* (Public Sector Management Group, LSE, 1993).

Pesh Framjee, partner in charge of Binder Hamlyn's Charity Unit which advises over 350 charities, has been involved with the voluntary sector for over fifteen years and writes and lectures extensively as a charity specialist. He has acted as finance director of a major international charity and is co-ordinator of the Charity Finance Directors' Group. Pesh Framjee is a member of the ICAEW Charity Accounting Group and of the Charity Law Advisory Group of the National Council for Voluntary Organisations, and was involved in the briefing of the House of Lords committee that discussed the Charities Bill. He is also visiting fellow in charity accounting and audit at South Bank University and was a member of the Charity Accounting Review Committee which revised the Statement of Recommended Practice on Accounting by Charities.

Chris Hanvey is director and secretary of the John Ellerman Foundation, a trustee of the National Council for Voluntary Organisations and a member of the executive committee of the Association of Chief Executives of Voluntary Organisations. He has worked in local government and as director of policy and information at NCH Action for Children. He has published widely, is joint editor with Terry Philpot of *Practising Social Work* (Routledge, 1993) and author of *Social Work with Mentally Handicapped People* (Heinemann, 1981).

Jeremy Hughes is director of public affairs, Leonard Cheshire Foundation. Over the past fifteen years he has dedicated himself to a career in the voluntary sector. He has worked in fundraising and public relations both in-house and as a consultant. He was a founder member of the Institute of Public Relations' voluntary sector group, 'Fifth Estate'. Elected a member of the Executive Council of the Institute of Charity Fundraising Managers in 1992, he currently chairs its Public Affairs Committee.

Ray Jones is director of social services, Wiltshire County Council. He has previously worked as a residential worker, field worker and manager in several social services departments and for a major national voluntary childcare agency; and as a university lecturer in social work. He is a visiting fellow at the University of Bath, and an honorary fellow of Cheltenham and Gloucester College of Higher Education. He is the author of five books, and numerous papers on social work and social services.

Kate Kirkland was appointed director of the Charities Group at accountants and management consultants BDO Stoy Hayward in April 1995. She became known as a leading author on charity governance in her previous post as head of the National Council for Voluntary Organisations' Trustee Services Unit. Her publications include *The Good Trustee Guide* (2 vols, NCVO, 1994, 1995) which has become a standard reference work. She was a trustee of Oxfam from 1987 to 1994 and is currently a trustee of the Family Welfare Association.

Joan Langan is a research fellow, School for Policy Studies, University of Bristol. She worked as a local authority social worker for a number of years before moving into research in the area of health and social care. Recent issues include the financial affairs of elderly people with dementia and issues of choice and control in mental health.

Quintin Oliver is director, Northern Ireland Council for Voluntary Action; the voluntary sector development agency in Northern Ireland providing information, support, training and representation to over 400 local groups. He worked for Strathclyde Regional Council's social work department as the United Kingdom's first benefits bus welfare rights adviser and driver and as adviser to the director of social work for ten years. He returned to Northern Ireland in 1985 to work for NICVA, from where he became a founder member and first president and secretary of the European Anti-Poverty Network (1990–4). In 1991 Quintin Oliver was appointed to the Council of State of Ireland by President Mary Robinson.

Terry Philpot is editor of *Community Care* magazine. He has edited several books, including (with Chris Hanvey) *Practising Social Work* (Routledge, 1993), and (with Linda Ward) *Values and Visions: Changing Ideas in Services for People with Learning Difficulties* (Butterworth-Heinemann, 1995). He is author of *Managing to Listen: A Guide to User Involvement for Mental Health Service Managers* (King's Fund Centre, 1994) and *Action for Children* (Lion, 1994). He is a member of the council of the NSPCC. In 1990 he visited Czechoslovakia, as a British Council fellow, to look at services for people with learning difficulties. He has won a number of awards for journalism.

Jill Pitkeathley, chief executive, Carers National Association, joined the association in 1986 from the National Consumer Council.

Nigel Siederer is director of the Association of Charitable Foundations. He has worked in the voluntary sector for over twenty years, starting out at the National Council for Civil Liberties in 1974. Most of his experience is with co-ordinating and resource bodies, of which he has been variously a committee member, development member, chief officer, and funder's representative. From 1978 to 1990 he co-ordinated the local advice centres in Lambeth, and played a part in setting up the national federation of Independent Advice Centres. From 1986 to 1990 he ran the Local Development Agencies Fund at the National Council for Voluntary Organisations.

Marilyn Taylor is reader in social policy, University of Brighton. She worked in the voluntary and community sectors for twenty years. She has written widely for a policy and practice audience on voluntary and community activity, on the impact of policy change and on the relationship between local government, service users and local communities.

Mike Whitlam has been the director-general of the British Red

Cross Society since January 1991. He was previously chief executive, Royal National Institute for the Deaf, deputy director, UK childcare and director UK operations, Save the Children Fund, project director, Hammersmith Teenage Project, National Association for the Care and Resettlement of Offenders, and assistant governor, HM Borstal, D C Hollesley Bay and Brixton Prison. He is co-founder of the Association of Chief Executives of Voluntary Organisations.

Roger Winfield is a partner in Wood Winfield, solicitors. After articles and then partnership in a large City firm he left to work in criminal defence and other legal-aid work. He started Wood Winfield with a partner in 1979 and now acts for charities, businesses and individuals in a broad range of work. Roger Winfield has long experience as a volunteer lawyer for a variety of organisations and is currently honorary legal adviser to a national charity.

Introduction

Chris Hanvey and Terry Philpot

We hold two conflicting views of charity. In the first it is perceived as 'cold', uncaring and covered in the barnacles of nineteenth-century workhouses, watery gruel and mean-spirited care. The second recognises this as a largely outmoded view, arguing that, despite a checkered past, a vibrant voluntary sector is a complementary part of any welfare state. This is witnessed by, for example, the place of children's charities in providing childcare (and increasingly so), as much as in the National Trust's place in the conservation of both buildings and countryside. This book largely accepts the second view and looks, in detail, at those diverse elements which go to making up a complex charity. At the heart of this is an altruism which might spring from a spontaneous donation, dropped into a Royal National Institute for the Blind collecting tin or from a day a month given, unstintingly, to the Woodland Trust by a volunteer, or from a trustee on the management committee of a local branch of the Samaritans. All of these represent a major strand in British social policy which has, at its core, an explicit acceptance that whatever the role of the state, there will always be a significant part to be played by a wide range of individuals brought together by a common desire to improve life for others through the gift of time, money and personal resources.

This book is about both the infinite complexity of this relationship and also the way it is being challenged, modified and moulded by an increasingly complex world. For the winds of change that have, in the last decade, transformed commercial life so fundamentally have also blown fiercely across the face of charities. To some extent the wheel has come full circle. In Lewis (1995), the author traces the role of the former Charity Organisation Society (now the Family Welfare Association) from its roots in 1869. She records that, as recently as three years before the start of World War I, the gross annual receipts of registered charities exceeded all public expenditure on the Poor Law. It was only as state services grew that the work of many charities declined – particularly in the field of social welfare – until today when, with a contracting state sector (in both senses of the word), the power of welfare charities is again being strongly felt.

In order to understand the complex interplay between state and philanthropy this book looks at the environment in which charities operate. It, therefore, becomes necessary to describe their organisation, the interests they represent, their increasingly complex funding, the legal requirements that govern them, and the influence which the growing importance of the European Union will bring to bear on them.

Much of this seems a considerable distance from an Elizabethan world in which certain purposes were regarded, by the law, as worthy of favourable treatment. Although no strict legal definition of charity exists even today, there is now acceptance of the preamble to the 1601 statute of Elizabeth I that charitable purposes can be classified in one of four ways: the relief of poverty; the advancement of education; the advancement of religion; and other purposes beneficial to the community (Quint 1994: 1).

While charity law is littered with fiercely contested legal debates as to whether, for example, a trust established to search for a Shakespeare manuscript, one to increase the present alphabet of 26 letters to 40, or another to pay pensions to poor employees of Dingle and Co. Ltd (Martin 1989: 410) were indeed charitable, there is some broad, if unspoken, unanimity across the sector, and the role of the Charity Commission is often that of increasing supervision to minimise abuse and maladministration. Of course, where conflicts do surface, as in the case of *McGovern* v *Att. Gen.* [1982], where a non-charitable body, Amnesty International, sought to obtain charitable status for part of its activities by setting up the Amnesty International Trust, then this can raise vital questions about the place of such organisations in a diverse world (*ibid.*).

Today the voluntary sector is indeed a house with many rooms and this complex architecture needs to be borne in mind throughout the following chapters. In 1991, the total income of registered charities was approximately £9,100 million. Charities' total expenditure was £8,500 million (93 per cent of total income) and 93 per cent of expenditure from charities went on goods and services. Significantly, this is vitally important when authors examine the way in which government pressures to contract out services are considered in relation to the charitable sector. Statistics reveal that the majority of charities are small. Eighty-eight per cent of charities have incomes up to £100,000, with only 0.2 per cent of the sector having an income over £10,000,000 (*Dimensions of the Voluntary Sector* 1995: Introduction).

With 390,000 full-time (equivalent) employees working in voluntary organisations in 1990 (*ibid.*), the charitable sector has also become a major employer. But this represents a very small percentage of the overall 'work force', as it were, who operate and maintain the voluntary sector. A report by Halfpenny and Low (in *Dimensions of the Voluntary Sector* 1995) reveals that, in one random survey, 21 per cent of respondents were involved in some kind of charitable work of one kind or another. Numbers of hours per month varied from 1 to 180, with the survey revealing a growing pattern of fewer volunteers working longer hours.

Against a backdrop in which voluntary income raised from donors is now measured in millions of pounds and volunteering remains an essential element of the British psyche, we also see a pattern of growing central and local government funding for the sector. In 1992–3 central government support to the voluntary sector amounted to £395 million and has increased in real terms by 172 per cent between 1979–80 and 1992–3 (*ibid.*). It is partly the sheer scale and diversity of the voluntary sector (and the complexity of some charities) that helps to make it attractive for some business enterprises to agree secondments to the voluntary sector in order that their job experiences may be enhanced. Similarly, local authorities provided an estimated £127 million in 1992–3 for grants and contracts; again an increase of 20.9 per cent in real terms since the previous survey of 1989–90. The way in which both central and local government funding has grown is a significant theme in the book and is also highlighted below.

The remaining part of the financial backcloth against which voluntary organisations function is provided by money donated to charities, through individual and corporate giving. It is estimated that between January and December 1993, the British adult population gave between £4.3 billion and £6.3 billion to voluntary organisations. This ranged from door-to-door collections, jumble sales, raffles; to television and radio appeals, corporate events, sponsorship, and sales in charity shops, and so on. Again the increasing sophistication required to tap public generosity successfully is a major theme of later chapters of the book. In brief, with the voluntary sector now accounting for 1.5 per cent of gross domestic product for England and Wales, its significance to daily life should never be underestimated (Mulgan and Landry 1995). Indeed, it helps to explain why some organisations are calling for a separate minister for the voluntary sector.

While these statistics help to provide a framework within which the voluntary sector can be examined, they fail to capture the sea change currently being experienced by all charities. Four major themes are clear and these will be traced in a variety of ways by contributors to the book.

First, it is acknowledged that in the last 200 to 300 years, charities have been significant players, to varying degrees, in the delivery of, for example, welfare services. Evidence for this was seen above in Lewis (1995). But today, the very nature of the long-established patterns of this role is changing. In 1739, for example, when the Thomas Coram Foundation was established, state provision for the abandoned children of London simply did not exist. Through sheer dint of personal charisma, hard work and, one suspects, mule-headedness, Thomas Coram established the Foundling Hospital in the face of, at best, public apathy and, at worst, callous disregard for human life (McClure 1981). But today the state (as represented by local government) is increasingly paying the voluntary sector not only to fill the gaps in statutory provision but, through purchasing services, to act as its agent. This poses profound questions about the future, and indeed the nature, of charitable organisations. What is happening to some charities is that, as voluntary income declines (that is, the money given by supporters), the money from local or central government (as a result of contracts) increases.

But should voluntary organisations provide this role, either plugging gaps in the welfare state or, increasingly, providing these services that the state has, until recently, seen as its own responsibility to fulfil? And how will the voluntary sector sustain its long-cherished position, not only as providing those services which the state cannot offer, but as pioneering new and innovative services which, in the fullness of time, the state may emulate? Last, as part of this theme, how will the voluntary sector be able to continue campaigning against the state (be this central or local government) if it is dependent upon these very sources for its funding? How also, as a corollary to this question, will donors feel about giving charitable money simply to plug inadequacies in state provision? We have already seen examples of disquiet where publicly donated money has gone to teaching hospitals which have subsequently closed.

The second major theme affecting charities today arises from the earlier statistics on the size of voluntary organisations. Gone, very largely, are the days of rattling tins on windy corners to raise significant sums of money for the voluntary sector. Fundraising is now a professional activity. Its practitioners have their own association and it is developing a growing reliance upon the corporate and business sector, trusts and the arrival of the National Lottery Charities Board. But while the larger charities (which, as we saw above, represent a very small percentage of the overall voluntary sector) can afford major poster campaigns and public relations initiatives, smaller organisations can no longer compete. Are we, therefore, going to see a gradual contraction in the number of voluntary organisations with Darwinian rules of survival operating, as the large get richer and the small go to the wall?

The last two themes, which recur in the book like variations on a familiar melody, are inextricably linked. The first of these is the role of volunteers, who play a vital part in the running of the voluntary sector, whether as trustees, unpaid fundraisers, direct service providers or advocates. Drawn by a healthy mix of personal need and altruism they are the undoubted life blood of charities. Yet they are being asked to perform a growing and sophisticated task. This is particularly evident in relation to the ever complex role of the trustee. On the one hand trustees are, by their very nature, volunteers who, throughout the United Kingdom, give their time generously to guide the strategic direction of large and small organisations. Yet, increasingly, the Charities Acts, with their emphasis on the financial responsibilities the trustees' roles carry, are demanding a degree of accountability and sophistication that may eventually become intolerable to many volunteers. With some charities now operating budgets of millions of pounds, the trustee carries an onerous responsibility and this poses a fundamental question as to how long it will continue to be the case that people will come forward to perform this role. Such a question is particularly apposite, if we are to believe the evidence of one *British Social Attitudes* survey that more than half the population agree that society relies too much on volunteers (*Dimensions of the Voluntary Sector* 1995).

Closely related to this is the fundamental issue of accountability. In many ways voluntary organisations are even less accountable than, say, local authorities. For those which are fundamentally membership organisations, there may be a constant, if *ad hoc*, check, that the activities of paid staff fit in with the needs and wishes of the membership. But for many voluntary organisations where, for example, the trustees are drawn from a broad cross-section of the population, accountability may become a crucial issue. This is particularly the case in a Britain which is refreshingly multi-racial and diverse in its aspirations. Since some of these organisations are, for reasons outlined above, becoming larger providers of services than the state, the issue of accountability is one which must rightly tax the interests of all of those concerned with fundamental democratic processes.

All of these are major themes which will, as well as being debated in the book, preoccupy the voluntary sector into the new millennium. But as these themes continue to be debated, one underlying assumption, perhaps shared by all of the authors, remains. This is the belief that our willingness to respond to need in a charitable way is one profound yardstick for the health of a society.

REFERENCES

Lewis, J. (1995) *The Voluntary Sector, the State and Social Work in Britain*, Aldershot: Edward Elgar.

McClure, R. (1981) *Coram's Children: The London Foundling Hospital in the Eighteenth Century*, New Haven and London: Yale University Press.

Martin, J. E. (1989) *Modern Equity*, Hanbury and Maudsley, London: Stevens.

Mulgan, G. and Landry, C. (1995) *The Other Invisible Hand: Remaking Charity for the 21st Century*, London: Demos.

Quint, F. (1994) *Running a Charity*, Bristol: Jordans.

Saxon-Harrold, S. and Kendall, J. (eds) (1995) *Dimensions of the Voluntary Sector*, London: Charities Aid Foundation

Chapter 1

To the millennium
The changing pattern of voluntary organisations

Stuart Etherington

The voluntary sector is a complex animal. It spans multi-million-pound philanthropic charities through to small, local community groups. Analysing what will happen to the sector over a period even as short as five years is inevitably daunting. The starting point of this chapter is that social trends inevitably impact upon the sector in a variety of ways. The economy influences funding, government policies change the context of voluntary action, and broader cultural change will also shape its development.

Any starting point for an analysis of the voluntary sector has to be a consideration of the likely broader environmental trends. These trends can be analysed by reference to the UK economy, demographic change, technology, government policy and cultural shift. How are these likely to change in what remains of the twentieth century?

First, the economy. There is no sign that any fundamental strengthening of the UK economy has yet been achieved, and forecasts suggest an average growth rate of approximately 2.3 per cent. Government consumption is likely to rise as a proportion of gross domestic product and personal income will grow slightly less than GDP as more overall national expenditure will be devoted to exports and investment. There is likely to be a slow rise in the number of self-employed people, and a continued departure of staff from major corporations causing a rise in the number of small consultancy-based groupings and numbers of individuals contracting back their services to major organisations. This is likely to be as true of the public sector as it is for the private sector. It may even be a characteristic of the larger voluntary organisations.

But perhaps most important for the voluntary sector, is what will happen to people's expenditure patterns, for this certainly impacts on the sector's voluntary income. Most forecasts suggest the following: consumers will continue to spend on housing, and this is likely to increase, particularly in relation to appliances, DIY goods, insurance and mortgages; and negative equity is likely to reduce, but will still be a major issue over the next five years. It is likely that people will increase their spending on leisure activities and that, most importantly, more elderly people's income and assets will be used up to provide long-term care for themselves. There will be greater private provision of medical care, pensions and social insurance generally. It is estimated that the percentage of personal disposable income used in 'informal taxation' will rise from 3.5 per cent to 5.1 per cent between 1989 and 1999, representing £22 billion, by the end of the century. Increasingly, as there are larger numbers of unemployed young people, there may be more significant intergenerational transfers of income and wealth, as middle-aged people are forced to assist their children beyond levels previously seen.

Employment patterns, too, will change. The number of young people in work will not change greatly if the proportions staying in education and training remain roughly the same. There is likely to be a greater number in further and higher education, although the trends for 1995 show an unexpected fall. The number of young adults aged between 25 and 34 will fall by 15 per cent. The number of people aged over 65 in the work force will fall by a half. More women will re-enter the labour market, but the increase will be less than from 1970 to 1990. Increasingly, employment will move to the service sector and there will be a continued decline in manufacturing and agriculture. There will be an increase in part-time and contract working, an increase in more flexible forms of organisation, and an increase in professional jobs requiring higher-level skills. There is likely to be an increase in home-working. Minimum wage legislation may well be introduced, and its effects on employment patterns are as yet unpredictable.

So in general, what can we say about economic trends during the period in question? First, it is likely that there will not be substantial growth. Resources may not be available for increased investment in either the public or the voluntary sectors. Within the overall limited growth of GDP, changes will take place and perhaps the most significant are an increasing amount of insecurity in the workplace and a higher percentage of personal disposable income being spent on services that were previously provided by the public sector. In short, there will be less disposable money available and this must inevitably impact on voluntary income of charities over the next five years. I will discuss the exact nature of this impact later on in this chapter.

Turning to demography, this will change the demand equation, particularly for those charities and voluntary organisations concerned with the provision of human services. First, the total population is forecasted to increase by 2.6 million. The working population will remain greater than the dependent population. It is estimated that 30 per cent of the working population will be in full-time work, 30 per cent in part-time work and 40 per cent dependent. The number of children is expected to be about the same. The number of young adults will fall by 2.4 million, leading to a higher average age in the working population. The number of people aged 65–79 will not change greatly, but significantly, the numbers over 80 will increase by 600,000.

What can we deduce from demographic change? There are perhaps two significant conclusions to be drawn. The first is that there will be less people in work to support a greater dependent population; and second, there will be a significant increase in the number of people over the age of 80. The demands that they will place, both on statutory and voluntary sectors, will be higher than the general population.

Let us now turn to the impact of technology. This, too, will change the way in which organisations work: in particular, it is likely to lead to higher degrees of productivity. For example, there will be continued rapid advances in computer performance, combined with falling hardware costs, and these will further extend the use of IT-based equipment. The parallel development in telecommunications will provide improved business links and a wider range of home-based services. The use of new technology may well lead to reductions in the work force, or higher degrees of productivity, and possibly an increase in home-working.

What then of government's reaction to some of these economic and demographic changes? First, no government or opposition spokesperson appears to be talking about substantially increasing levels of taxation. With limited growth in GDP, an increasingly dependent section of the population and more money being used on a dependent population, it is unlikely that there can be any significant increase in government spending on the voluntary sector. Indeed, there has not been in the recent past. Central government spending on the voluntary sector has been falling with one significant exception, housing associations. If these are seen as part of the voluntary sector, then government spending has increased substantially, for housing association spending constitutes over 85 per cent of central government spending on the voluntary sector. Indeed, some would argue that has gone too far, and what was previously part of the voluntary housing movement has become state agency, with all but its governance being determined by central government policy. This may also be a trend in social care as a result of contracting. What is clear, however, is that the voluntary sector can expect no major increase in the amount of money available from central government.

There are other governmental trends which may influence events. One is a possible movement from nation-states to region downwards, and superstate upwards. This may depend on whether Europe widens or deepens. All the signs are that it will widen. Regionalisation, however, will continue, even if only on an administrative basis. This significantly affects those parts of the voluntary sector which are concerned with regeneration and with employment and training. Local government spending will only marginally increase. The other significant development, which may well continue for the next five years, is the growth in the number of quangos. This is part of a continuing fragmentation of government. If government changes, there may be pressure to democratise some of these new governance structures. The state, however, is less likely to play a significant role and will continue to contract out work through a variety of different agencies. There is some suggestion that the population is reacting to governmental trends by some movement to more voluntary forms of organisations. Single-issue campaigns and self-help responses to social problems may well be a result of this. This has been true in the environmental movement, but is increasingly true among certain black and ethnic minority groups, who are turning away from the state for solutions. This trend may continue as the general dissatisfaction with democratic politics increases. The voluntary sector may therefore find itself once again an instrument of civil renewal, outwith the actions of the state – returning to its traditional homeland.

So what can we say then about the influence of government?

First, the voluntary sector can expect little extra money. Second, there may be an increasing fragmentation of administration into a variety of quasi-governmental bodies, and third, new forms of associational organisation may form around specific issues where individuals may place more of their energy, rather than in more formalised political activity.

Another area where trends will impact heavily on the voluntary sector is health and social care. While this is only one segment of the voluntary sector, it has continued, nevertheless, to remain large and influential. Since the creation of the NHS, the sector has never been particularly active in the field of acute health care, although it has made some in-roads in complementary medicine. It is in the area of long-term care where it has been more significant, and here the voluntary sector is likely to play a greater role, providing contracted services to the state. In this sense, it will cease to become the voluntary sector. Perhaps the most significant definition of the voluntary sector is that it draws its governance, its rationale, and a reasonable proportion of its money from outside the state. Organisations which are earning 80–90 per cent of their funds from the state have reached a level of dependency which makes them more part of the state than part of civil society. This is not necessarily wrong, but it should represent a conscious choice by the leadership of voluntary organisations. The move from the civil to the state raises important philosophical issues which contracting organisations ultimately have to answer. While their governance is still drawn from outside the state, the accountability of their managers is increasingly to those who prescribe the contract terms.

The final trend, which may well be important in terms of voluntary sector development, is cultural. This is the most difficult area to forecast. However, some tentative conclusions can be suggested. First, there is likely to be an increasing impact from broadcasting. The growth in the number of television channels and radio outlets is likely to be of significance. Getting your message across will be easier, and at the same time these activities will become more pervasive. There is likely to be an increase in home-based activity. More important, there is significant survey evidence of a decline of confidence in established institutions. This is true of politics, as I have mentioned earlier, but it is also true of a range of other institutions. The only place that there has been increase in confidence in British institutions between

1983 and 1993 is in trade unions, possibly a reaction to changes within the workplace. Patterns of attachment are switching to the family from established institutions, and there is a trend towards a more atomistic society, driven by both technology and a decline in support for institutions.

There is, however, a paradox within this issue of cultural change. It appears that society is becoming more atomistic, but at the same time, there appears to be a yearning for new forms of association around arts, sports, heritage and types of political campaigning. It is impossible to determine which of the drive to new associational forms or the drive to atomism will ultimately be more significant. The voluntary sector must hope that the continued desire of people to come together prevails. To this extent, it must remain concerned with the social changes implied by certain technological development and changing patterns of economic behaviour and work.

The first part of this chapter has sketched out some significant systemic changes which are likely to be of importance over the next five years. Five years is not a long time in terms of some of these developments, but nevertheless, some of the trends are already beginning to have their impact. The exact effect on the sector, and the way in which it may respond, is the subject of the remainder of this chapter.

First, let us look at the economy and the sector, and, in particular, the impact that economic changes may have on voluntary income. This is the story of how individuals may alter their behaviour in relation to the voluntary sector as a result of wider economic change. The first thing to note is that voluntary sector income tends to follow the pattern of GDP. It grew throughout the 1980s and early 1990s, but with the growth rate slowing since the mid-1980s. The voluntary sector is relatively small, it constitutes 4 per cent of GDP. Individuals' expenditure patterns may change as the state withdraws from certain key areas, leaving individuals to pay for themselves, and leaving less available to donate to charity. Greater insecurity at work may lead to higher savings levels, with less available to give.

What impact might this have on individual giving patterns? The trends are already obvious. Planned, tax-efficient giving has not increased proportionally at all over the last five years. It has remained at approximately 10 per cent of total giving. This is unlikely to increase without increased tax concessions and large-scale marketing. The Charities Aid Foundation has spent much of its history encouraging government to provide increased tax concessions, and indeed encouraging individuals to give through these methods. While this work has been important, the general lack of recognition by the public of a civil responsibility to give may ultimately have resulted in limited change. The public has very clear views about what charities should provide. British Social Attitude Surveys have continually revealed that charities have a distinctive role that is not connected with basic provision. This may ultimately be a major constraint on the public's propensity to give. Certainly more could be done in the area of tax-efficient giving. The important thing to note is that this is unlikely to happen. It is difficult to see how, over the next five years, there can be any significant increase in the numbers of people giving by tax-efficient means. Donations have in fact fallen. The average donation fell from £1.40 per month in 1987 to £1.28 per month in 1993. Given increasing economic security, limited growth rates and a propensity to spend on other activity, it is by no means clear that this will change beneficially.

A significant change in giving patterns has been brought on by the National Lottery. There is much misunderstanding of the effects on charity of the National Lottery. It is very early days, but consumer research, both before and after the advent of the lottery, has shown a consistent fall of approximately 11 per cent of people giving as a result of the lottery. This could represent up to £300 million of lost donations, particularly to those charities which are involved in discretionary fundraising, raffles and street collections. These charities tend to operate in social and health care, environment, overseas aid and medical research. The lottery, however, represents a net gain for the sector as a whole. New monies are available to the arts, sports and environmental fields for capital projects. There will, therefore, be winners and losers. Winners will be those organisations particularly in the arts, sports and heritage field, who previously received little money, but can now apply to their relevant lottery boards for, what is, essentially, new money. Other, fundraising charities, particularly in the areas identified above, will lose money as a result of reductions in their fundraising income. There is not enough available to them through their distribution boards to compensate them for this loss. So within an overall difficult fundraising environment, an additional factor has arrived on the scene which distorts the picture of charitable giving. Whatever happens to fundraising, it is interesting to note that £1 billion created by the lottery, £250 million of which is likely to go to charities who were previously directly fundraising from donors, is now being dispensed by government-appointed boards: quite large-scale nationalisation of the charity industry for certain segments.

The other major area of individual giving is provided by direct-mail activity, and there is growing evidence that returns on investment in this area are diminishing and that donor acquisition is becoming more expensive.

Dwarfing these problems, however, is the mainstay funding of philanthropic charities, legacy income. Legacy income is important to established charities in two respects. For one group it represents a huge proportion of their income which allows them to continue to function independently of any government intervention. For others, legacy income represents money which is used for activity which is not contracted for, in particular the transactions costs associated with contracting, and indeed, maintaining a campaigning and policy stance independent of their state funders. What happens to legacy income is therefore important. Legacies have in fact been buoyant in the 1980s. However, there is some suggestion that as a result of the economic trends identified earlier in the chapter, this may not be true for the next five to ten years. What factors might drive this? First, there is a stagnant housing market. Charities derive much of their legacy income from properties that are left to them. Second, people are now required to pay more for their care in old age. This may mean simply that they have fewer assets when they die. This alone could cause a catastrophic reduction in the amount of legacy income. But, as has been suggested earlier, there are other trends which may impact on this form of income: the fragmentation of household structures, the economic insecurity of middle-aged and middle-class people, who are increasingly transferring any money that they have either into paying for the young adults in their families, or indeed making their own provision for health and social care, together with an increasing propensity to spend amongst older people. Many people die without leaving wills. Nevertheless, more of nothing is nothing, and it may well be that substantial areas of individual giving may decline over the next five years, causing major problems for certain forms of charities.

Thus, voluntary income is certainly not going to be an easy

ride for the next five years: tax-efficient giving is static; individual giving has been declining as a result of the economic recession and may decline further as a result of the lottery. Direct mail is becoming increasingly expensive for charities, and legacies may well plummet. Therefore, there are likely to be downward income trends for voluntary organisations from this broad source of voluntary funding over the next five years.

What, then, of state funding? We have already seen that, if housing associations are excluded, central government funding for the sector is declining. There has been a reduction in urban-regeneration funding and voluntary sector activity has reduced. Funding for adult training has been cut by 38 per cent and often the voluntary sector is subsidising training places for disadvantaged groups. European funding is delayed each year, causing major cashflow problems for participating voluntary organisations. There is a distinct move from core to project funding and an increased fragmentation of government funding programmes. Overseas development had increased during this time, but recent announcements suggest that this may now decline.

Overall then, with the exclusion of housing association funding, central government's contribution to the sector has been declining across most government departments. Taxation is not forecast to increase, the amount of money available to government is relatively static, and it is therefore unlikely that the voluntary sector can look to central government for succour.

Local government funding of the sector has, however, been rising. In 1992 it provided £588 million for voluntary organisations. By 1995, this had risen to £687 million. Within this overall growth, significant changes have taken place. There is a particular growth in social services funding for the sector as a result of community care changes. The Special Transitional Grant increases mask no growth in most other areas of local authority funding to the sector. There is a shift from grants to fees for service, and there is some evidence that local authorities look to voluntary organisations to use voluntary income to subsidise price. However, it is fair to say that the community care changes have led to increased amounts of money available to the voluntary sector through contracting in community care services.

The future is particularly difficult to predict. It is by no means clear what will happen when Special Transitional Grant conditions cease. Will local authorities continue to fund the voluntary sector to the same extent? Perhaps most important, however, is likely to be increased private sector competition. Local authorities are increasingly interested in constructing markets for the social care services that they provide. There is some evidence that the voluntary sector will be competing directly with private sector provision and that local authorities may shift to scale economies above the area of locality where voluntary organisations are effective, in order to create more efficient markets. So what can we say about state funding for a voluntary sector which may be increasingly hit in terms of the voluntary income available? First, central government has reduced its funding to the sector. Second, while local authorities have increased their funding they have shifted to contracting and specifically to the social care arena.

There are two other avenues available to voluntary organisation to raise money: companies and trusts, and trading. As far as corporate and trust fundraising is concerned, the picture is not particularly rosy. Corporate giving by the top 400 companies increased marginally between 1990 and 1992 and since then has decreased in real terms. It is also becoming much more sophisticated. It used to be that companies made donations in small amounts at the whim of the chairperson. Increasingly, we are seeing annual budgets established in blue-chip companies in a specific department that deals with this. Increasingly too, charitable donations are being integrated with business objectives, in particular, employee development and affinity marketing. But given the limited GDP growth, this sector of funding is unlikely to grow in significant ways over the next five years. As far as trust funding is concerned, it rose until 1991, but thereafter reached a plateau. There are not significant amounts of money available here. The distortion within the trust picture is the result of the Wellcome Trust giving more in the area of medical research. This is a result of changes within the company and the trust. It is likely that the Wellcome Trust and the lottery boards will emerge as gigantic players. The lottery boards are state appointed. Each of the lottery boards and the Wellcome Trust will be as big as the total trust-giving sector. Trading has grown, but the rate of growth has slowed.

In general, then, the next five years are not likely to represent a period of substantial growth in the funded voluntary sector. The sector's rate of growth may continue to decline. It is difficult to see how individual giving will rise, and indeed how statutory funding will increase except in the area of social care contracting. But within this the market structure of the voluntary sector may well change. What tentative conclusions can be drawn about changes in market structure? As far as social care organisations are concerned, there may be a growth in small organisations. These are better placed to take advantage of the contract culture. If this continues to be a significant area of work, smaller local organisations or the federal parts of larger national organisations will continue to grow in response to contracting. In childcare, there has been a reduction in the percentage growth of organisations. There is no suggestion that this will change. For overseas-aid charities, the larger organisations have done much better than the smaller ones. As we have seen, central government funding has played a part in this, as has increased fundraising for emergency aid. Larger organisations have been able to market more effectively and the larger ones may well dwarf the smaller ones if current trends continue. As far as medical research is concerned, larger organisations have grown faster in the last five years. The lottery may have an impact here, which may be offset by monies available from the Wellcome Trust. As far as environmental charities are concerned, they may well continue to grow at a fast rate. They have monies available from other lottery boards. There may be net gainers and these may grow fast, given continued public support for environmental issues. As far as animal welfare charities are concerned, they may see a reduction. As for arts and sports, there may well be continued capital growth as a result of the lottery, but it is likely that revenue growth will not be sustained at the same levels. There will, therefore, be changes in the market structure of the voluntary sector as a result of the wider environmental shifts outlined earlier.

In general, as far as funding strands are continued, the voluntary sector is in for a shaky time over the next five years. Within this, certain voluntary organisations will do well, others will do badly, but the general trend will be lower levels of growth.

What of the other environmental changes? How will they impact on the voluntary sector? The environmental analysis identified the growing fragmentation of government and the growth of quangos as governmental instruments. As the voluntary sector grows in areas which are more concerned with public policy, then the question of governance of these organisations may well be drawn into the public arena. There is growing public and political concern about general governance issues which may be translated to the voluntary sector. The Nolan Committee is now beginning to look at quangos and non-governmental organisations and there is increased media interest in the cost effectiveness of voluntary organisations. There are two possible responses to this. The first is to strengthen the regulatory environment; the second is to look more at the area of standards and quality. Certainly, the regulatory environment is not without fault. Whether charitable purposes are drawn in the right way is under question. Since it includes religious groups but excludes groups concerned with human rights, the law fails to address effectively the issue of beneficiaries being appointed as trustees. Issues surrounding the effectiveness of charities have been raised, but have not been approached systematically within the law. Constraints on the remuneration of trustees can be argued to limit a charity's ability to attract them from all walks of life. The regulatory environment says little about the accountability of trustees to a wider group of stakeholders. The existing definition may not be flexible enough to contain the wide range of activities now undertaken by the voluntary sector. Unincorporated trusts cannot address the issue of limited liability. There may be moves to improve the legal framework to encourage easier transnational working in Europe. Membership- and self-help-based organisations may develop as a significant response to increased associational forms and yet charity law may have problems in dealing with this. The list of potential charity law reforms is large, but we have only just had a new Charities Act which essentially tightened up the law and increased the transparency of reporting. Although there may be moves to change the regulatory environment, they are unlikely to be successful. Charities, a major part of the voluntary sector, are still attempting to come to terms with the new law and the new changes. Charity law reform and changes in the regulatory environment are unlikely to be high on the agenda of the present government. So, while there may be a case for reform, it may have to wait.

This means that people are likely to be focusing on the development of quality standards rather than regulatory changes. Much work has been done in other sectors on the development of these standards, and some voluntary organisations borrowed these standards and have attempted to apply them in their own spheres. Given that there may be increasing public and political scrutiny of voluntary sector activities, it is likely that they will turn much more vigorously to the development of quality standards than to regulation. This is likely to be a major area of development over the next five years.

In the first part of this chapter, I speculated on the impact of cultural change. This may have some effect on the voluntary sector. The increase in broadcasting outlets may affect fundraising, public relations, campaigning and information within the sector. As the number of outlets grows, it will become easier for voluntary organisations to get their message across. Given increasing participation patterns, heritage, environment, overseas-aid and sports-based voluntary sector activity should grow, but established institutional charities may decline as a result of the declining confidence in institutions, especially among young people. They may turn to new styles of voluntary activity of a more associational form. The biggest evidence for this comes from the environment movement, although there is some suggestion that this is broadening out into other areas, with particular growth in the self-help movement.

Technology may also have its consequences, although this is as yet unclear. There is little research data on current uses or developments around information technology within the sector. However, given the environmental analysis, both information technology and telecommunications are likely to impact increasingly on the sector, both in terms of the running of its business activities and, in particular, in advice-giving. There is an early beginning of some Internet usage and some networking, particularly in the environmental field. It is a new area for the voluntary sector and one which may see some growth over the next five years. Employment policy and volunteering may well be significant areas of policy development over the next five years. Recent estimates suggest that the registered charities sector has 440,000 full-time equivalent and 2,000,000 volunteers. There is, however, no systematic information on the sector's work force and no single body with the authority to represent the sector to government on training issues. Much of the training in the sector is currently *ad hoc* and there is little recognition of the value of training as a strategic function.

Volunteering may well emerge as a significant area of government policy, whatever colour that government is. It is interesting to note that between 21 and 34 per cent of the population volun-

teers. Volunteering is mainly concentrated on children's education, health and social services, and there is a debate beginning
about the role of volunteers in contracted services. The number
of people volunteering appears to be increasing and the debate
about active citizenship generated by the Conservative government, but taken up with interest by Labour, is clearly emerging
as important in the political environment. There are two reasons
for this: first, volunteering is seen as a way of acquiring skills and
perhaps feeding secondary labour markets; second, and perhaps
more important, it is seen as central to the debate about active
citizenship. It is likely that this debate will continue to be important in the voluntary sector over the next five years.

In conclusion, it is difficult to predict exactly how the voluntary
sector will react to the changes I have described in this chapter.
What we clearly see is that there will be no substantial growth in
the funded sector into the next millennium. The economy will
grow at a relatively limited rate. It is unlikely that government
will increase the level of taxation. Individuals will expect over
the next five years to pay for more things which previously the
state had provided. The disposable income available to them, or
indeed for them to leave, is likely to decline. Hence, voluntary
giving may well not grow at the levels that we saw in the early
to mid-1980s. Similarly, state funding, with the exception of social
care funding from local authorities, shows limited signs of
increasing.

Renewal within the voluntary sector is therefore unlikely to
come from increased funding. The market structure of the voluntary sector may well change, but overall there can be no expectation of major growth. Set against this, there may however be
some growth in active citizenship which will find itself renewing
aspects of the sector. This may happen in two ways: first, the
level of volunteering may well increase and this may impact on
more informal voluntary organisations. Second, and perhaps more
important, the decline in support for established institutions may
lead people to come together in looser associational forms independent of the state for a whole range of responses from self-
help to quasi-political activity. This may lead to a renewal of
associational civil activity outwith the state. In fact, the sector
may divide structurally, if not legally, into three distinctive groups.
First, contracting organisations: these organisations, particularly
in the social care arena, but also prevalent elsewhere, will be

almost totally dependent on state funding. Their accountability structures increasingly will be to their funders and the role of trustees as independent instruments of governance will be increasingly questioned. Whether these organisations are part of the voluntary sector or whether they will join others approaching from a different direction, such as training and enterprise councils and health trusts, is yet to be seen. The second group will be those more traditional philanthropic charities. They will be under enormous cost pressure as the sources of their independent funding, particularly legacies, but also individual giving, decline. These are also likely to be more institutional, therefore will not attract support from a younger generation. The third part of the sector may well be associational forms not highly dependent on the state for funding, representing more of a civil tradition and utilising new media to a greater degree.

The sector's flexibility is its asset. It has adapted itself throughout its history. For example, internationally, former Communist states are hoping that they can develop their own voluntary sectors as a demonstration of a civil bastion against the state. The sector will constantly change, as much into the next millennium as within the last. Of that we can be sure.

Chapter 2

Map of the new country
What is the voluntary sector?

Marilyn Taylor and Joan Langan

In an old story, asked to describe an elephant, one person compares it to the trunk of a tree, another to a snake. No doubt a third might have described its ivory tusks. The point of the story is that the same thing looks very different according to where you come at it. That certainly applies to the voluntary sector. Some describe it in terms of large household-name charities; others refer to the countless small community and self-help groups, run purely on voluntary effort. Still others see it mainly as campaigning organisations. Each would have very different expectations of what it could do and where it fits in society.

The voluntary sector, however we describe it, has been part of UK society and welfare provision over the centuries, adapting to the changing political environment. But recent developments have brought the sector into the limelight, as policies seek to reduce the role of the state, especially in the delivery, but also in the financing of welfare. Voluntary and community organisations are attractive not only to advocates of the market. The growing interest in communitarian approaches from Left and Right would like to see both the moral responsibility for welfare and its delivery brought 'closer to the community'. Voluntary and especially community organisations would be a major vehicle for this vision.

How well equipped are these various organisations to meet the changing demands of current policy and what can they bring to the mixed economy of welfare? To answer this question we need to put together a picture of the whole 'elephant' but also to understand what its constituent parts contribute to the whole. Drawing on recent research (Taylor, Langan and Hoggett 1994, 1995), therefore, this chapter takes stock of the voluntary and community sector, focusing particularly on its organisations at local level.

Shore *et al.* (1994: 113) comment: 'Much more is known about Britain's large charities than about the [*sic*] myriad small voluntary organisations which are to be found in every urban and rural community.' However, the local picture is slowly being pieced together. The Community Development Foundation has carried out a range of research on local community organisations and estimates as a result that there are some 300 groups per 100,000 population (Community Development Foundation 1995). Kendall, Knapp and others have also carried out local studies as part of their research on the UK voluntary sector (Shore *et al.* 1994; Kendall and Knapp 1995). A major local mapping exercise is now under way at the Home Office, and Knight (1993) has described the voluntary sector in fourteen very different localities. Our own research[1] mapped the sector in three localities with different political traditions: one rural, one urban and one outer London Borough (Taylor, Langan and Hoggett 1994, 1995).

Comparing local studies is fraught with difficulties. It is, however, possible to suggest a few generalisations from these studies.[2] In both Shore *et al.*'s Liverpool study and our own research, half the organisations had been formed since 1980, with only one in eight founded before 1946. Well over half the organisations in each sample were local – in the sense of describing themselves as neighbourhood, locality or city-wide rather than county-wide, regional or national. They spanned an enormous range of activity between them. A significant proportion operated on a shoe-string – nearly a third of our sample had incomes of less than £5,000 and national figures suggest that two-thirds of all registered charities in England and Wales have an income of less than £10,000. Nearly three-quarters of the organisations in our sample used volunteers.

Although fitting formal definitions of the voluntary sector, only 70 per cent of our sample and 60 per cent of the Liverpool sample described themselves as such. Knight (1993) found that only 43 per cent of organisations in his local studies had charitable status, compared with 55 per cent in ours and three-quarters of the Liverpool study.

Commentators on the sector have suggested a number of ways of classifying its organisations; most commonly by function, size, values (for a summary, see Kendall and Knapp 1995). Most emphasise a distinction between large professional services providing organisations with paid staff, and small mutual or community-based organisations with few or no paid staff (Paton 1992; Chanan 1991; Knight 1993).

In our own study, which covered the field of community care, we developed a map of the sector which took into account both size (large, medium and small) and what we called 'ownership'. Dividing our sample between organisations run By Us for Us, and those run By Us for Them (Bishop and Hoggett 1986), we identified: user-run or self-help organisations and community-run organisations in the first category; and organisations run by people giving their time or money to others ('donor organisations') and not-for-profit organisations, essentially run by professionals (mainly housing associations and not-for-profit trusts) in the second.

The characteristics of the organisations in our study varied considerably across this map. Only one in five self-help organisations had paid staff. These organisations were the least likely to have a formal constitution, and had the smallest (usually elected) management committees. They were also most likely to have been formed after 1980; had smaller budgets (75 per cent had less than £5,000); and were less likely than others in the sample to get money from government, generating their money from donations, fundraising and subscriptions. The income and staffing profile of the smallest 'donor' organisations (lunch clubs, social and leisure clubs) was similar, although they were more likely to have a formal constitution. The larger 'donor' organisations had the widest range of activities and the widest variety of funders. Along with community-based organisations, they had the largest and most complex management committees – formed through a mix of election, co-option and appointment. The not-for-profits were the largest organisations and most likely to cover an area wider than the locality. 'Donor' organisations providing residential services had the oldest age profile in the sample.

While the vast majority of 'donor' and community organisations defined themselves as part of the voluntary sector, a third of those providing residential care preferred to call themselves part of a not-for-profit sector. The same proportion of housing associations and user-based organisations also defined themselves in this way. Our case studies suggested that, at one end of the scale, housing associations increasingly see themselves as part of the business world (Roof 1992), while at the other, user-based organisations do not always wish to align themselves with what they see as 'charity'. In areas where voluntary action is sparse and there is no local umbrella organisation, people running small voluntary organisations are likely to see themselves as part of informal systems of care, just doing what is expected of them in their locality, with no sense of being part of a 'sector' at all.

Some commentators stress the associational roots of the sector (Billis 1993). Two-thirds of the organisations in our study had members. While all user-based organisations had members and two-thirds of small 'donor' organisations, only half of the larger 'donor' organisations claimed to have members and only one in seven not-for-profits.

The organisations in our study were set up in the following ways:

Individual 'entrepreneurs': people seeing a need and taking the initiative to get the people and financial resources together to meet it. These included a day centre for older people, a Christian residential-care organisation, a Muslim women's organisation.

Collective action: a group of people with common problems joining together. These included a branch of a national welfare charity, set up by local parents; a residential home for people with learning difficulties set up by parents; organisations of service users; a range of black and ethnic minority community centres, including a number of Afro-Caribbean organisations that all grew out of a Caribbean cricket club set up in 1950 where it was said: 'It was racism that drove us to set this up. It wasn't conducive for us to mix in community centres. It was the same as in the churches. They said we were too loud.'

Other local voluntary or church organisations acting as the catalyst for an independent local initiative. This was the start for a neighbourhood-care scheme set up by an ecumenical council; an independent user-led mental health advocacy project that grew out of a branch of a national charity; a black association for mental health set up by a local Afro-Caribbean organisation.

Local public sector professionals who saw the voluntary sector as a place where they could meet needs that could not be met within the public sector. Examples included an organisation

for people with dementia; a group of parents
learning difficulties that grew into a residential
operative for mental health service users.

a project to develop carers' services set up by a forum
untary and statutory organisations; a management train-
network set up by a consortium of local voluntary organisations.

National organisations taking the initiative to set up a service in
the area. These included a day-care service set up by one
national charity when it closed down a residential home; a local
organisation for older people set up during the last war.

Statutory bodies: two organisations set up by government during
the last war to meet welfare needs; much more recently, two
trusts to provide residential care set up by local or health
authorities wishing to divest themselves of their residential-care
provision in response to current policy. Both still had strong
statutory links in the form of premises or seconded workers
and neither had much in common with any organisation in the
rest of our sample, even the housing associations, which we
classified under the same 'not-for-profit' heading.

Theorists argue that voluntary organisations are set up to fill
gaps that cannot be met either by the public sector or the market
(Weisbrod 1988). They also argue that the sector arises in
response to the diversity both of need and supply (James 1987)
and the desire of certain stakeholders to have more control over
the services they use (Ben Ner and van Hoomissen 1992). The
organisations in our study were sometimes set up to meet needs
that could not be met in any other sector (e.g. mutual support)
or that were not a high priority on crowded statutory agendas
(e.g. the support service for people with dementia set up by
professionals). Some were set up because other systems failed to
meet the needs of particular populations (black and ethnic minority groups) or because although services were available, they
were not run in ways that met the needs of their users (care
organisations set up by parents or service users). Some were set
up to promote alternative ways of meeting needs (a counselling
centre, some user organisations). Others were set up because
statutory alternatives were no longer viable.

Milofsky and Hunter (1994) call attention to the 'background
communities' from which voluntary organisations grow. The

above descriptions show how many voluntary organisations are embedded in communities of interest, religion, race or professional and voluntary sector networks. The profile of voluntary organisations in any locality is also influenced by local traditions and politics (see Taylor and Lansley 1992). We found many more self-help, community and voluntary sector support organisations in the urban area we studied, where there was a long tradition of community development in the local authority and a relatively well-resourced council for voluntary service. Although the ethnic populations in two of the areas were similar, it was in the area with the strong community development tradition that black and ethnic minority organisations existed in any numbers.

Altruism is a commonly recognised force behind voluntary activity and the urge to help others was clearly a major factor in a number of the organisations in our study. A concern for social justice – getting a better deal for people – also drove organisations in the sector. Community and self-help organisations were often based on solidarity (the organisation mentioned above that was set up in response to racism; user organisations set up to challenge professional attitudes and provision; an organisation of Muslim women who felt marginalised both within their community and beyond). Religion was a powerful motivator (Taylor, Langan and Hoggett 1994), not only for the Muslim women and some other minority ethnic organisations, but for a Methodist discussion group that grew into a housing association or other organisations set up to fulfil values and obligations of serving others. Professional values were another motivating force, most obviously where statutory workers were involved in setting up organisations, which then continued with or without their help, but also in an independent counselling centre, which had grown out of a local branch of the Family Welfare Association and which now acted as a training organisation as well as providing services.

Many have described the voluntary sector as value-led (Hodgkin 1993; Jeavons 1992). People running organisations in other sectors might wish to dispute this definition. We found no shortage of values in the private sector organisations in our research, as we have argued elsewhere (Taylor and Hoggett 1994a; Taylor, Langan and Hoggett 1995). Indeed several owners and managers had backgrounds in volunteering or in the public or voluntary sectors. While there may be cowboys in the residential-care trade, there are also people who have more in common with what Marceau (1990) has called 'craftsmen-entrepreneurs'. They would probably identify as little with the commercial sector and a profit-seeking stereotype as most voluntary organisations. If voluntary organisations do not have a premium on values, however, it is still possible to see them as predominantly 'value-rational' organisations (Rothschild-Whitt 1979; Paton 1996). Ultimately, they gain their legitimacy, not from the bottom line, nor from an electoral mandate, but from the mission to which their donors, volunteers and members subscribe. Rothschild-Whitt, studying 'collective' organisations, argues that in such organis-ations, while there is 'little attempt to account for decisions in terms of literal rules [or, we might argue, the bottom line], con-certed attempts are made to account for decisions in terms of substantial ethics' (1979: 513). This is a description many volun-tary organisations would recognise.

Evers (1993) argues that the voluntary sector mediates between the three major operating spheres in society: the state, the market and the personal. This position is reflected in the complex make-up of voluntary sector management committees, representing the multiple constituencies that go to make up many voluntary organ-isations. Some user organisations based on solidarity confine their membership to fellow users, but many of the larger self-help organisations bring together users, carers and sympathisers from many walks of life, while donor and community organisations typically have a wide spread of management committee members. Within this, some constituencies may dominate (Harris 1993), but the opportunity exists, in principle, for a wide range of stake-holders, including users, to become involved.

This complexity can lead to tensions between different constitu-encies. It also leads to accusations of inefficiency. A worker in a national charity spoke of the difficulties of convincing 30-odd trustees of the need for change, while for a period in another organisation, when there was no director, staff found that any one of four committee members could be telling them what to do. One of the private sector providers in our sample rejected the very thought of operating as a voluntary organisation because of 'all those committees'.

Another characteristic associated with voluntary organisations is *trust*. As the worker for a coalition made up of a number of organisations said: 'There's no supervision, no tight management, but good trust.' Although a number of organisations have paid staff (two-thirds of our questionnaire sample), a lot depends on the energies, commitment and goodwill of volunteers and management committee members. Some organisations vet volunteers, others don't. One Christian organisation said that it relied upon local knowledge. It was embedded in local networks and could usually find someone to vouch for a potential volunteer.

Organisations in our study saw themselves as generally flatter in structure than organisations in other sectors, with their functions more integrated, at least in comparison with the public sector. Thus, one of the not-for-profit trusts commented:

> People are turning their hands to all sorts of different skills – the accountant looks at transport issues and one of the community liaison workers does secretarial work – if we can't provide a quick response, we are no better than a statutory organisation.

Flatter structures are a consequence of funding as well as values. Most of the organisations in our study commented on how little money was available for core management functions (Taylor, Langan and Hoggett 1994), while one local director with responsibility for sixteen staff commented on the wide range of functions he had to carry out, compared with his previous position in the private health sector – including mending the boiler!

Compared with other sectors, some felt there was also a much less rigid line between helpers and helped. One manager commented that a lot of the volunteers who worked with them were lonely or bereaved people, themselves in need of support and the self-esteem which being a valued member of an organisation could bring (Rogers, Pilgrim and Lacey 1993), while in a drop-in centre for older people, the helpers were only a few years away from being the helped. In a user organisation a volunteer commented that 'as a volunteer, I'm under the paid workers, as a management committee member, I'm their boss'.

Voluntary organisations are supposed to be closer to the user and community. The voluntary sector as a whole offers a potential for users and marginalised communities to become actively involved as volunteers and management committee members which is not available elsewhere. User organisations are themselves part of the sector although, as we have seen, they do not always define themselves as such.

In our sample, user involvement varied considerably and even where users were in the majority on a management committee, some felt that the views of professionals still dominated, while others felt paid workers or professionals did not always appreciate the power their position gave them. One organisation had brought two carers on to a largely professional management committee, but failed to appreciate how difficult it was for the carers to have an impact on a tight-knit professional group. On the other hand, it was professional staff in three organisations who had introduced more user participation into organisations run by parents. While several smaller organisations felt that they offered the informal opportunity for more face-to-face contact between those running the organisation and those using it, this did not guarantee an empowering, as opposed to paternalistic, approach. By comparison, some of the larger organisations (particularly the housing associations) had the most explicit systems for involving users.

A number of the organisations in our sample were committed to participatory ways of organising. Several user and community organisations said they made decisions after as wide a consultation as possible. Many donor organisations had open and accessible structures, though sometimes by default rather than design. One residential-care organisation was described as a 'family' with everyone diving in to help and 'hands-on' management, which allowed people to learn by practical example rather than by directives from above (this was also true of some private organisations).

Participation is not easy. Two organisations commented how interest waxed and waned and a management training organisation in one locality described how it was 'doing the same training again and again because people burn out'. A user organisation spoke of people moving on when they became empowered, while others who are 'up to their eyes in their own problems' need nurturing if they are to contribute. Many organisations found themselves treading a fine line between inclusive structures, where everyone had access to decisions, and structurelessness, where everyone went their own way or where, although the language was of participation, it masked the power and influence held by paid staff or the few most active people.

It is important to recognise that not all voluntary organisations are inclusive and participatory (Taylor and Hoggett 1994b).

Rothschild-Whitt argues that in collective organisations, 'since personal and moral appeals are the chief means of social control, it is important to select members who are unlikely to challenge the basic assumptions upon which they are built' (1979: 513). In our study (Taylor, Langan and Hoggett 1995), we identified five main ways of organising, three of which were 'top-down' and only two 'bottom-up' (Table 2.1).

Table 2.1 Organisational forms

		Top-down		Bottom-up	
Charis-matic (7)[a]	Hierarch-ical (3)	New manag-erialist (4)		Partici-patory (9)	Devolved, federal (2)
One or two founding individu-als retain the dominant influence or, by default, the work falls on one or two shoulders	With clear responsi-bilities at different levels of the organisation	Decentralised in structure but with strategy, budget and standards dictated from the centre		Open access to decision-making – may be intentional or by default	Local autonomous units with a central umbrella body

Source: derived from Taylor, Langan and Hoggett 1995: 25–8
Note: (a) Indicates the number of organisations in our sample fitting this description

It is tempting to distinguish between national organisations and local organisations, seeing the former as the most bureaucratic, least likely to have a participatory, community base and least 'voluntary'. But this is not the case. Chanan (1991) has distinguished between 'professional non-profit organisations' (with a head office running local branches) and 'voluntary service organisations' (where the national office acts as a resource for autonomous local groups). Local groups which are members of voluntary service organisations may be less formal than wholly independent local organisations, because they can rely on the services of head-office staff and operate on an entirely voluntary basis rather than having to employ professional staff themselves. Indeed, some local organisations in our study decided to affiliate to national bodies in order to benefit from their experience and resources. In an example from outside our study, a local branch of a national organisation had grown quickly and was finding the support and resources offered by headquarters inadequate. It was thinking of going it alone and buying in the support it wanted.

We noted earlier how voluntary organisations are often embedded in local networks or 'background communities'. What is interesting about Milofsky and Hunter's model (1994) is the dynamic picture they paint of how organisations grow, overlap and sometimes die. They argue that the diversity of interests in most localities generates a rich variety of organisations representing different and sometimes overlapping interests. Sometimes organisations will plough their own furrow, at other times they will come together to meet common aims. The local mental health festival in one of our study areas was led by a users' organisation but brought together all organisations in the field. Organisations may remain close to their 'background communities' or they may grow and formalise, with others in the background watching their progress as a kind of 'Greek chorus' (Milofsky and Hunter 1994) to which they owe 'responsive' accountability (Leat 1988)[3] or forming new organisations to fill the gap.

Our classification (see p. 23) was not a static one. Organisations were moving across it: from small to large; from statutory to not-for-profit; even from user- to predominantly donor-based. Some branches of national bodies had become completely independent and two organisations had grown out of the demise of others. They were also changing their organisational forms from charismatic to participatory or hierarchical; from participatory to hierarchical or vice versa. Several were experiencing what one respondent called the 'birth pangs' of moving from a smallish to a larger organisation: 'It has expanded so much the cracks are showing.' One user organisation, where growth had already led to major problems in communication and co-ordination, was struggling with the dilemmas of whether to appoint a co-ordinator or not and the change in culture this would bring.

Milofsky and Hunter's background communities underline the importance of networks, not only in the origins of voluntary organisations but in their later operations. Often, especially in black and rural communities which have not had the opportunity to develop their resources, it is the same people who get involved in different initiatives. The chairperson of one volunteering scheme was also assistant co-ordinator for the local victims' support scheme, while the worker in a small black mental health project was wanted on everyone's committees. Several people cropped up on each other's management committees, were involved jointly in new ventures or met in joint planning meetings. Networking is an increasingly fashionable term, but for many of the smallest organisations in our study it had long been essential to survival. In one area, three one-person agencies offering services to carers provided a network of services together which they could not possibly have achieved separately.

Milofsky and Hunter's background communities also recognise the intermeshing of the voluntary with other sectors, particularly the public sector. As we have reported elsewhere (Taylor, Langan and Hoggett 1994), we found strong links with the statutory sector and some with the private sector. These links were variously through management committee membership, through support in kind from statutory sector workers, through joint working and alliances, through statutory workers working as volunteers out of hours. In the black voluntary sector, where resources were limited, we were told that the line between statutory professionals and voluntary activity could be very blurred.

The sector which we have described in this chapter is one that is characterised by its diversity, which draws on a range of different motivations and 'background communities'. Although individual organisations vary considerably, common organising principles within the sector include: operating on trust, accountability to values rather than rules or profit margins, with a measure of participation, integration and user and community involvement. What does all this have to contribute to the patterns of welfare which will be required into the twenty-first century?

One of its strengths is its diversity. If the demands of welfare are to be met into the next century, organisations will be needed that can cater for the diversity of need in a way that the market alone cannot, especially in areas where people cannot afford to purchase their own care. If the necessary resources and imagination are to be released, organisations will be needed that can provide a channel for the many different motivations which encourage people to contribute to welfare. A system of welfare that depended solely on voluntary organisations would perhaps be patchy and inequitable. But within a mixed economy, its diversity and the energy it releases have a great deal to offer.

There are many changes facing the voluntary sector today: population change, changing needs, changing demands and policy change (Taylor 1996). For organisations in our study, the most significant policy changes were the community care reforms introduced in the NHS and Community Care Act 1990 along with the more general advance of what has been called the contract culture, with its demands for a more businesslike approach. Though our research was conducted early in the implementation of the recent reforms, concern was already being expressed about increased regulation, increasing constraints on funding and the effects of market competition (Taylor, Langan and Hoggett 1995). There were fears that these pressures could squeeze out smaller organisations and volunteers as well as discouraging user and community involvement in management. One key issue for the future is likely to be balancing the desire to involve service users in the planning and management of services at the same time as responding to the pressure to become more businesslike and professional. (For a fuller discussion of pressures for change, and particularly the effects of regulation, see Langan and Taylor 1994; Taylor, Langan and Hoggett 1995: 38–41).

The voluntary sector will certainly survive – after all it survived the arrival of state welfare, which took over many of its earlier functions. But will it retain its ability to act as a home for a diverse range of organisations and motivations? There is a growing tendency to differentiate between large and small, the institutional sector and associations (Knight 1993), and to see the former as losing their claim to be truly 'voluntary'. This is nothing new. William Beveridge complained of the formalisation of the sector in the 1940s (Beveridge 1948). While it alerts us to the dangers of co-option, however, such a stark dichotomy ignores the many thousands of organisations who are neither small nor big, who struggle to survive in the medium ground of the sector. It also oversimplifies the national–local relationship. In our research, some large organisations at least have had an important role to play in supporting autonomous local initiative and in contributing weight and resources to coalitions and campaigns with smaller organisations. To fracture this sense of identity and responsibility – however tenuous it may sometimes be –

could remove essential support from local voluntary, community and user networks.

The dangers of co-option are very real and some will succumb. But the signs may not be as bleak as some commentators would suggest. As user and community organisations are struggling with pressures to professionalise, so some of the more traditional organisations are getting users on to management committees and other decision-making forums. As some voluntary organisations seem to be pulled further and further into an agency role, the emphasis on consultation with communities and users and the need to support the organisational channels for these consultations provides others with new opportunities.

What is most important is to ensure that the diversity and dynamism of the sector is maintained. This requires continued support for new and smaller organisations, both from government and from the larger, better-resourced organisations in the sector. This will ensure that as existing organisations change, formalise or die, there are new organisations to take their place as 'movers and shakers' and, perhaps as Milofsky and Hunter's 'Greek chorus' (1994), holding established organisations to account. But there is also a need to experiment with new kinds of support and new organisational forms. This is especially so for medium-sized organisations who face critical decisions about growth and structure, so that they have real choices and can continue to pursue their aims and maintain their culture while contributing to wider networks and coalitions of welfare advocacy and provision.

In the late twentieth century, the boundaries between public and private responsibility are shifting – in the United Kingdom and elsewhere. A new institutional environment has emerged (Stewart and Taylor 1993), reflecting the diversity of need and choice in society, but risking ever greater fragmentation. As a group of organisations which are both public and private, voluntary and community organisations both act as a barometer of these changes and reflect contradictions and challenges which will become more and more common. More and more organisations are now moving to the fringes of what has, in the past, been voluntary sector territory. The language of networks, partnership and alliances is more and more common. We have already commented on the parallels between concepts of trust and integration in the voluntary sector and leading-edge thinking in industry. Organisations from across the sectors will have to recognise the demands of a variety of stakeholders and to negotiate agreed territory on which to move forward if needs are to be met. In these circumstances, the debates and concerns of voluntary and community organisations will be increasingly shared in the wider world.

NOTES

1 This research was carried out by the authors with Paul Hoggett and funded by the Joseph Rowntree Foundation. It studied voluntary and private organisations in three localities and consisted of a questionnaire survey, followed by more detailed case studies on 33 organisations, of which 25 were voluntary or community organisations.
2 These comparisons are mainly based on our own research and Shore et al. 1994. The Home Office studies were not publicly available at the time of writing and the Knight studies are too varied to allow comparison. Given the difficulties of identifying the smaller organisations – they are less easy to trace and less likely to fill in questionnaires if they are traced – these figures are likely to be skewed towards the larger organisations.
3 Leat (1988) distinguishes between: accountability-with-sanctions; explanatory accountability, where an organisation is required to give an account; and responsive accountability where there is no requirement or sanction, but the organisation still has a sense of responsibility to give an account.

REFERENCES

Ben Ner, A. and van Hoomissen, T. (1992) 'Non-profit organisations in the mixed economy: a demand and supply analysis', *Annales de l'économie publique, sociale et coopérative* 62: 519–50.
Beveridge, W. (1948) *Voluntary Action*, London: George Allen and Unwin.
Billis, D. (1993) *Organising Public and Voluntary Agencies*, London: Routledge.
Bishop, J. and Hoggett, P. (1986) *Organising Around Enthusiasms*, London: Comedia Press.
Brenton, M. (1985) *The Voluntary Sector in British Social Services*, London: Longman.
Chanan, G. (1991) *Taken for Granted: Community Activity and the Crisis of the Voluntary Sector*, London: Community Development Foundation.
Community Development Foundation (1995) *Regeneration and the Community Guidelines to the Community Involvement Aspect of the SRB Challenge Fund*, London: Community Development Foundation.
Evers, A. (1993) 'The welfare mix approach: understanding the pluralism of welfare systems', in A. Evers and I. Svetlik (eds), *Balancing Plural-*

ism: New Welfare Mixes in Care for the Elderly, Aldershot: Avebury, pp. 3–31.

Harris, M. (1993) *The Power and Authority of Governing Bodies: Three Models of Practice in Service-providing Agencies*, Working Paper no. 13, London: Centre for Voluntary Organisation, London School of Economics.

Hodgkin, C. (1993) 'Policy *and* paper clips: rejecting the lure of the corporate model', *Nonprofit Management and Leadership* 3(4): 415–28.

James, E. (1987) 'The non-profit sector in comparative perspective', in W. W. Powell (ed.), *The Nonprofit Sector: A Research Handbook*, New Haven: Yale University Press, pp. 397–415.

Jeavons, T. (1992) 'When the management is the message: relating values to management practice in nonprofit organisations', *Nonprofit Management and Leadership* 2(4): 403–17.

Kendall, J. and Knapp, M. (1995) 'A loose and baggy monster: boundaries, definitions and typologies', in J. Davis Smith, R. Hedley and C. Rochester (eds), *An Introduction to the Voluntary Sector*, London: Routledge, pp. 66–95.

Knight, B. (1993) *Voluntary Action*, London: Home Office.

Langan, J. and Taylor, M. (1994) 'Bending the rules', *Community Care*, 22–8 September.

Leat, D. (1988) *Voluntary Organisations and Accountability*, London: National Council for Voluntary Organisations.

—— (1995) *Challenging Management: An Exploratory Study of Perceptions of Managers who have Moved from For-profit to Non-profit Organisations*, London: Centre for Voluntary Sector and Not-for-Profit Management, City University Business School.

Lewis, J. (1993) 'Developing the mixed economy of care: emerging issues for voluntary organisations', *Journal of Social Policy* 22(2): 173–92.

Marceau, J. (1990) 'The dwarves of capitalism: the structure of production and the economic culture of the small manufacturing firm', in G. Redding and S. Clegg (eds), *Capitalism in Contrasting Cultures*, Berlin: de Gruyter, pp. 355–79.

Milofsky, C. and Hunter, A. (1994) 'Where non-profits come from: a theory of organizational emergence', paper presented to the Association for Research on Nonprofit Organizations and Voluntary Action, San Francisco, Calif., October.

Paton, R. (1992) 'The social economy: value-based organisations in the wider society', in J. Batsleer, C. Cornforth and R. Paton (eds), *Issues in Voluntary and Non-Profit Management*, Wokingham: Addison-Wesley, pp. 3–12.

—— (1996) 'How are values handled in voluntary agencies?', in D. Billis and M. Harris (eds), *Voluntary Agencies: Challenges of Organisation and Management*, Basingstoke: Macmillan, pp. 29–44.

Rogers, A., Pilgrim, D. and Lacey, R. (1993) *Experiencing Psychiatry*, Hong Kong: Macmillan Press.

Roof (1992) 'No sign of movement', November–December: 21–5.

Rothschild-Whitt, J. (1979) 'The collectivist organisation: an alternative to rational-bureaucratic models', *American Sociological Review* 44: 509–27.

Salamon, L. M. (1994) 'The nonprofit sector and democracy: prerequisite, impediment, or irrelevance?', paper presented to the Aspen Institute Nonprofit Sector Research Fund Symposium on 'Democracy and the Nonprofit Sector', 14 December.

Salamon, L. M. and Anheier, H. K. (1994) *The Emerging Sector: An Overview*, Baltimore: Institute for Policy Studies, The Johns Hopkins University.

Shore, P., Knapp, M., Kendall, J. and Carter, S. (1994) 'The local voluntary sector in Liverpool', in S. Saxon-Harrold and J. Kendall (eds), *Researching the Voluntary Sector*, Vol. II, Tunbridge Wells: Charities Aid Foundation, pp. 113–28.

Stewart, M. and Taylor, M. (1993) *Local Government Community Leadership*, Luton: Local Government Management Board.

Taylor, M. (1996) 'What are the key influences on the work of voluntary agencies?', in D. Billis and M. Harris (eds), *Voluntary Agencies: Challenges of Organisation and Management*, Basingstoke: Macmillan, pp. 13–28

Taylor, M. and Hoggett, P. (1994a) 'Quasi-markets and the transformation of the independent sector', in W. Bartlett, C. Propper, D. Wilson and J. Le Grand (eds), *Quasi-markets in the Welfare State*, Bristol: School for Advanced Urban Studies, pp. 184–206.

—— (1994b) 'Trusting in networks? The third sector and welfare change' in P. 6 and I. Vidal (eds), *Delivering Welfare: Repositioning Non-Profit and Co-operative Action in Western European Welfare States*, Barcelona: CIES, pp. 125–49.

Taylor, M. and Lansley, J. (1992) 'Ideology and welfare in the UK: the implications for the voluntary sector', *Voluntas* 3(2): 153–74.

Taylor, M. and Lewis, J. (1993) 'Contracting: what does it do to voluntary and non-profit organisations?', paper presented at the conference 'Contracting: Selling or Shrinking', University of the South Bank and the National Council for Voluntary Organisations, 20–22 July.

Taylor, M., Langan, J. and Hoggett, P. (1994) 'Independent organisations in community care', in S. Saxon-Harrold and J. Kendall (eds), *Researching the Voluntary Sector*, Vol. II, Tunbridge Wells: Charities Aid Foundation, pp. 129–43.

—— (1995) *Encouraging Diversity: Voluntary and Private Organisations in Community Care*, Aldershot: Arena.

Weisbrod, B. A. (1988) *The Nonprofit Economy*, Cambridge, Mass.: Harvard University Press.

Chapter 3

Swimming together
The tidal change for statutory agencies and the voluntary sector

Ray Jones

The storm tides of the Thatcher years have created a radically different context for statutory and voluntary organisations, and although the currents of change may now sometimes seem less strong, there is still a feeling of trying to build and maintain relationships across the sectors upon foundations of shifting sand.

The Thatcher years were certainly a time of radical change:

> When Thatcher came to power there was a consensus that education, health, the public utilities, the criminal justice system, the civil service, and to a much less extent housing, were public services to be publicly provided. By the end of the 1980s, in just a decade, that was not the case. It was then possible, indeed desirable, to separate the aims of service outcomes from the means of delivery. Publicly owned aims (mass education, clean water, etc.) could be achieved through a range of providers in the public, private and independent sectors.
>
> (James 1994: 60–1)

The extent and depth of the changes introduced by the Conservative governments of the 1980s really were dramatic. Commentators who certainly are not sympathetic to the New Right ideology have still recognised positive as well as negative aspects of the new agenda:

> It would be churlish to ignore the positive contribution of the New Right advocates. Their criticisms of the waste and bureaucracy within the government's civil service have been justified. Some of the reorganization planned or being carried through may well be beneficial. They have had the courage to attack the power of the legal and medical professions.
>
> (Holman 1993: 16)

Even within the trade union movement there has been an increasing willingness to be open and reflective, and to acknowledge past sins while continuing to fight hard to continue to challenge exploitation and to seek social justice. For example, in a text sponsored by Unison it is commented that 'state workers have often acted in controlling and even abusive ways' and that 'professional power meant this oppression was often disguised as help, even when it was imposed against the will of those receiving it':

If employed workers are to build new and effective alliances with users, they must acknowledge that in the past trade unions have been accomplices in such an indefensible system, and bear their share of responsibility for the slow progress towards community care before the 1980s.

(Carpenter 1994: 6)

The 1980s and the 1990s have indeed seen dramatic changes in most public services. The changes relate to changes in power, control, funding and responsibilities and have redefined the 'market place' (indeed even the terminology!) in which we understand the role of the state and of public services. While the power, control, funding and responsibilities for public authorities may all be seen to have changed (usually by being reduced), the focus on consumer choice and on performance and value for money has increased. This has been effected in a number of ways through:

- *funding mechanisms* which allow central government to determine local agendas and which often favour the provision of services within the voluntary and private sectors (e.g. funding for grant-maintained schools; funding for health 'waiting list' initiatives; funding to housing associations for new housing; additional funding for placements in private and voluntary sector residential care and nursing homes)
- *regulatory (but not direct service provision) responsibilities* remaining with national and local government (e.g. the National Curriculum; residential-care standards)
- *residual responsibilities* remaining with public sector agencies (e.g. homelessness; public health; special education; child protection)
- *public reporting of performance* against national standards and formats (e.g. school league tables; health authority waiting lists;

Citizen's Charter initiatives; Audit Commission performance
indicators)
- *consumer choice and empowerment* (e.g. choice of schools;
  choice of residential and nursing homes).

Much of this is potentially very positive. The emphases on consumer choice and empowerment, on public accountability, and on
standards and performance all challenge some of the worst
aspects of traditional public-sector monopolistic bureaucracies
reflecting a 'dissatisfaction with large, bureaucratic organisations
which have now been divided into accountable units in most parts
of the welfare state' (Flynn 1990: 69).

There are, however, also a number of dangers which include
the increasing power held by unaccountable quangos and 'arm's-
length' agencies (e.g. Further Education Funding Council; Housing Corporation; Benefits Agency), and central (and local)
government passing responsibilities to the private and voluntary
sectors without making available the resources to fulfil those
responsibilities.

The way in which voluntary organisations operate in the 1990s
is partly a reflection of the changes wrought in the public sector.
The interdependence of the state and voluntary sectors has in
many ways increased, with voluntary organisations (especially
within the field of social welfare) becoming mainstream providers
of services commissioned and funded by state agencies. However,
as noted by Wistow and colleagues (Wistow *et al.* 1994: 86), 'the
development of local authorities as purchasers of care was not
entirely a new one in the sense that the statutory sector had
never been the sole provider of social care'. But the changing
political and ideological context of the 1980s and the 1990s, the
'Thatcher years' and the 'Thatcher legacy', have offered many
opportunities for voluntary organisations to expand and to
increase their 'market share', although as well as opportunities
there are also perceived threats from the changes.

The relationships between the state and voluntary sectors have
become more complex, both in terms of the scope of the relationship and also regarding the rules and processes which determine
and facilitate the relationship. The scope of the relationships
includes:

- the purchaser relationship – state agencies purchase services
  from voluntary organisations

- the regulatory relationship – state agencies inspect and regulate (against performance standards) voluntary organisations
- the competitive relationship – services directly provided by the state (e.g. local authority home-care services) compete with voluntary sector providers for business
- the collaborative relationship – state sector service providers work with voluntary sector service providers within a complementary relationship to seek adequate service coverage (e.g. local authority home meals services jointly planned and provided with, for example, WRVS volunteers delivering the meals)
- the commissioning relationship – state sector agencies (such as local housing authorities) strategically commission services from the voluntary sector (such as housing associations)
- the agenda-setting relationship – (rather like the commissioning relationship in reverse) voluntary organisations develop new patterns of service which then are added to the commissioning and purchasing agendas of state agencies (for example, new services for people with AIDS might fit within this category)
- the resource-creating, resource-stimulation, resource-harnessing and resource-supporting relationship – state sector organisations fund and support voluntary sector development agencies as a means of supporting voluntary action (often by unpaid volunteers) within the community to add to the total resource of assistance and commitment available
- the advocacy relationship – voluntary organisations seek to advocate for individuals with regard to state agencies, or through collective advocacy attempt to influence how and what resources are available and deployed.

All of these categories assume a direct relationship, a direct interaction, between voluntary organisations and state agencies, but of course for many voluntary organisations (such as some leisure, recreational and cultural organisations) their link with any statutory organisation may be very limited. It would be very arrogant and, indeed, inaccurate for any public sector manager (such as myself) to assume that all voluntary organisations and all parts of the voluntary sector had an immediate and direct relationship with the state sector. Not only does the nature of the relationship vary but its very existence and extent also vary.

Before moving on to explore the roles and processes which shape and maintain the relationships between the state and voluntary sectors, it is necessary to reflect on the disparate nature of the voluntary sector. The voluntary sector might see state organisations as very varied and indeed inconsistent, creating difficulties in particular for those voluntary organisations who work across the boundaries between statutory agencies, such as voluntary organisations who work with many local authorities, or with local authority and with health service organisations. However, there is also considerable variation within the voluntary sector, creating a richness of diversity but also a complexity of differentiation and 'it is a significant feature of the current times that defining the voluntary sector is becoming an increasingly difficult thing to do' (Gutch, Kunz and Spencer 1990: 6).

The voluntary sector can be characterised along a continuum based on size and organisational complexity (from local unpaid good neighbours to large voluntary sector bureaucracies) and it can also be differentiated through typologies relating to geographical focus (local–national–international), purpose focus (welfare, leisure and recreational, cultural, religious, political, and so on), style focus (campaigning, service delivery, social and mutual support, and so on), and funding focus (funding contributed by participants, by voluntary public donations, by payments for service from individuals or public agencies, and so on).

It is the diversity of the voluntary sector which enriches and which is to be fostered (not controlled), but it is also the diversity and differentiation which makes the voluntary sector difficult to conceptualise. Different types of voluntary sector activity require and demand different relationships with statutory agencies, but it is possible to characterise along three major, and interrelated, dimensions major attributes of voluntary organisations within the social welfare sector which are likely to be influential in determining the relationship required with statutory agencies (Figure 3.1).

Figure 3.1 suggests a linkage between the main role of the voluntary organisation (e.g. giving advice and information), the style of its relationship with statutory agencies (e.g. greater dependency on statutory agencies for funding and for establishing and maintaining its main role), and its major orientation (e.g. towards service users or towards the direct management and provision of services).

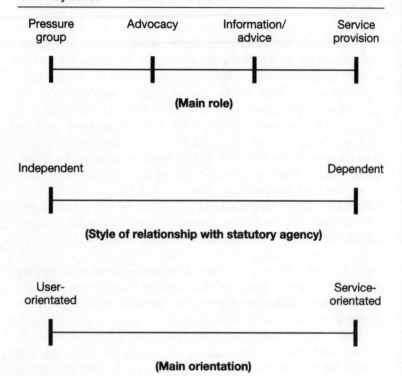

Figure 3.1 A typology of voluntary organisations

It is important to be clear, however, that voluntary organisations and the voluntary sector are not the same as service user
(or carer) organisations. Some voluntary organisations may be
user organisations or carer organisations, but many are not. There
can be a mistaken assumption, particularly within social welfare,
that voluntary organisations represent and speak for service users
and for carers. Voluntary organisations, like all organisations,
have their own vested interests and agendas (to protect and
expand, for example, the services they directly manage and
provide) and they may be no more (or less) sensitive and responsive to the views of users and carers than statutory organisations.
This issue is increasingly recognised within the voluntary sector:

> What is the biggest challenge facing charities in the build up
> to the Millennium? The Lottery, the contract culture, lack of

funding or political campaigning? I would argue that it is the challenge of user involvement. The phrase has become part of the voluntary sector's jargon, but the reality has not even begun to touch many parts of the sector.

(Gutch 1995: 1)

It is possible, therefore, to characterise social welfare voluntary organisations along a further continuum (as in Figure 3.2), this time focused on the relationship between the voluntary organisation (and indeed statutory and private organisations) and service users (and carers).

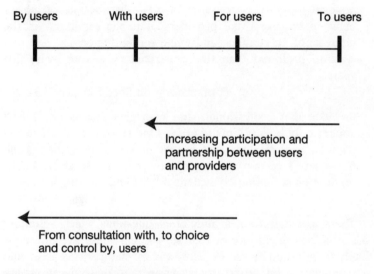

Figure 3.2 Organisational orientation to service users

Figure 3.2 depicts a continuum where social welfare organisations range from being user-controlled, where actions are determined 'by' service users to organisations which do things 'to' service users with service users having no control or say over what happens to them. In between are organisations which, often paternalistically and sometimes patronisingly, do things 'for' service users, and organisations which are not user-controlled but which seek to engage, and to negotiate with, service users.

Many organisations in the voluntary and statutory social welfare sectors see themselves moving along the continuum towards greater partnership and participation with service users often through processes of consultation, but many service users are now demanding real choice within, and direct control of, the services and assistance they may need. The move from large institutional confinement to residential care to community care is now being extended to independent living, with disabled people (and neighbourhoods as with community centres and family centres) wanting control as to how they receive assistance. This is a challenge made to the statutory sector (see James 1994: 8), but it is also now a challenge for organisations in the voluntary and private sectors:

> political viability ... requires a new distribution of power between the users and providers of public services – in the interests of an enabling and empowering democracy, one that is more profound than that generated by a vote every five years.
>
> (Commission on Social Justice 1994: 40)

> the idea that professionals and managers always know best applies only in very limited areas. One reason for the growing popularity of market ideas is that in a market exchange the buyer has a certain amount of power over the seller. Public services must find an equivalent way of empowering its users.
>
> (Flynn 1990: 187)

There are, therefore, a number of questions which voluntary organisations might ask of themselves, and these are questions likely to be asked by service users and by statutory agencies who are purchasing for service users. Answers to these questions are likely to influence the attractiveness and acceptability of the voluntary organisation to service users:

- Is the organisation paternalistic and patronising towards service users?
- Is the organisation participative, enabling users to have their views heard?
- Does the organisation allow within its structure for formal representation by users?
- Is the organisation user-led and user-controlled?

The agenda of consumer influence, consumer choice and consumer control is not only, as noted at the beginning of this chapter, an emerging 1990s issue for statutory public services. It is also now firmly on the agenda for the voluntary sector.

Also firmly on the agenda for the voluntary sector is the requirement to be more explicit and clear about the major roles and functions for voluntary organisations. For example (and referring back to Figure 3.1), voluntary organisations which have expansionist ambitions and aspire to grow as direct service-provider organisations, with a developing bureaucracy, are likely to become more and more dependent on generating year-on-year and growing funding from statutory organisations through grants and fees. Although these voluntary sector provider organisations may still strive to be innovative and to pilot new patterns of service, their main organisational goal may become organisational survival, with survival to be achieved by receipt of continuing payments for service from statutory organisations.

These growing voluntary sector provider organisations may also come to find themselves less able or willing to challenge central and local government agencies because of their (real or unreal) fears about antagonising their funders. Their advocacy and pressure group roles may be seen or experienced as compromised, and indeed they may certainly find it difficult to directly encourage individual and collective advocacy which might itself be targeted on the types of services provided by the organisation and which have become its core function and identity. All of these dangers have been recognised by a number of commentators within and outside the voluntary sectors, such as Gutch (1992: 83) and MacFarlane (1990: 16), and by Carpenter, and Davies and Edwards:

> At the same time as the voluntary sector becomes more bureaucratic, and involved in mainstream provision, it is also likely to become less accessible, innovative and diverse.
>
> (Carpenter 1994: 80)

> What will be the long-term effects on the voluntary sector of a shift from looser funding arrangements to relatively tightly specified service agreements and contracts? Fears have been expressed about voluntary organisations losing their independence and autonomy, and being tied ever more tightly to the statutory funders' services priorities.
>
> (Davies and Edwards 1990: 12)

Voluntary sector organisations, as service provision organisations, do, however, play an important role in extending the range
of services, and the range of organisations providing services,
from within which service users can make their choice as to what
services they want to receive and who they want to provide
the services. Many voluntary sector provider organisations also
continue to bring with them a tradition of service innovation,
often initially funded by their voluntary income rather than by
grant and fees from statutory agencies. However, as service providers, the voluntary sector is in competition with the statutory
and private sector service providers, and, as will be noted, this is
likely to determine their relationship with statutory public sector
organisations, including their funding relationship.

One cluster of roles, however, which voluntary sector organisations might fulfil, and which is much more difficult for statutory
public sector agencies themselves to undertake, are the advocacy,
pressure-group and lobbying roles. Voluntary sector organisations
might specialise in these roles and, as noted above, it is a function
they are more likely to accept and successfully undertake if they
are not encumbered themselves in trying to protect and guard
their own direct provider services. It is also a function which the
voluntary sector is much more able to fulfil than statutory agencies, as integral to the budget-holding and budget-management
task of statutory organisations is the task of rationing to keep
expenditure within budget.

Voluntary organisations themselves also clearly have to keep
their own expenditure within the money they have available, but
potentially they have greater political freedom to canvas for more
funding for services overall and to challenge the rationing
decisions and processes. As well as using voluntary income to
fund the advocacy, pressure group and lobbying roles, it is also a
legitimate call on statutory agencies to fund this type of activity,
especially individual and collective advocacy to assist and
empower vulnerable service users. Statutory agencies themselves
are likely to be compromised if directly seeking to provide advocacy opportunities which would need to challenge the statutory
organisation.

The type of funding relationship, however, which might be
more appropriate between statutory and voluntary organisations
differs depending on the functions of the voluntary organisation.
The funding made available for a voluntary organisation which is

primarily a direct provider of care services is likely to be on different terms from the funding for a voluntary organisation where the main focus is individual or collective and individual advocacy (e.g. advocacy schemes), mutual support (e.g. co-operative befriending and social clubs) or voluntary sector support and development (e.g. many councils for voluntary service).

When, for example, is it most appropriate for statutory agencies to fund voluntary organisations through the payment of an annual grant and when to fund through payment of a fee for services provided? When is it appropriate to think about a service agreement between a statutory and voluntary organisation? Should funding be an annual decision or, for example, a rolling three-year commitment? To what extent should statutory agencies formally specify the specific services and service standards to be provided by voluntary organisations? How should performance against the specification be monitored and measured? When is competitive tendering appropriate compared to preferred partner status? How are year-on-year (and within-year) cost changes to be calculated and captured? How to decide between block and spot individual one-off purchasing? What about the funding requirements for a newly established organisation commissioned to fill a gap in the market (but with no initial cash flow guaranteed by payment for existing services being provided) compared to those of a well-established organisation with an established fee-based income and cash flow?

The 1990s world of the contract culture is certainly not simple. The question is: can it be more efficient and effective, with a focus on value for money, performance and outcomes, than the benevolent, but often conservative and historic, arrangements of the past which focused on the payments of grants but with little accountability to the funding organisations?

The contract culture has generated its sceptics and critics, and some of their concerns have already been noted. But it is important to understand, as described earlier, that the changing culture and context is not something being imposed by statutory organisations on the voluntary sector. It is a sea change for all the sectors. It is a part of the 1990s context in which both the statutory and voluntary sectors are now increasingly required to operate. A strong focus on value for money, performance, effectiveness and accountability (including a public accountability and an accountability to direct consumers) has not been heavily and traditionally ingrained in the culture of statutory public services or much of the voluntary sector. The new requirements require new relationships.

It is important to recognise the immense scale of the sea change, for both the statutory and voluntary sectors, but that the flow of change has been as great, if not greater, for statutory agencies as for the voluntary sector. It can sometimes feel that the past ten years have flooded the public and voluntary sectors with new agendas and that we are all awash (indeed sometimes all at sea!) with change. But there is no future here for King Canutes in either sector. We still have a shared responsibility to channel the changes so that the positive opportunities rather than the potential negative consequences of the 1980s changes are achieved, and the political changes of the 1990s are not unhelpful:

> Margaret Thatcher did Britain two favours. First, the scale, speed and consistency with which she applied her policies in the public sector created the potential for nothing less than a paradigm shift in thinking about delivery of human services. Second, she ceased to be prime minister at a point at which the process of implementing that paradigm shift was incomplete and therefore both process and tomorrows were still malleable. The challenge of the 1990s is one of using the space created by Thatcher's paradigm shift, at least to improve service and service delivery, at most to build healthy communities.
>
> (James 1994: 1)

Change may be invigorating or demoralising, it is often threatening, but it can also present new opportunities. Change is rarely, however, comfortable, and so it is for the changes for statutory and voluntary organisations.

For managers in the public sector it can feel like they cannot win whatever they do:

> The social services department which avoids risk in contracting may be damned by central government, and by disappointed private and voluntary sector suppliers for failing to promote competition, and damned by consumers for failing to allow choice. But the social services department which contracts with those it does not thoroughly know and trust, with those who do not have a long and unimpeachable track record, will, if anything goes wrong, be damned by the media, by consumers,

by the taxpayer and by central government for taking risks and failing in its duties both to those in receipt of care and those who fund care.

(Leat 1993: 66)

The picture painted by Leat also suggests that the experience for service providers, including managers in the voluntary sector, is hardly likely to feel any more comfortable if 'choice, quality and value-for-money is to be achieved by the creation of a competitive market in care' which will require that 'supplier organisations awarded contracts will be kept in a state of creative insecurity, responsive to the demands of purchasers and users, by the "threat" of new competitors' (Leat 1993: 58).

The higher profile now given to managerial accountability is emphasised by Norman Flynn (1990: 68), and the increased accountability held by managers in all sectors can create tensions across the sectors. For example, a former chief executive in one local authority, while recognising the 'undoubted benefits in support channelled through the voluntary sector', then asks: 'Does a voluntary organisation make a genuine contribution to help need in the area? Or has it become an introverted oligarchy? Does it genuinely do good works? Or does it consist of those who ride on the authority's financial band wagon?' (Brooke 1989: 80). He goes on to note that:

There are also drawbacks to voluntary organisations. They can be unprofessional, unaccountable and undirected. . . . There is a loss of control over the service and the ultimate (and perhaps only) sanction of cutting grant can be unacceptably controversial. In such situations the buck tends to stop with the local authority, despite the independence of the voluntary organisation.

(Brooke 1989: 81)

The heightened accountability and responsibility for managers in all sectors clearly affects the relationships across the sectors, and this is often most apparent in discussions about money. So, some thoughts on when different types of funding relationships and processes might be appropriate between the statutory and voluntary sectors.

First, the payment of *grants*. Traditionally, voluntary organisations tended to receive their funding from statutory agencies through the payment of annual grants. The payments continued year-on-year with little information being collected about the efficiency and effectiveness of the organisations receiving the grants. At a time of general budget growth during the 1970s and indeed the early 1980s new organisations received grants without funding having to be redeployed from existing grant recipients or from other service areas.

The position now has certainly changed. No longer are statutory agencies working with growth in real terms, and indeed the experience for many statutory agencies is actual budget reductions. If new grants are to be awarded to voluntary organisations the money has to be found from within existing, previously committed expenditure. Many voluntary organisations are, therefore, along with their statutory agency funders, finding that their annual grants are not even increasing in line with inflation, and those voluntary organisations (like local authorities) that have financial reserves are having to use their own declining reserves to maintain levels of service.

The capping of budgets and expenditure has instilled a new discipline in the funder–recipient relationship. Voluntary organisations are being asked to monitor and to demonstrate their efficiency and effectiveness by measuring performance against business-plan targets and the standards set within service specifications. This requires voluntary organisations (along with statutory and private organisations) to be more businesslike and more organised. For some voluntary organisations this is a major culture change and requires the availability of business and management skills along with a continuation of the voluntary motive and ethic.

Voluntary organisations may be held more accountable (to funders and to the public) for the grants they receive, and may also be competing for funding in a more stringent environment. But the degree to which voluntary organisations are held to account for the grant they receive and the complexity of the accountability mechanisms needs to be sensitively tailored to the size of the grant, the stage of development of the organisation, and the nature and function of the organisation.

For example, the small grant paid to a newly established mutual support social club which meets once a week in a community centre and is attended by people who have had a mental illness or who are socially isolated clearly should require less complex monitoring and accountability procedures than an established voluntary organisation with paid employees receiving tens of thousands of pounds in grant aid each year which might be delivering a range of services. Indeed for the larger organisation it would not be unreasonable to be seeking a service agreement which makes explicit what services are to be provided, to what extent, and at what standard, and for performance to be measured against the requirements of the service agreement. As well as being a means of establishing and maintaining an accountability to the funders, the service agreement also provides a safeguard for the voluntary organisation in having a clear understanding about the (negotiated) expectations and requirements of the funders.

Payment of a grant without the rigours of a service agreement would seem more important for small local community-based voluntary organisations which do not have, and probably do not require, the full organisational structure and commitment to produce full-blown business plans and the like. However, it is still important to have adequate reporting (such as audited accounts) to demonstrate probity and that services have been provided and taken up (for example, through giving activity indicators). These small voluntary organisations, in particular, are likely to benefit from assistance and advice provided by the voluntary sector development and support agencies (such as councils for voluntary service), and as well as funding voluntary sector service providers. It is important, as noted by Leat (1993: 60), to continue to fund those agencies which support the voluntary-sector network.

For many voluntary organisations (including the development agencies) the payment of grant should increasingly be within the context of a service agreement, and the service agreement should also be an indicator of a longer-term funder–recipient relationship. Local authorities, for example, may have yearly financial uncertainty, but they expect, quite reasonably, to receive government grant and council tax income each year. The same should hold true for voluntary organisations through service agreements with grants paid annually but with, say, a rolling three-year funding commitment, albeit with the necessary escape routes should organisations dramatically fail to meet the terms of the service agreement.

But the payment of a block annual grant, even when paid in relation to agreed service standards and agreed volume of service to be provided, is not always the most appropriate funding process. The payment of *fees* in respect of specific services provided relates increasingly in social welfare to residential care (and sometimes domiciliary and day-care) services, where block purchasing through grant payment may be less sensitive than individual fee-based spot purchasing, in promoting user choice, and in encouraging organisational responsiveness and flexibility in the overall market place of provision.

Managing an organisation with a fee-based income is clearly more complex than managing an organisation with a grant income paid at the beginning of the year, as it raises issues in relation to cash flow and in needing to market and sell services to users and purchasers. This dynamic may be threatening to the providers but it is likely to encourage efficiency and responsiveness. It also offers the opportunity for the voluntary-sector provider to grow, and indeed to innovate, if the services provided are those which users and purchasers increasingly want to have available and to purchase.

There will be times, however, when a combination of *grant and fee* payments may be appropriate. For example, a voluntary organisation may receive a grant but then be approached about providing an additional service (e.g. leading a major policy consultation). The cost of this additional activity may not be subsumed within the grant already paid but may be met through the payment of a fee for this particular activity.

There may also be times, especially for new organisations, when they need the security of being able to meet their core organisational premises, administrative and managerial overhead costs while developing and marketing their services which will in future draw in a fee income and possibly generate a cash reserve. The funders might, therefore, look to fund through grant payment the core organisational costs for, say, a three-year developmental period; and might also agree to block purchase (again possibly for a limited period) a number of services, but with additional services being purchased through spot fee purchasing (maybe at a marginal cost). Over time the funding might move away from core grant and block purchasing to an emphasis on spot purchasing. The stages in this relationship, their timing, and the decision whether to move to an emphasis on spot purchasing, are likely to be determined by the purchaser view about the purchaser's responsibilities to commission this new service to meet an identified service shortfall. The purchaser will also need to take a view about the future risks it is reasonable to leave with the provider taking into account, for example, the implications and likelihood of the service not remaining viable.

Finally, with respect to funding processes and relationships, there is the formal and legal relationship which might be established through issuing contracts for services, and in particular contract relationships which might follow from a tendering process.

Compulsory competitive tendering is certainly not new for government agencies. Within local government, for example, blue collar manual services (such as building maintenance, cleaning services, refuse collection, and so on) have been subject to such tendering for many years. It now looms large for white-collar local authority activities, such as personnel, legal and financial services, with the Department of the Environment requiring that a proportion of these services be subjected to compulsory competitive tendering during the next three years. There are also the tendering requirements within European Union regulations where contracts may have to be advertised in the European journals and open to competitive tendering.

For voluntary (and private) organisations, opportunities are arising to bid through a competitive tendering process to provide a wide range of services purchased by local authorities. Within the field of social welfare, for example, a number of local authorities have invited competitive tenders to provide domiciliary care services and others have sought competitive tenders for the provision of specialist residential accommodation.

The contract culture, therefore, might be experienced as a threat by the voluntary sector, compromising its independence and freedom, but it does also provide opportunities to secure funding for expansion and growth, and in particular opportunities to receive funding and provide services previously largely reserved and retained within public sector monopolies. However, in addition to the opportunities and the accountability (and indeed security) which may be developed through the contract culture, it is also important to recognise and maintain, as noted by Richard Gutch (1991: 13), the flexibility which is still required in the funding relationships between the statutory and voluntary sectors.

The changes of the 1980s and the 1990s have been as much for the statutory sector as for the voluntary sector, and the changes are not the creation of either sector. The requirement to manage constructively the changes, and to seek positive opportunities and outcomes for the users of services, is however firmly within the remit and responsibility for managers in the statutory and voluntary (and private) sectors, but with the increasing demand (and the increasing acceptance) that service users take centre stage and direct services.

The political and ideological seascape has indeed changed dramatically since the election of a Conservative government in 1979, and it is important to recognise that the new agendas which have been set are similar for all the sectors. We are all swimming together within the same sea, coping with the same current of change. We should also have shared ambitions to keep services afloat for service users albeit with service users increasingly determining the shape of these services and the strokes and style which should be used (through user consultation, user choice and user control) in making services available. If the choice is between sinking or swimming together there is really only one choice to be made.

REFERENCES

Brooke, R. (1989) *Managing the Enabling Authority*, Harlow: Longman.

Carpenter, M. (1994) *Normality is Hard Work: Trade Unions and the Politics of Community Care*, London: Lawrence and Wishart.

Commission on Social Justice (1994) *Social Justice: Strategies for National Renewal*, London: Vintage.

Davies, A. and Edwards, K. (1990) *Twelve Charity Contracts*, London: Directory of Social Change.

Flynn, N. (1990) *Public Sector Management*, Hemel Hempstead: Harvester Wheatsheaf.

Gutch, R. (1991) *Contracting In or Out? The Legal Context*, London: National Council for Voluntary Organisations.

—— (1992) *Contracting: Lessons from the USA*, London: National Council for Voluntary Organisations.

—— (1995) 'User involvement is next challenge for the sector', *Third Sector*, 6 April.

Gutch, R., Kunz, C. and Spencer, K. (1990) *Partners or Agents?* London: National Council for Voluntary Organisations.

Holman, B. (1993) *A New Deal for Social Welfare*, Oxford: Lion.

James, A. (1994) *Managing to Care*, Harlow: Longman.

Leat, D. (1993) *The Development of Community Care by the Independent Sector*, London: Policy Studies Institute.

MacFarlane, R. (1990) *Contracting In or Out? The Impact on Management and Organisation*, London: National Council for Voluntary Organisations.

Wistow, G., Knapp, M., Hardy, B. and Allen, C. (1994) *Social Care in a Mixed Economy*, Buckingham: Open University Press.

Chapter 4

A mixed blessing?
How the contract culture works

Norman Flynn

The NHS and local authorities are making increasing use of the
voluntary sector in the provision of community care services (see
Mocroft 1995). The regulations covering the implementation of
the National Health Service and Community Care Act 1990 made
it compulsory for local authorities to spend 85 per cent of the
Special Transitional Grant on services other than those provided
by themselves. At the same time, the rules on residential care
made it financially disadvantageous to refer older people in local
authority elderly persons' homes.

Authorities were faced with a choice of the private sector and
the voluntary sector. The private sector was well established in
residential care, which had grown as a result of the entitlement
which elderly people previously enjoyed to social security payments to cover their residential and care costs in private homes.
There was a private homecare market, consisting of a range of
types of company offering care at home to private clients paying
their own bills with some provision to local authority service
users, especially at times when the in-house providers were not
available. This market consisted almost entirely of companies
operating as agencies, providing a link between customers and
self-employed workers.

There was also a voluntary sector, consisting of a variety of
organisations. There were local voluntary associations of unpaid
volunteers providing a range of support services. In addition there
were national charities, employing paid workers, supplying
services either to people with particular needs (different forms of
disability, particular conditions) or for particular groups (women,
children, older people). These organisations may or may not also
have been involved in lobbying and campaigning on behalf of

'their' group, or on issues such as disability rights. As well as these service providers, there have also been organisations whose purpose was purely to campaign and lobby and not provide services. (To see the scale of the voluntary sector in the United Kingdom, see *Henderson's Top 2000 Charities* 1995, or *Dimensions of the Voluntary Sector* 1995.)

The statutory sector had, before the NHS and Community Care Act, made extensive use of the voluntary sector for service provision, especially for specialist services for people with multiple disabilities, people with problems whose incidence was so low that any authority would be unlikely to have sufficient demand to provide its own services for those people.

However, the implementation of the Act brought with it some concerns about the impact of increased contracting on the voluntary sector. There has been a long history of state contracting in the social services field in the United States (Kettner and Martin 1987; Bernstein 1991; Gutch 1992; Smith and Lipskey 1993). Commentary on this process has been critical of the bureaucratic nature of the contracting process but positive about the impact of the use of the voluntary sector on innovation and flexibility. Smith and Lipskey (1993), writing about US experience, were concerned that the increase in the use of contracting was part of the Reagan and Bush regimes' policy of federal withdrawal from social programmes. They warned particularly about the potential impact on entitlements and equity of having workers for voluntary organisations as the 'new street-level bureaucrats' making decisions about eligibility to services rather than publicly accountable, state-employed street-level bureaucrats. One of their other concerns was that as salaries and conditions of employment were depressed as part of the process of competitive contracting, the non-profit organisations would not be able to attract and retain staff of sufficient calibre and service standards would be eroded.

Richard Gutch made a study tour of the United States in the spring of 1991 and brought back some lessons for the UK practice (Gutch 1992). He concluded, among other things, that:

- voluntary organisations became less, rather than more, financially secure as a result of short-term renewable contracts
- the process was very heavily bureaucratic and involved a lot of paper

- there was no strong conclusion that organisations became distorted by the process of contracting
- there was strengthening of the power of professionals and full-time workers, compared with volunteers
- small organisations were tending to be squeezed out as the larger organisations could better afford to 'play the contracting game'
- there had been an increase in the commercialisation and competitive behaviour among non-profit organisations
- competition had been used to reduce costs and contracting has concentrated on the purchase of provision rather than outcomes.

Gutch's work, and other work by the National Council for Voluntary Organisations (including the periodical publication *Contracting In or Out?*), set the agenda for the development of contracting in the United Kingdom. The themes recur: the growth of dependency and its impact; the squeezing out of small organisations because of high transaction costs; fears about the impact on innovation; the impact of contracting on the financial health of the organisations involved; the impact on the democratic and structural nature of the voluntary sector.

This chapter looks at some of the positive and negative effects of contracting on the organisations in the voluntary sector and on the relationship between them and the statutory sector. It concludes with a review of some of the remaining issues.

Some charities are heavily dependent on public grants and fees and charges for their income. Table 4.1 shows the amount of income which comes from these two sources in a selection of charities in the care field. The proportion of income from these sources, in this sample, ranges from 29 per cent (MIND, which was set up both to campaign on the issue of mental health and to organise self-help and other services) to 99.4 per cent (Community Integrated Care, which was established to provide services under contract).

In some cases, the proportion of funding from these sources has grown. For example, Scope's income from fees and charges grew from 53.7 per cent in 1991 to 64.1 per cent in 1994, and Sense's from 51.4 per cent to 68.9 per cent, by adding £6 million of fee and grant income over the same period. However, this growth of income is not without its problems

One result of the increased reliance on state funding is that

Table 4.1 Sources of income for charities

	Total income (£ million)	Public grants, fees etc. (£ million)	Other fees (£ million)	Grants, fees as per cent of total
MIND (1993)	3.25	0.49	0.46	29
Age Concern England (1994)	14.80	3.72	1.75	37
Barnardo's (1994)	72.80	33.60	—	46
Scope (1994)	55.50	—	35.60	64
Cheshire Foundation (1993)	52.80	41.40	—	78
Community Integrated Care (1994)	17.80	8.10	9.59	99

Source: derived from *Henderson's Top 2000 Charities* 1995

voluntary organisations could become dependent on the statutory sector. At a meeting of a national charity's management team, one member said: 'We are simply the servant of the statutory authorities.' In the discussion which followed, some members expressed the view that it was possible to maintain their values and ways of working, while others felt that they were being forced to adapt to the wishes of their funders.

This discussion epitomised one aspect of the dependency problem: that contracting forces people to do what they would not otherwise wish to do. In one of the organisations studied in research for the Joseph Rowntree Foundation (Common and Flynn 1992) the voluntary organisation had changed the sorts of people for whom it provided services. However, this fear of distortion is based on anticipation and anecdote or the results of case-study work.

There is a fear that concentrating on acquiring contracts can distort the organisation in three ways. First, that contracts will hand over control of the services provided to the purchasers. Those voluntary organisations which are controlled by their members and whose services are therefore under user control fear that services defined by purchasers would loosen their democratic organisational form.

There is also a possible distortion of the clientèle of the organisation. One drug and alcohol charity, for example, has now moved into the field of caring for people with long-term mental health problems. In this case, the move was motivated by the offer of contracts, rather than the founding principles of the organisation. This move from an internally generated motivation to a market-orientation changes the 'market segment' in which the organisation operates.

A third fear was identified by James Richardson whose survey (1995) tried to test the hypothesis that purchasers created dependence by asking which party to the contract had written the specification. Only 11 per cent were written by the funders, while 155 were written by the service provider and the rest were developed jointly. While there had been some change in the nature of the services provided, these were caused by the changes in need or demand and not by the imposition of unwanted contracts: 'None of the results provided support for the hypothesis that contracting has led to significant interference in the nature of service provision through the medium of contracting... the survey suggests that fears of widespread mission distortion have not been fulfilled' (1995: 7).

It could be argued that this is not a perfect test of the effect of dependency on the services provided by the voluntary sector. Once the process gets to specification-writing stage, the puchasers have already decided roughly what sort of services they wish to purchase. The other aspect of distortion could be that organisations which contract to provide services are unwilling or unable to engage in other aspects of their work, either lobbying and campaigning or individual advocacy work. Richardson, again, found no evidence that charities were discouraged from engaging in these activities: 'There was no evidence to support the hypothesis of greater restrictions being imposed on campaigning organisations' (1995: 8).

In a study of innovation in voluntary organisations, Osborne (1994) found that organisations which were mainly funded by public money were no less likely to be innovative: '74% of those organisations which received the major part of their income from central or local government had developed innovations; only 39% of those organisations who relied upon voluntary contributions or fees had developed innovations' (1994: 2). Osborne also found that innovation was more likely in organisations with paid staff than in volunteer-based ones. Richardson (1995) found similar results in relation to innovation. 'While this evidence cannot be said to be conclusive, it is indicative that contracting has not led to a significant deterioration of the role of volunteers' (1995: 11).

Richardson found some evidence, however, of the squeezing out of organisations which dealt with 'unpopular causes' (1995: 13). There may be a financial reason for the exclusion of less than mainstream voluntary organisations, which is that the transaction costs for the purchasers are higher, the smaller the contracts which have to be negotiated and monitored. It is both cheaper to negotiate large contracts and apparently less risky to manage the process of service delivery through contracts with large, established, national bodies (Russell, Scott and Wilding 1995). It is this distortion, of the sector as a whole rather than of individual organisations participating in contracting, which will be the main impact of contracting. Purchasers have limited management resources to invest in the contracting process. Work with small local organisations takes more time than signing a few large contracts with large organsations. In any case, dealing with an organisation which has an infrastructure of professionals and advice is more comfortable and less time consuming than dealing with volunteers in local organisations.

It would seem at first sight that income growth from contracts would represent an improvement in the financial health of the voluntary sector. There are several reasons why this might not be the case. We found, in a series of seminars during 1994, that competitive tendering sometimes results in unrealistic bidding. This phenomenon is not confined to the voluntary sector: the competitive process leads people to want to win contracts, even if they are uncertain that they will be able to deliver within the bid price. This can lead the providers to try to renegotiate the contract or to cut costs to such an extent that quality suffers. In subsequent rounds of competition, people are more realistic about their costs, but it does mean that new entrants also have to go through the learning process.

Another of the financial pitfalls of contracting is that the flow of service users may be unstable. If people are contracting on the basis of cost per case they have to make some assumptions about future workload. While this may be a predictable flow of funds, the incidence of need or the priorities of purchasers may change. Richardson (1995) found that charities have been urged to change their services not because of the preferences of the purchasers but because of changes in demand.

There can also be a reliance on referrals. Even if there is a contract with a statutory purchaser, decision-making about what services are used is done by the person making the assessment in conjunction with the service user. It is possible that services will remain unused, even if there is a contract. In some cases, the contract depends on referrals to the service from a third party. This simply adds to the uncertainty of workload.

Another financial aspect concerns fixed costs. The standard way of covering fixed costs is to add a percentage to the direct costs of providing a service. This additional amount is supposed to cover such things as head-office costs, administration and management. In practice, fixed costs are 'lumpy'. As organisations grow, they add staff to carry out functions previously done as part of someone else's job. As individuals and sections are added, they are unlikely to be covered by the additional contract percentage in the short term. In addition, there are cases in which the additional administrative cost simply did not cover the administration of the contract: many invoicing, monitoring and checking mechanisms require a large amount of administrative effort which may not have been anticipated at the contract negotiation stage. Russell, Scott and Wilding found one example of a contract with a voluntary organisation in which the purchaser refused to cover any management costs (Russell, Scott and Wilding 1995: 40).

Cashflow can itself add a financial burden to an independent provider of services. Sometimes payments are delayed for mechanical reasons, such as accounting systems not working. In other cases, payments are temporarily withheld for the purchasers' cashflow reasons. There have been cases of independent suppliers of community care services having to resort to the courts to ensure payment.

Last, so far as finance is concerned, short-term contracts create an unstable career pattern for employees. The uncertainty generated by the constant need to renegotiate makes it difficult for the voluntary organisations to develop their staff and to retain them. There is a conflict between buyers' desire for flexibility and providers' need for stability. Guaranteed long-term contracts create an environment in which staff can be offered development opportunities, while locking purchasers into particular services.

The other impact of contracting is that organisations become opportunistic, in the sense that they will make a short-term decision to bid for a contract because it appears to be an opportunity to generate revenue. It is possible for organisations to accrue a series of contracts which in a relatively short period can skew the portfolio of activities away from the original intentions of the founders or trustees. If they are very opportunistic, there is little possibility of any strategic thinking or planning. Russell *et al.*'s survey (1995: 37) showed that this was the case in their sample:

> None of the sample appear to have defined a strategic view of their future role in response to this changing environment. The question of whether the organisation had a development plan elicited a negative response in all but one case. Given the voluntary sector's history of having to work from year to year, this is perhaps hardly surprising.

Richardson (1995) found that even where there were long-term contracts, they contained 'break' clauses which allowed the purchaser to withdraw from the contract at any time during the period, with notice.

These, then, are, or may be, some of the negative consequences of contracting. There are, of course, various arguments in favour of contracting, from the point of view of the voluntary sector. The first is that multiple sources of funding offer protection; if there are contracts with many purchasers, dependency is reduced. For this to be true, it would require the voluntary organisation to balance the loss of income in one area with a gain in income in others. This is not always the case. Some national charities are, in effect, federations of local branches, which may or may not pay a levy to the central organisation. In these circumstances, the fact that the organisation as a whole has a range of purchasers across the country is of no interest to the branch which has just lost its contract. However, some charities have a monopoly, especially locally, in the provision of very specialist care. In these cases, purchasers and providers are mutually dependent and are forced to find collaborative ways of working.

If there is to be a long-term partnership between the statutory and the voluntary sectors in community care, various aspects of the relationships need attention. We have seen that the evidence from the various surveys mentioned above is generally positive on the questions of innovation, the retention of the capacity to lobby, the ability of voluntary organisations to maintain their independence. However, both sides of the partnership need to pay attention to the following issues.

There needs to be a balance between the flexibility required for purchasers and individual service users and the stability of funding required by the providers. Contracts which combine a cost per case approach with underwriting of a certain level of volume would represent a sharing of the risk of low volumes between the purchasers and the providers.

Another source of risk is that of a service innovation being unsuccessful or unpopular with purchasers. New services take time to establish and build up a volume of service users. Almost by definition, if they are genuinely innovative, there is a risk that they will not be what is required. The issue is who accepts that risk. The NCVO/Association of Directors of Social Services' joint policy statement (1995) recognises this problem: 'if VOs [voluntary organisations] are to develop new services then they may seek some specific assurances about contractual opportunities so as, for example, to provide them with the necessary confidence to make capital investments' (para. 14 (f)).

The pursuit of contracts can also make an impact on the structure of voluntary organisations: centralisation of specification writing and contract negotiation can take away the autonomy of local branches or groups. This can be avoided if the head office acts as a supporter for the local branches rather than a controller. However, there are cases where the organisation as a whole is standardising the services it offers as part of the process of professionalisation which it sees as a necessary prerequisite of entering contracts.

One of the issues we identified in our study of contracting (Flynn and Hurley 1993) was the inherent contradiction between the purchasers' desire for flexibility and the providers' need for stability. This problem remains and the increase in stability in the providers can be achieved only by longer-term contracts.

There are still problems in calculating the costs of providing services, especially in the allocation of shared costs and estimating administrative costs, as the volume of contracting grows. While some contracts explicitly exclude management costs, it is still important to know what these costs are, because they have to be covered from some source of revenue or other.

A key question is what to do with the voluntary income that a charity raises, when contracting with local and health authorities. 'Top-up payments' in residential care, or not receiving the full cost of care as part of the contract, could be seen as a substitution for services which really should be provided by statutory funding or could be seen as supplementation of state funding, which is a legitimate role for a charity. Tendering on quality may allow the voluntary sector to be the benchmark on quality which will set the standard for the private sector and show the purchasers how it can be done. However, if this is only possible through subsidy from voluntary income, what does it mean? A benchmark of services at a price which the purchasers cannot afford is not a usable standard.

There is no doubt that contracting costs time and money for both sides of the bargain. There seem to be administrative economies of scale, where organisations with a basic infrastructure find it easier to contract than smaller ones. This poses a continuing danger to small organisations. The only solution is to recognise and compensate the costs of contracting. The economies of scale of the contracting process may lead to the continuing growth of the large voluntary organisations, as we have seen already. This may occur simply through the continuing growth of contracting or it may occur through a voluntary sector version of mergers and 'acquisitions', as smaller organisations are displaced and their larger counterparts attract their volunteers as well as the contracts which they would potentially have won.

Dealing with these remaining issues points to the development of more relational or obligational contracting processes: longer-term contracts; contracts which share risk; and contracts in which purchasers recognise the cost and other difficulties which providers face when entering the contracting process.

Some of the difficulties which were anticipated both by charities and commentators have been less severe than expected. The explanation for this may be that the compulsion imposed on local authorities to spend Special Transitional Grant funds with the non-statutory sector placed the providers of services at an advantage over the purchasers, and in those authorities in which the elected members preferred to deal with the voluntary sector, placed charities at an advantage over the private sector. However, it would be prudent for the voluntary agencies to continue to be wary about the dangers predicted, of distortion and loss of independence in particular. Such prudence requires the development of a sufficiently robust strategy of development to enable managers to take the opportunities offered by contracts without unforeseen or undesirable consequences for the services offered and values represented by the service-providing organisations.

REFERENCES

Bernstein, S. R. (1991) *Managing Contracted Services in the Non-Profit Agency*, Philadelphia: Temple University Press.

Common, R. and Flynn, N. (1992) *Contracting for Care*, York: Joseph Rowntree Foundation/*Community Care*.

Dimensions of the Voluntary Sector (1995) ed. S. Saxon-Harrold and J. Kendall, London: Charities Aid Foundation.

Flynn, N. and Hurley, D. (1993) *The Market for Care*, London: London School of Economics.

Gutch, R. (1992) *Contracting: Lessons from the USA*, London: National Council for Voluntary Organisations.

Henderson's Top 2000 Charities (1995), London: Hemington Scott Publishing.

Kettner, P. M. and Martin, L. L. (1987) *Purchase of Service Contracting*, London: Sage.

Mocroft, I. (1995) 'A survey of local authority payments to voluntary and charitable organisations 1992/3', in *Dimensions of the Voluntary Sector*, ed. S. Saxon-Harrold and J. Kendall, London: Charities Aid Foundation.

National Council for Voluntary Organisations (1991) *Contracting In or Out?*, London: NCVO.

National Council for Voluntary Organisations and Association of Directors of Social Services (1995) *Community Care and Voluntary Organisations: Joint Policy Statement*, London: NCVO.

Osborne, S. P. (1994) *The Once and Future Pioneers?*, Birmingham: Aston Business School.

Richardson, J. (1995) *Purchase of Service Contracting: Some Evidence on UK Implementation*, London: National Council for Voluntary Organisations.

Russell, L., Scott, D. and Wilding, P. (1995) *Mixed Fortunes: The Funding of the Local Voluntary Sector*, Manchester: University of Manchester Press.

Smith, S. R. and Lipskey, M. (1993) *Non-Profits for Hire: The Welfare State in the Age of Contracting*, Cambridge, Mass.: Harvard University Press.

Chapter 5

From those who know
The role of service users

Clare Evans

Voluntary organisations have a tradition of providing more flex-ible and responsive services for their users than statutory organis-ations, and of having an advocacy role in campaigning on behalf of users and their needs. However, the rise of the consumerist ethos and the growth of the disability and user movements have challenged these traditional assumptions and voluntary organis-ations need to change and adapt if they are to continue to form strong alliances with service users. At the same time the develop-ment of user-controlled organisations shows they have a com-plementary part to play in the diverse voluntary sector. With appropriate support and resources they can become a significant force in bringing about change, addressing the power imbalance between service users and service providers and purchasers, and in developing innovative examples of good practice in service delivery.

Much has been written particularly by non-users, seeking to define the term 'service user' and related issues of representation. Indeed, at times, such diversions appear to the more cynical of us as a welcome distraction from the real challenges of hearing and responding to the views of service users. For the purposes of this chapter the term 'service user' will be used broadly to describe those people who need to use services over a long period of time and are dependent on services for their life chances. Those speaking from this perspective, however, may at any one time not be in receipt of services – it includes those, for example, who may be recovering from emotional distress or alcoholism, and disabled people with physical impairments who may currently live in the community without receiving services.

The emphasis in the National Health Service and Community

Care Act 1990 on developing needs-led services presents a challenge to purchasers and providers working in a system which has grown up piecemeal without the overall planning of services based on an assessment of people's needs. As social services and health authorities become more focused in their purchasing, the traditional pattern of annual renewal of grant aid to long-standing voluntary organisations has died away and voluntary organisations must produce new funding proposals for providing services, based on evidence of need and on the continuing expectation by funders of user involvement in providing feedback about the service. The results of early research suggested voluntary organisations seemed 'to be responding to the challenge and were ahead of statutory services in involving their users' (Beresford and Harding 1990). However, the picture is not uniform, and just as voluntary organisations have diverse philosophies so their performance on user involvement appears very varied.

Service users perceive voluntary organisations by their function in relation to themselves individually or collectively. The function of the voluntary organisation also defines the kind of role service users play in relation to it. Voluntary organisations' functions for service users can be categorised under the following broad headings.

Service delivery organisations: in this broad category there is a wide range from large national service providers to small local organisations such as a small day centre. As from other service providers, service users individually seek flexibility, quality of service, and choice and control from the voluntary sector service provider. Through the care-management process, for example, we can expect to be given information about a range of service providers to enable us to choose the one which best meets our assessed needs. A chance for other opportunities to experience user empowerment is also important to many users. Users' expectations from a 'good' voluntary sector service provider are that there should be:

• straightforward accessible and jargon-free information, widely distributed, about the service – for example, the geographical area covered, the charging policy, the reliability of service including crisis cover and a clear contact point. This empowers

us to make a choice about service based on clarity and showing diversity between services
- evidence of the centrality of users' views in defining 'quality issues' and of the mechanisms the organisation has for evaluating its service; developing a variety of feedback loops for service-user views can ensure that the service is continually developing and responding to user need and is therefore much more likely to be individually empowering in the way it is delivered
- personnel involved in the organisation, whether as volunteers or as paid workers, who recognise user expertise and relate to us in an empowering way, enabling us to achieve the goals we seek. Unfortunately, for too long some voluntary organisations' personnel like some statutory services have been characterised by paternalistic and patronising attitudes and assumptions about what users need instead of recognising service users' knowledge about how to have our needs met. Perceiving users as the customers and the focus for the style of service delivered can present a significant challenge for both large service deliverers with strong bureaucratic structures and small local organisations where the organisation may be delivering services based on out-of-date assumptions. Training, particularly involving users in the training process, offers the most hopeful way of responding to the challenge and it is important voluntary organisations budget for, and funders recognise the need for, ongoing training. The systematic involvement of service users as equal participants with professionals in all care-management training in Wiltshire was found by managers 'to affect significantly the way professionals perceived their role in relation to users' needs' (Evans and Hughes 1993: 23)
- a commitment to involve users structurally within the organisation to maximise their expertise, to enable them to support each other to give their views and play a representative role.

While funders may have crude tools to encourage user involvement such as a requirement in service agreements to show evidence of how users are involved in the management and planning of the service, it is to local development agencies in conjunction with trainers from user organisations that voluntary organisations can look for the opportunity of developing this aspect of their organisation. Thus, for example, the Kennet Rural Development

Agency in conjunction with the Wiltshire Users' Network brought workers, committee members and users of small voluntary organisations in a rural area together to share their experiences and develop new ways of involving users. A particularly useful focus for these workshops was users' views in relation to quality. Those present were able to identify a variety of ways of collecting users' views including, for example, the valuable role of volunteers in encouraging users' views. The recognition of the value of the opportunities for collecting users' views as the service was delivered enabled the voluntary organisations to realise the need to collect systematically those views and feel more confident they could justify their organisation to funders. The informal comments of users in transit as they are given lifts to hospital as part of a local community transport scheme can, for example, give a fuller picture of the service in relation to quality than a standard questionnaire designed without the involvement of users. As the culture of voluntary organisations slowly changes so that users' views are valued as central to the organisation, service users will feel more confident to participate in the wider aspects of the organisation.

Such participation requires sensitive support and encouragement from staff and volunteers. Service users' full participation on a voluntary organisation management committee, for example, requires not just the commitment to ensure two committee places are kept for the purpose but the development of various support systems and perhaps a change of style in committee procedures: inaccessible jargon dropped by other committee members; the payment of users' costs to attend; committee papers presented in a medium accessible to users (such as on audio tape for visually impaired users); and opportunities created for the users on the committee to relate back to the wider constituency of users. A day centre, for example, may set aside part of a session prior to the committee for centre users to come together to give their views on centre policy in relation to the agenda of the forthcoming committee meeting, for the user representatives to take forward.

Voluntary organisation staff and volunteers sometimes fail to recognise the important role they can play in supporting users of their service to participate in wider opportunities for involvement in the planning of community care. Often publicity about such opportunities remains firmly on the workers' desk so that they act as gatekeepers for information. In contrast, those workers who understand the importance of supporting individual users to give their views have shown how users' confidence and active participation can be encouraged by their interest and by practical support, such as help in arranging transport and provision of enablers as well as the passing-on of information.

Development agencies: these can be both geographically specific (e.g. councils for voluntary service) and specialist (e.g. Age Concern and the Pre-School Learning Alliance). Such agencies can enable the empowerment of service users in two ways. First, they can encourage voluntary sector providers to become more user-led in ways similar to that described above. A large co-ordinating organisation for older people, for example, with several hundred small day centres on its circulation list can help to change the culture of these small organisations by providing them with information about the new consumer ethos, opportunities for training and community development support.

Second, such agencies encourage the development of self-help and user groups. Most service users come from a position of isolation and disempowerment within their communities and have difficulty in getting their views heard. The contribution gained from meeting together and sharing experiences in a small group changes people's lives by acting as the first step leading to a fuller participation in service development. 'I've never felt safe to say things before' and 'I thought I was the only one who felt like that' are the comments users make as they experience for the first time the empowering effects of sharing experiences with others in a similar situation.

At times such small self-help groups of vulnerable people, who may seek confidentiality to combat society's prejudices against them – for example, recovering alcoholics or those who have experienced sexual abuse – feel unsupported by local development agencies. They can easily become invisible as larger, more structured voluntary organisations become prominent, and are easily left off mailing lists for information about opportunities to give their views or to gain funding.

Community voluntary organisations: these organisations are seeking to play a campaigning and advocacy role on behalf of service users but are not made up of service users. Such organisations are often set up by volunteers or carers with a particular interest in a specific care group or condition and can play an effective part in putting pressure on purchasers to meet an identified need.

However, these advocacy and campaigning organisations can create tensions with user groups as such organisations appear to speak on users' behalf and make assumptions about their needs. This tension can be increased by users' perceptions that statutory agencies choose to resource, and be more influenced by, such groups than user groups themselves. Certainly it has been important in Wiltshire to clarify and establish with health and social services that while voluntary organisations have a legitimate role to play in representing community views and campaigning about issues of concern, they do not directly represent the views of users in contrast to user-controlled organisations. Consultation on the community care plan in January 1991 after the legislation required social services departments to consult with 'organisations representative of users and carers' consisted of a day conference at an inaccessible venue attended by voluntary-sector workers and volunteers. Five years later there is far more understanding of the diversity of the voluntary sector and the need to give priority to hearing the direct voice of users in addition to traditional representation from the voluntary sector.

Self-help and user groups: the importance of these for service users has already been described above. Sadly, professionals in both the statutory and voluntary sector often fail to recognise the importance of informing users about self-help groups at the appropriate time – for example, at the point of diagnosis. Too often users speak of being lost, isolated without knowing what the future holds, and deprived of information about learning to live with a condition. It is not surprising that eventual introduction to a self-help group can significantly change the way users perceive themselves and their situation. Jenny Morris says that social services as planners and purchasers value self-help groups which place a high value on personal experience and create a sense of unity and self-identity among service users (Morris 1994). Such groups, too, are cost effective for funders. Very small grants to cover, for example, the costs of meetings and publicity enable groups to grow strong. These groups can be open to negotiation to give them views on services and thus put their user expertise at the disposal of those planning services.

It was the isolation experienced by a service user who, as a volunteer, attended the community care plan conference described above which led eventually, in November 1991, to the formation of the Wiltshire Community Care User Involvement Network. The voluntary-sector local development agencies were active at this early stage in enabling users and voluntary sector allies to come together in their first meeting in line with the community development principle of encouraging and enabling people to organise and take action for themselves. As time went on, however, and the Network was perceived as taking power and resources from other parts of the voluntary sector, tensions developed and some service users sought to dissociate from the voluntary sector while others counted it as their natural home. Certainly, as a user organisation fighting for the first time to get our voice heard, it was not easy, as we became empowered, to recognise the possible feelings of powerlessness in the voluntary sector as statutory agencies presented the challenges of the new contract culture, and the pressures for change led some voluntary sector workers to become threatened and defensive about user participation. Paul Reading (1994) shows how easily there can be conflict and difficulties even where there are shared goals between voluntary sector workers and users for increased user participation.

As the Network grew it became clear that to develop an effective model of an organisation which users controlled required a combination of a traditional community-development approach, with a new style of relationship with funders, a new legal model of organisation and a distinctive role in the voluntary sector.

It was important to follow a community-development approach of building on the strength of local groups of users and enabling them to empower themselves to participate, while at the same time lobbying for opportunities for users to be involved in as many ways as possible in the planning, delivery and evaluating of services. There were few strongly established user groups or groups of disabled people to link with but it was important to recognise that the process of empowerment starts in small self-help groups and other places where users gather to share their views. The confidence gained from this experience enabled them to participate in more focused user involvement opportunities such as staff training, care-management development workshops,

and developing detailed policy proposals such as those for
Wiltshire Independent Living Fund.

From the start, the Network was managed by a committee of
sixteen people of whom 75 per cent were service users. The other
25 per cent of places were reserved for allies as part of our
commitment to joint working. As such, the Network follows in
general the model of a 'supportive organisation' described in Judi
Chamberlin's typology (Chamberlin 1988) while on occasion
adopting a separatist model with the right to hold some events
for users only. We decided not to become a registered charity
partly because we thought it might inhibit our role as a campaigning organisation and partly because the rules about beneficiaries
from charities not being permitted to be trustees conflicted with
our vision of the Network owned and managed by service users.
In order to demonstrate that user expertise was valued, we were
committed to payment to service users for their participation and
it was inequitable that the users taking responsibility for managing the organisation should not have their expertise recognised.
Instead we chose to register as a not-for-profit company limited
by guarantee which gives the management committee the legal
status of company directors.

Eighteen months after our formation, having had small
amounts of funding for users' meeting costs and administration,
we negotiated a service agreement with the social services department funded from community care infrastructure funding. The
purpose of the agreement for £55,000 was twofold – to provide a
network of support to service users; and to facilitate direct links
between users and the department. Maintaining independence in
providing a service which challenges funders, in the same way as
individual advocacy support, is sometimes perceived as a difficulty
by those outside the organisation. However, the nature of the
funding relationship is somewhat different from that of other
voluntary sector organisations. Unlike other organisations, we
requested that the service agreement should be legally binding so
that funding was not threatened by knee-jerk reactions to challenges we made. We also wrote our initial service specification
based on our understanding of the activities we could provide for
our funding. In addition, there was an understanding between
funders and the Network that the model of an independent user-
controlled organisation negotiating user involvement and setting
in some measure its own agenda was an effective way to develop

user involvement in community care and to avoid tokenism. Beyond this, confidence about our independence grew from the fragile relationships of trust and recognition of user expertise growing between the Network and senior managers in social services.

It is not only a new kind of funding relationship that user-controlled organisations develop with statutory organisations. Many user-controlled organisations have to grow quickly and can lack the infrastructure and experience of long-standing voluntary organisations with a tradition of paid managers. In this situation, therefore, they should be able to rely on statutory allies to provide appropriate support when requested. Thus, when we sought office premises to rent, we purchased the services of a member of the property services section of the county council to arrange site visits and negotiate a suitable lease after we, as users, had had complete control over the choice of premises. When we recognised the need for a better financial information system to manage our increased funding we secured the services of a consultant for small computer systems employed by the county council. Paying for these services maintains our independence but enables us to secure the most appropriate help.

Realistically funded user-controlled organisations can play an effective role as a specialist development agency enabling more marginalised users to become empowered to participate. In one area of Wiltshire, users in the Network joined with social services and health purchasers and providers to create an opportunity for mental health service users to come together to give their views. The users' workshops were facilitated by mental health user consultants. After gaining strength from meeting together on their own as users to share experiences and identify the key issues of service delivery for them, the service users are now ready to invite those they seek to influence to their forum to lobby for change.

In another area, a specific piece of development work to enable older people to have a voice was jointly planned with a local social services team, and a multiple-agency project established to develop an older people's care strategy. An older member of the Network worked with development workers to bring older people together to identify issues of concern. After eight months, it was possible to hold a meeting of these older people and others together with service providers to hold them to account to answer the queries they raised. The older people present were enthusiastic to meet again with the providers six months later to see what progress had been made concerning their requests.

There are two major values in such a pattern of development work. The service users being contacted for the first time gain confidence from dealing with service users already able to speak out, and feel safe to give their views. Meetings which are independently facilitated also give service users the opportunity to set their own agenda by viewing their lives holistically. It was significant that the issue most commonly identified by the older people was the lack of a pedestrian crossing near the post office and a member of the highways department attended the meeting to take the matter forward.

As users become confident and recognise their expertise drawn from experience, they aspire to develop their own alternative pattern of service delivery. By this they seek to avoid the traditional pattern of service delivery where too often services are perceived as being delivered in a patronising way with professional expertise and decision-making taking precedence over user expertise and self-assessed needs. Users particularly recognise their expertise in delivering services in the areas of information, advocacy and support for independent living. Such aspirations to develop user-controlled service provision are part of an international pattern in both the psychiatric survivor movement and the disability movement.

It is important such provision is fully evaluated in users' terms so that the implications for good practice in mainstream provision can be identified. Peter Beresford identifies 'the development and testing of self-run and user-controlled alternatives to existing services as a basis for change in mainstream provision' as a priority focus in user-led research (Beresford 1994).

The philosophy of independent living with its emphasis on disabled people's rights to have control over their personal assistants through cash payments has led to some innovative support-service schemes being developed by disabled people's organisations. With legislation expected soon to enable local authorities to make cash payments to disabled people to buy their own care, social services departments will be looking for partnerships with disabled people's organisations to contract with them to provide peer support schemes to maximise the effectiveness of cash payments. Innovative and well-established schemes such as at the

Greenwich Association of Disabled People will form the models on which to build other schemes. A comparatively new support service to accompany Wiltshire Independent Living Fund has been used by 90 per cent of applicants to the fund and shows the popularity of systems based on peer support.

As part of the support service it was possible to establish a time-limited Living Options Partnership Project which sought to enable African-Caribbean and Asian disabled people to gain access to Wiltshire Independent Living Fund and other services. By using an outreach approach, contact was made with people in ethnic minorities isolated in rural areas who had not previously had contact with services. The perceived independence of the user-controlled organisation, where the project was based, gave these service users confidence to gain access to services for the first time.

'Information is power' is as meaningful for service users as for others in society. 'Word of mouth' and 'soft information' from other users is often identified by service users as the most effective means of obtaining information. Two disabled people in the Network with a particular commitment to this project made a successful funding application for a city centre information drop-in centre for service users of all kinds. Here the divisions between service recipients, volunteers and workers fade away as the atmosphere established at the centre empowers everyone to participate. Thus, for example, people with learning difficulties can improve their literacy skills enabled by a mental health service user.

Underlying the change in culture that voluntary organisations must make in order to empower their users, is the need for a change in attitude by voluntary organisation personnel, from the charity model of disability to the social model of disability. The charity model is deeply ingrained in some charity organisations both at national and local level and the images presented in their advertising materials, for example, can perpetuate attitudes where recipients of services are expected to be grateful and deserving. David Hevey sees the cultural task for disabled artists as one of 'shifting disability representation off from the body and into the interface between people with impairments and socially disabling conditions' (Hevey 1993). While collecting users' views as customers and changing services in line with views expressed is a move away from this, the more significant step of recognising the value of users' expertise and building it into all levels of the organisation requires more of a long-term change in the culture of the organisation. However, there are signs that where there is sufficient commitment at senior-management level it is possible to turn traditional organisations round to become user-led. Arthritis Care, for example, uses the criteria of 'experience of arthritis' as part of the essential person specification for some paid posts as well as encouraging active participation of people with arthritis on its management council and at local branch level (Gutch 1994).

A number of dilemmas remain for service users as they seek out a distinctive role in the voluntary sector. Michael Oliver explores the political dimension of these dilemmas for organisations of disabled people in the disability movement as they develop a relationship with the state (Oliver 1990).

For many groups of service users there is still not a level playing field on which to compete for funding to develop effective user involvement or alternative services. Evidence from Wales (Drake and Owens n.d.) shows that user-controlled voluntary organisations were far less likely to receive adequate resources than other voluntary organisations. User-controlled organisations are perceived by many local authorities as too risky for them to contract with for services. Yet where users have had the opportunity to be realistically resourced the expertise, energy and urgency they bring have enabled them to be effective in working for change in the services. Without adequate funding user-controlled organisations remain marginalised and reflect the marginalisation of their membership by society as a whole, perceived as deviants and only able to play the dependency role.

Meanwhile in the wider voluntary sector, users' views are increasingly sought as the consumerist ethos becomes part of the contract culture in which we must all operate. Voluntary organisations can no longer rely on users' unquestioning acceptance of their role as advocates and campaigners. Instead service users will judge them by their flexibility and responsiveness to user need in line with service providers in the private and statutory sectors. Moreover, the expertise of service users must be recognised, and opportunities to learn from it built into the voluntary organisation's culture and structure. The distinctive strengths of the voluntary sector such as innovation and flexibility and independence, however, make them potential allies as service users seek to establish their right as citizens to participate in society and as stakeholders in the planning and provision of services.

REFERENCES

Beresford, P. (1994) 'Commentary on future community care research', *Community Care Management and Planning* 2(2).

Beresford, P. and Harding, T. (1990) 'Involving service users', *NCVO News*, October.

Chamberlin, J. (1988) *On Our Own*, Mind.

Drake, R. F. and Owens, D. J. (no date) 'Consumer involvement and the voluntary sector in Wales: breakthrough or bandwagon?', *Critical Social Policy*.

Evans, C. and Hughes, M. (1993) *Tall Oaks from Little Acorns: The Wiltshire Experience of Involving Users in the Training of Professionals in Care Management*, Wiltshire Community Care User Involvement Network/Wiltshire Social Services Department.

Gutch, R. (1994) 'What are we managing?', *Voice*, June.

Hevey, D. (1993) *Disability Barriers – Enabling Environments*, ed. Swain, J., Finkelstein, V., French, S. and Oliver, M. Milton Keynes: Open University Press.

Morris, J. (1994) 'The shape of things to come? User-led social services', *Social Services Policy Forum*, Paper 3.

Oliver, M. (1990) *The Politics of Disablement*, London: Macmillan.

Reading, P. (1994) *Community Care and the Voluntary Sector*, Venture Press.

Chapter 6

Standing up to be counted
Campaigning and voluntary agencies

Francine Bates and Jill Pitkeathley

Few would deny that charities ought to be able to campaign on behalf of those they represent. They need to be able to lobby for changes in policy and practice which would benefit their client group. However, the publication, in 1994, of the *Political Activities and Campaigning by Charities* (which was modified and reissued in 1995) (Charity Commissioners for England and Wales 1995: 7) shows how sensitive an area this is. According to the guidelines, a charity can engage in political activity if:

- there is reasonable expectation that the activity concerned will further the stated purpose of the charity, and so benefit its beneficiaries, to an extent justified by the resources devoted to the activity;
- the activity is within the powers which the trustees have to achieve these purposes; ...
- the views expressed are based on a well-founded and reasoned case and are expressed in a responsible way.

The guidelines also state that 'whether a charity can properly engage in campaigning will therefore depend upon the nature of its purposes, its powers, and the way in which it contributes to public debate'.

Working as a campaigner and not overstepping the rules of political neutrality is difficult enough in itself. But there is more to being an effective campaigning organisation than simply not breaking a set of rules, helpful though these are, especially in making it clear that campaigning is acceptable in pursuit of one's aims.

Our experience leads us to believe that to be an effective lobby a charity needs four things: a constituency; a clear and simple message; respect; and some success.

You have to be clear about the group on whose behalf you are campaigning and you have to be seen to represent them. This does not, of course, mean that every one of them has to be a member of your organisation or to subscribe to its views – that would indeed be a tall order where there are nearly 7 million carers. Rather it means that you must be in touch with sufficient numbers and a sufficiently wide group to ensure that your role as a representative is credible. Carers National Association (CNA) does this through both its membership and its board of trustees, which is elected directly from the membership, so that any carer member can stand for election and become involved in the governance of the organisation. The importance of an active membership or local networks driving the policy and direction of an organisation is crucial to the success of any campaigning that a charity wishes to undertake. CNA has around 12,000 members. We keep our members informed by producing a lively magazine which they receive six times a year. We tell them about our latest campaigns and encourage them to get involved as much as they can within the constraints of their caring responsibilities. This can either be on an individual basis – by asking them, for example, to write to their MP – or by encouraging them to become involved locally. Many carers have told us how powerless they feel about their situation and this often gives rise to considerable anger. We try to harness that anger in a positive way by urging and helping them to express their feelings to those national and local politicians who make the decisions which affect their lives. There is no doubt that writing to one's MP is still an effective method of drawing attention to a problem. Most MPs are far more likely to respond favourably to a constituent rather than to what they may judge as a 'whingeing pressure group'. Often, individual members of CNA write to us asking us to take up a particular issue that they feel very strongly about and which may be affecting others. For example, a carer recently contacted us to see whether we would mount a campaign to amend the Road Traffic Act to allow carers to park in 'residents only' spaces when they visited relatives living in a sheltered-housing scheme or residential-care home.

We also have a large network of local branches and groups and are in touch through a specialist worker with hundreds of carers' workers – staff employed by the statutory or voluntary sector who have a specific remit to work with carers. Our five-days-a-week helpline service too keeps us informed about the problems which carers are facing. We place great importance on all of these means of keeping us up to date about the areas of concern to carers as well as those issues which distress particular groups of carers, such as those from minority ethnic backgrounds. It is also vital to realise that the organisation's constituency goes beyond the actual users of its campaigning service, and extends also to the other organisations working in the area or with the body. CNA, for example, convenes the Carers Alliance and works closely with all the organisations who are its members. We have also tried to build a positive relationship with disability organisations. This has not always been easy, given the inevitable tension that can sometimes arise between the needs of disabled people and the needs of carers. But we have joined forces together to highlight the blatant discrimination that many disabled people experience and support the Rights Now campaign, which attempted to introduce civil rights for disabled people through a series of private members' bills.

In 1994, as a result of an extremely effective campaign by this coalition, mostly of charitable organisations, the government was forced to introduce its own anti-discrimination legislation to end discrimination for disabled people. While the Disability Discrimination Act has many flaws, it does signify a major step forward for both disabled people and the charities who campaigned on their behalf.

The message of a campaign must be clear and simple, without being simplistic. In summary, CNA wants to make the lives of carers 'better', but that is not a sufficiently focused message for campaigning. The message must be more specific. One kind of campaign is centred around a specifically political objective: a change in legislation. Another starts from a broader base and is aimed more generally at policy-makers and service providers. One example of this is the campaign called 'A fair deal for carers', which aims, on the one hand, to make carers more aware about how community care can benefit them and, on the other hand, to make service providers more sensitive to the needs of carers. The campaign is backed by well-researched documents about the current situation of carers which have proved to be very attractive to the media and started the campaign off with a bang. Materials are then produced which are useful to local authorities and to carers and gives us opportunities, as the campaign progresses, to keep reinforcing the message.

CNA has taken policy decisions not to become involved in direct service provision because it has proved easier to keep the campaigning stance if we are not service providers. Many other charities do successfully combine the two roles, but we have found that our message is more easily understood if we keep the two roles quite separate. At times this has been a difficult message to get across to our branches and groups. For example, it is not always easy for a local group, anxious to improve things for carers in its area, to refuse money offered by a local authority to provide a respite care service. However, the message is now clearly understood and accepted throughout CNA. This is an issue which increasingly must concern charities as more of them go down the contracting route. How will they keep their cutting edge when their very survival may depend on not rocking the boat lest the contract goes to another agency?

No organisation can possibly succeed in campaigning unless it commands respect. Of course, it has to be respected by those for whom it campaigns. But it is equally important to be respected by those whose minds, hearts and wills you are trying to change. This means walking the difficult tightrope between being strong and being strident. Treading that tricky path between speaking with a confident voice and shouting so loudly that no one can or will listen to you is a skill which must be acquired. This balancing act is not only about being politically neutral, although that is hard enough. Politicians and the political machine hold traps for the unwary such as being invited to speak to a 'think tank' to put the carers' point of view only to realise it is seen as the voice of the Right and that speakers at group meetings are automatically given membership. The next day a politician of the Left, with whom you are sharing a platform, invites you to join him in condemning government social security policy.

However, gaining and achieving respect is about more than political neutrality. Arguments must be well researched; they must be put strongly and with passion, but also with logic and fact. There must be allies who will back you and argue the same case and you must avoid, however great the temptation, public disagreement with charities which have similar aims to your own. Any public falling-out only gives those you are trying to influence the opportunity to point out that you are not to be taken seriously.

While doing all this, often at the cost of great personal frustration, you have also to be able to resist those in your own charity who will be urging more radical action and cannot always understand that change does not usually happen simply as a result of making a lot of noise. A member of CNA once suggested that the only way we were going to achieve an increase in the Invalid Care Allowance (ICA) was for all the staff to barricade themselves in the office of the Secretary of State for Social Security and refuse to emerge until he had increased ICA up to £100 per week!

We have spent literally years building up good relationships and though we have the advice and help of an honorary consultant, who used to work for a lobbying company, we have preferred to employ a full-time member of staff rather than employ an agency. We have always found it more helpful to be positive about any concession which is made, however small and however late. Ministers sometimes have a hard time too, and like all of us, prefer to be recognised rather than reviled when they make a change which benefits the group campaigned for. Also, ministers move departments and it is wise not to breathe a sigh of relief when the one who has given you a hard times goes to pastures new. He or she will very likely be back and you would do well to remember that as you write your letter of congratulations and say how much you hope he or she enjoys his or her new position.

Some see this view of how you achieve respect as sycophantic. Some organisations achieve their objectives in a short time and by simply building a voice so strong it cannot be denied. But most charities which have campaigning as their aim have to keep a velvet glove over that iron fist, and make it clear that the power of the fist is there without necessarily brandishing it.

Those who support the aims of a campaigning charity, with their time, money and commitment, need some reward for their efforts. They need to feel they have achieved something and that their voice has been heard. Victories are necessary and if they can't be large ones, at least they should occur at regular intervals. Moreover, those who are funding the work, be they donors or sponsors, will need to see some 'return' in the form of objectives achieved.

Success is often measured by column inches, so ensure that you target the media. You must have news stories, feature stories and, above all, people. In our case, these are carers who are willing to speak to the media to offer the human interest angle.

You have to divide up your objectives into packages and, within those packages, into goals which are achievable. You may not be able to achieve them all. Some may have to await a change of government, a shift in national thinking, a win on the National Lottery. But there will be some which can be reached, given a following wind and perhaps some negotiation and compromise. This will depend in part on timing. There may be a tide in the affairs of men which leads on to victory, but there is certainly one in the affairs of a charity which has to be taken at the flood. Opportunities may occur in a particular set of circumstances which will not happen again and which offer a chance to bring about change. Campaigning agencies need to grab their opportunities. When they occur, you must be ready for them and have your campaign ready to go. The opportunity may present itself in the form of an unexpected amount of money; a rare conjunction of people and policies; a shift in public opinion; or a sympathetic voice where you usually meet opposition. Whatever the opportunity, you have to seize it and push your agenda. In rare cases, all four of the above happen together. Such was the position of CNA in November 1994.

The organisation has always taken the view that lobbying to change, influence or promote legislation is an essential part of its campaigning work. This is predicated on our core belief that carers, like other groups in society, should be entitled to certain legal rights which ensure their role is both recognised and supported. In November 1994, we grasped an opportunity to give carers greater entitlements within the framework of community care legislation by drafting and promoting a bill for the Private Members Ballot. The rationale behind the bill was based on our early policy and campaigning work at the time of the Griffiths report in 1988 (Griffiths 1988) and the introduction the following year of the National Health Service and Community Care Bill. As that bill progressed through Parliament we argued strongly that carers as well as users of 'community care services' should also have a right for their needs to be assessed by social services authorities. During this process, the association was successful in raising public and political awareness about the needs of carers but we were unable to convince the government to support our

amendment to give carers the right to an assessment. Nevertheless, from that year the foundations were laid, enabling us to
pursue this objective as our major political goal. The National
Health Service and Community Care Act was implemented in
April 1993. We monitored its impact on carers from the beginning. This resulted in our publishing a hard-hitting research
report, *Community Care: Just A Fairy Tale?* (Warner 1994) which
revealed that 80 per cent of carers felt that the introduction of
community care had made no difference to their lives. The report
provided us with major evidence that the much-trumpeted
reforms, far from benefiting carers, were actually making matters
worse. The research also showed that the vast majority of carers
wanted a separate right to an assessment and believed that respite
care should be a legal right.

Having waited patiently to see whether community care would
live up to its expectations and provide the recognition and practical support to carers which they had been promised in numerous
documents and ministerial speeches, it was blindingly obvious
that this was most likely to be achieved by drafting our own
legislation. We had already begun to consider how this could be
done as early as the autumn of 1993 by engaging the minds of a
number of lawyers who were interested in this growing area of
law.

The Carers (Recognition and Services) Bill began life as a
simple two-clause bill placing a duty on local authorities both to
carry out an assessment of carers and to provide services to them.
We sought to raise awareness about the Bill (despite the fact it
only amounted to no more than a sheet of A4 paper at this stage)
in all our work. In September 1994, we secured a commitment
from the Labour Party to introduce the provisions of the Bill in
its policy document, *Making Carers Count* (Labour Party 1994).

In October 1994, the NatWest Group's community relations
division, sufficiently enthused by our determination to amend the
law, agreed to help us fund the campaign for the Bill which we
called 'Give carers a break'. NatWest had supported CNA in the
past by establishing a NatWest Branch Fund to help develop
our growing network of branches. Our existing relationship with
NatWest, coupled with its awareness of its own employees
with caring responsibilities, led it to support the campaign for the
Bill as part of a wider programme aimed at empowering carers.

Funding from NatWest immediately enabled us to produce a

well-designed and persuasive leaflet which we sent to virtually all MPs, urging them to put their name forward for the ballot and to take up our Bill if they were successful. NatWest Group's vision and foresight in supporting our objective at such an early stage not only proved invaluable as the campaign progressed but was crucial to its ultimate success. NatWest's support is particularly important given the general reluctance of the corporate sector to finance charities to carry out work of this nature.

The Bill was taken up by the then backbench Labour MP, Malcolm Wicks, who came tenth in the ballot for private members' bills. This was a stroke of good fortune on our part. He is a well-known social policy expert with a particular interest in carers and community care. Before becoming an MP in 1992, he was director of the Family Policy Studies Centre. While working there, Malcolm Wicks was responsible for calculating the provoking statistic that the nation's carers saved the government somewhere between £15 billion to £24 billion per year. (This amount is now estimated to be between £30 billion and £40 billion per year (Institute of Actuaries 1993).)

Malcolm Wicks' genuine commitment to getting the Bill on the statute book was matched only by that of John Bowis, parliamentary under-secretary of state for health. It was clear from our meetings with the minister that he was moved by the plight of carers, especially young carers, and had a personal interest in ensuring that the Bill progressed. Indeed the Bill would not have succeeded without government backing including that from the leader of the House, Tony Newton, always an ally and a friend to the association. It was he who made sure that the Bill did not get bogged down in parliamentary procedure. Thus, we witnessed the relatively rare spectacle of a Bill which placed increased responsibilities on local authorities and created rights for a large section of the community, introduced by a Labour MP, co-sponsored by members of all political parties, including Plaid Cymru and a member of the Ulster Unionist Party, securing the active support of the Conservative government.

But we did not rely only on the goodwill of the politicians concerned. Two other factors assisted us: the growing public awareness of the problems in relation to community care; and the enormous sympathy, often arising from direct personal experience, that the plight of carers can generate. As part of our strategy, the association launched a high-profile campaign aimed at carers, the government, MPs and media. We actively encouraged carers to write to their MPs and to the then secretary of state for health, Virginia Bottomley. We did this by producing and heavily promoting a campaign resource pack aimed at carers, carers' groups and professionals working with carers. The pack consisted of a leaflet about the campaign; a briefing on the Bill (which we updated as the Bill progressed); an action sheet explaining how to write to an MP and what to say; a standard press release for issue by local groups; and brightly coloured adhesive lapel badges with our campaign slogan, 'Give Carers a Break'. We sent out over 4,000 packs in a few weeks, which resulted in MPs and the Department of Health being inundated with letters of support for the Bill.

Carers were also involved directly in the parliamentary campaign by arranging a tea party, sponsored by the NatWest Group, in the Members' Dining Room of the House of Commons, just a few days before the Second Reading of the Bill. The object was to enable carers to meet MPs over a cup of tea and a bun, talk to them about their experiences and tell them why the Bill was so vital. Carers came from as far away as Scotland, North Wales and Northern Ireland in order to lobby their MPs. Thanks to NatWest, we were able to pay travel expenses and, most crucially, the costs of providing alternative care for the person that they usually looked after. Over 200 carers attended the tea party, all of whom wore their badges, and clutched their briefings on the Bill as they trooped through central lobby. There is no doubt that this well-timed event affected the MPs who attended, including the Health Secretary who was the person largely responsible for deciding whether or not the government would allow the Bill to progress through its Second Reading.

Later, as the Bill approached its committee stage, the association arranged for a small group of young carers to come to Parliament to ensure that their needs were also included within the scope of the Bill. They met with Malcolm Wicks and John Bowis over lunch. Once again, the impact of meeting these young people, some of whom were undertaking considerable caring responsibilities, appeared to have a profound impact, particularly on the minister, who subsequently announced at committee stage that the Bill would include carers under the age of 18.

Over the course of six months, from December 1994 until June 1995, we secured maximum coverage in the national, regional and local press and media for the Bill. The press interest in carers and community care had never been higher. The Bill was introduced at a time when community care as a policy was failing in many areas. A number of local authorities had run out of money; several were being judicially reviewed because they had either withdrawn or reduced services to elderly and disabled people; and many users and carers were actively protesting that they were being means-tested to pay for services and residential care. There was no shortage of angry people willing to speak to the press about their particular stories.

However, there is no doubt that the problems carers face are enormous and many people including members of the government, civil servants and newspaper editors are deeply concerned by the social and economic implications of neglecting 7 million carers. They, too, for example, may have personal experience of the difficulties of coping with an elderly parent with Alzheimer's disease or have a child with Down's syndrome. And if they haven't – they know someone who has. It was only because we recognised these unique factors and sought to capitalise on the opportunities that presented themselves to us, that the Carers (Recognition and Services) Bill received Royal Assent on 28 June 1995 and came into force on 1 April 1996.

The Carers (Recognition and Services) Act will not change the world for carers. But it is a significant and important step. It was significant for CNA, too. It confirmed our role as an effective voice for carers, increased our public profile immeasurably and gave the staff and members of the association a great feeling of success and of achieving together the seemingly impossible. It is a great feeling to have won a battle, even though the war is not over. This success gives us all the commitment and the determination to fight on.

The voluntary sector must beware of becoming too like the corporate sector. True, we have much to learn from business and we must operate in a businesslike way. But those who work in charities are motivated by commitment to a cause in addition to their managerial objectives. Campaigning charities must never forget that.

Campaigning is an absolutely vital part of the work of the charity sector. It is where, in a sense, charity began in this country. Dedicated and passionate people saw a social injustice, often from their own experience, and set about doing more than just alleviating the problem by opening a school or feeding the poor. They turned a private trouble into a public issue to bring about changes in the law and in public opinion.

It would be all too easy at the present time for charities to concentrate on service provision and forget about their campaigning role. Certainly, the development of the contract culture means that an increasing number of charities are dependent for their very existence on providing services to the exact specification set out by the commissioning agency. It is not surprising, then, that much of the charitable sector may be in danger of embracing too wholeheartedly the language of the business world. We are all busy devising our mission statements and business plans, and concentrating on our outcomes and our throughput. But we do ourselves a disservice if we embrace too thoroughly the philosophy, as well as the language, of the commercial sector. While we may have a lot to learn from the corporate bodies, they have a lot to learn from us: about passion for an issue; commitment to a cause; but also about managing on a shoe-string, making imaginative use of limited funds; and, above all, about being tenacious and politically sophisticated when it comes to campaigning for a cause in which we believe.

REFERENCES

Charity Commissioners for England and Wales (1995) *Political Activities and Campaigning by Charities*, London: HMSO.

Griffiths, Sir Roy (1988) *Community Care: Agenda for Action*, London: HMSO.

Institute of Actuaries (1993) 'Financing long-term care in Great Britain', *Journal of the Institute of Actuaries* 121: 1–68.

Labour Party (1994) *Making Carers Count: A Labour Party Consultation Document*, London: The Labour Party.

Warner, Norman (1994) *Community Care: Just a Fairy Tale?*, London: Carers National Association.

Chapter 7

In trust
The changing role of trustees

Kate Kirkland

Voluntary organisations have, arguably, never had to operate in an environment as complex and volatile as that of today. The sector is having to adapt to the development of a mixed economy of social welfare provision, changing legislation and regulation, a massive restructuring of funding due to the impact of the National Lottery, and public pressure to become more businesslike. The organisations that survive will be those that learn to become masters, rather than victims, of change. Survivors will be those that respond competitively to change, such as the shift in funding from grants to contracts. They will view change as an opportunity, rather than an obstacle. Organisations that resist change, rather than welcome it, are likely to fail.

As organisations struggle to manage change and become more effective, the contribution made by boards of trustees to this process has inevitably come under the spotlight. It is becoming increasingly clear that, if organisations are to succeed, trustee boards cannot continue to operate as they have in the past. As Ken Dayton wrote: 'you cannot long have good management without good governance' (Dayton 1985: 1). Most boards work as they have always done, and they are so busy 'doing' that they do not take the time to assess their effectiveness. Those that have taken the time for a thorough self-examination – for example, Oxfam, Save the Children Fund and the Royal National Institute for Deaf People – have ended up making major changes to the role of their trustees, and to the size and structure of their boards.

Concern about the effectiveness of trustee boards dates back to 1990 when a committee chaired by Lord Nathan identified that trustees were becoming the weaker members of the leadership teams managing voluntary organisations, while staff were becoming increasingly professional (Nathan 1990). In 1992 research for the Charity Commission/National Council for Voluntary Organisations working party on trustee training found that two-thirds of trustees surveyed did not even realise that they were trustees (NCVO 1992a: 102). Yet calls for a new code of governance in the voluntary sector to improve public accountability, mirroring that conducted by Sir Adrian Cadbury into the standards of corporate governance (Cadbury 1992), were not taken seriously until October 1995, when NCVO's honorary treasurer, Chris Swinson, made the case for such an inquiry in his presentation at the Charity Commission's 'Definitive Guide to Charity Accounting' conference. If the public was to have confidence in charities, he argued, the sector should demonstrate its belief in the importance of high standards of governance and accountability for its actions.

In the last ten years there have been remarkable changes in the way public services are provided. The government's perception of the inadequacies of local authority provision, coupled with the belief that private sector practices would sharply improve performance, led to a rapid rise in the number of quangos, including NHS trusts, training and enterprise councils (TECs) and local enterprise councils (LECs). Housing provision has shifted from local authorities to housing associations, and many schools have opted out of local authority control. Many charities now contract with central and local government to provide a wide range of services.

With hindsight it is surprising that, at the time when so many quangos were being set up, there was no common philosophy about how they should be governed, by whom, and what standard of governance should be required. So, today, we have a situation in which members of the governing bodies of charities, TECs, LECs and housing associations bear personal fiduciary liability, while members of the boards of NHS trusts do not. Non-executive directors of NHS trusts are paid, but non-executive directors of TECs, LECs, housing associations and most charity trustees are not. The non-executive directors of NHS trusts are appointed by the Secretary of State for Health, or under delegated powers; members of TEC and LEC boards are drawn from categories determined by the funding authority; and housing associations and charities can usually determine their own board membership.

Some organisations have set up Cadbury-style audit committees, others have not.

These wide, and generally inexplicable, discrepancies in governance policy and procedures are among the issues that a review of voluntary sector governance should address. The housing association movement has made a start. In March 1995, the results of an inquiry, chaired by Sir David Hancock, into housing association governance were published (National Federation of Housing Associations 1995). Key recommendations included the need to strengthen accountability, by having smaller, more strategically focused boards, made up of people with a level of competence commensurate with the task they had to carry out.

Tomorrow's boards of trustees will need the vision to guide their organisations to achieve their goals at a time of increasing legislation and regulation, increasing competition for funding, and when being a charity is no longer an excuse for being amateur, unprofessional or unbusinesslike.

Regulation is certainly increasing. Although, contrary to public perception, the Charities Act 1992 made few changes to the responsibilities of trustees, it did, however, heighten awareness of them. Many trustees realised, for the very first time, that in agreeing to become a trustee they were not merely accepting a position of honour, but taking on a position of considerable responsibility.

The 1992 and 1993 Charities Acts have increased regulation in charity accounting and reporting, fundraising, the disposal of charity land, and the criteria for eligibility for charity trusteeship. But, in addition, trustees also bear responsibility for ensuring that their charity complies with changing legislation and regulation in other areas, such as employment law, health and safety legislation, advertising standards, PAYE and VAT. The introduction of contracting means that trustees are also responsible for ensuring that the quality standards for service delivery specified in contracts are adhered to. This can be particularly difficult if the charity depends on volunteers to deliver the services. Many long-standing trustees now feel reluctant to take responsibility for ensuring that their charity complies with mounting legislation and regulation that they may not fully understand, or even be aware of.

The introduction of the National Lottery has made it harder for most charities to make reliable estimates of their future income and, in turn, the level of services they can provide. There have been winners, including those charities that have received money from one of the distribution boards, and losers, especially those whose fundraising has been badly hit. But undoubtedly, some charities have been better than others at anticipating the likely impact on their fundraising and making plans accordingly.

It is in facing such challenges that trustees should perform a strategic leadership role. Boards should have tried to anticipate the impact of the National Lottery on their charity's fundraising ability, and directed plans to take advantage, if possible, of its introduction, or at least limit the potential damage. After all, the trustees are responsible for the organisation's long-term financial stability. But all too often they neglect this responsibility by wasting their precious time dealing with short-term operational issues, such as the purchase of a new fax machine.

Again, it is the trustees who should have taken responsibility for ensuring that plans were in place to reduce or expand service provision, according to the predicted impact of the lottery on the organisation's income. The differing degrees of success with which charities have coped with the introduction of the National Lottery may well provide some good examples of effective and ineffective governance.

Charities are increasingly being seen as small to medium-sized businesses. Competition, and the desire to achieve as much as they can with limited resources, is driving them to operate in a more businesslike way. The public have become intolerant of informality and amateurishness and focus now on performance, outcomes and impact, as both the Nathan report (Nathan 1990) and *On Trust* (NCVO 1992a) testify. Yet for many trustees this presents a dilemma, as traditionally they enjoyed their charity involvement precisely because its informality contrasted with the culture of their business lives.

In their leaflet *Responsibilities of Charity Trustees* are the Charity Commission who describe trustees as 'the people responsible under the charity's governing document for controlling the management and administration of the charity, regardless of what they are called' (Charity Commissioners 1996: 2). However, by defining the trustees' role in terms of responsibility for 'management and administration', the commission fails to distinguish sufficiently between the role of governing a charity, and that of managing it, leaving many trustees confused about what exactly their role should be, and unclear about how much of the charity's work it is permissible to delegate to staff.

Governance should not be thought of as different from management, but rather as a part of the system by which organisations are managed and controlled. As Richard Chait puts it: 'Governance is too complicated and too dynamic to be reduced to some inviolate division of labor' (1993: 2). In smaller charities the trustees will be both the governors and the managers, but as organisations grow larger, the trustees should increasingly focus on governing, or directing the organisation, providing strategic leadership and making the major policy decisions, and should delegate more and more of the other management tasks to staff.

Trustees do not have to manage organisations themselves. However, they are responsible for ensuring that they are well managed. So, as soon as trustees begin to delegate work to staff or volunteers, they must ensure that they have given clear instructions about the parameters within which the staff or volunteers are free to make decisions. They must monitor the work they have delegated, and they must hold staff and volunteers accountable for making progress towards the achievement of the organisation's goals within the parameters they have defined.

However, in the debate about voluntary sector governance, it is vital to remember that although the underlying principles of trusteeship and good governance apply to all organisations, the role trustees play in any one organisation will vary, and it should be developed in the unique context of that organisation. Voluntary organisations are not homogeneous. It is therefore difficult, and often dangerous, to make generalisations. The Imperial Cancer Research Fund and the National Trust are as different from each other as they are from a local community self-help group or an inner-city farm. Size, whether or not the organisation has members, whether it is operational or grant-making, whether or not it is community based, whether it is a new or long-established organisation, and the main sources of funding, are all key differentiators that will result in the development of different roles for trustees relative to those of staff, different sizes of governing bodies and different governing committee structures.

Theories about the emphasis of trusteeship being on governance rather than management bear little resemblance, however, to the current practice of trusteeship in the majority of organisations. If you ask trustees to describe their role, most invariably respond by listing all the activities they undertake for the organisation of which they are a trustee. They make the mistake of equating what they do with what the role should be.

Cadbury defined corporate governance as 'the system by which companies are directed and controlled' (Cadbury 1992: 15). The executive and non-executive directors are responsible for setting strategic aims; providing leadership; supervising the management of the business; and reporting to the shareholders. Similarly, the key responsibilities of charity trustees are to agree the organisation's mission or purpose; set its strategic aims; provide leadership to those managing the process of achieving the aims; monitor progress towards the achievement of the aims and ensure that assets are being safeguarded and managed efficiently and effectively; and hold themselves accountable to the charity's 'owners' – the donors and the tax-paying public – for how effectively the resources are being used to achieve the mission.

If you examine the current practice of charity boards it soon becomes apparent that many are failing to discharge these key responsibilities. Too many boards spend the majority of their time looking backwards, noting the activities that have been carried out, or duplicating work they have delegated to sub-committees or staff to do. They do not spend enough time questioning the extent to which the organisation's activities are making an impact on the problem that it was set up to address, or looking at the changes that are happening in the outside world and creating a vision of how the organisation should adapt its programme to take account of them. They should be questioning whether the organisation's services are still relevant to the beneficiaries' needs, or if new services should be developed; deciding if the organisation should be devoting more of its assets to campaigning to change the underlying causes of the problems they are seeking to address; or whether the organisation should be working more closely with others who have similar aims.

There are several reasons why many charity boards perform less effectively than they should. One is the lack of a commonly accepted model of good charity governance, that makes clear the difference between governing an organisation and managing it. Another is because trusteeship is a voluntary activity that people undertake in their leisure time. When people join a charity board they tend to conform to that board's existing practice and culture. Unless they feel very strongly that there should be a change, and have the time and energy to bring it about, they settle for the status quo. Some individuals sit on several boards, each with its own culture and way of working, yet they rarely import good board practice from one organisation to another. Ineffective boards are also a reflection of the inadequate arrangements for the guidance and training of trustees noted by both the Nathan report (Nathan 1990) and the *On Trust* report (National Council for Voluntary Organisations 1992a). A large-scale survey of trustees, commissioned by NCVO's Trustee Services Unit in 1994, found that the number of trustees being offered any form of updating or training was still only 36 per cent (Sargant and Kirkland 1995: 32). It is therefore not surprising that trustees are commonly the weaker partners in the leadership team and boards fail to ask for the information necessary to challenge staff decisions.

Worse still, when surveyed by the National Council for Voluntary Organisations, two-thirds of trustees did not even realise they were, in law, charity trustees (National Council for Voluntary Organisations 1992b). This does not necessarily mean that all of this large fraction were not performing their role effectively – in many instances they had simply never been referred to as 'trustees' but called 'the management committee', the 'council', the 'executive', or some other term – but it is probable that many were not. Some trustees had been appointed to comply with rules in the charity's governing document about the number of trustees required, but with no expectation that they would play an active role. But the lack of awareness may also have been symptomatic of the changes that take place as organisations grow and employ increasing numbers of professional staff.

In the founding phase of an organisation's life cycle, the trustees are usually the charity's operational staff as well as its directors and managers. If the charity grows, the trustees begin to delegate some of the work to paid staff. However, they rarely reappraise how their own role should now change and develop, so their agendas continue to focus on management issues and they continue to view themselves as the managers of the organisation, rather than as its directors. Or, in an alternative scenario, many trustees eventually reach the point where they feel their paid, full-time professional managers are better qualified than they are to make strategic decisions about the organisation's future, and see their role becoming increasingly symbolic. They take a less and less active role in running the organisation's affairs and think they can discharge their trustee responsibilities by merely turning up to a few meetings a year and giving formal approval to decisions already taken by staff.

Trustee boards can generally be classified as one of four main types: 'approving' boards, 'leadership' boards, 'representational' boards and 'involved' boards. Approving boards are usually found in well-established organisations with goals that are stable and widely accepted, and that are serviced by well-qualified professional staff. The board regards the staff as 'being in charge' and relies heavily on them for advice and information. It rarely rejects a staff recommendation for action and normally the only situation in which it takes the lead is in the appointment of a new chief executive. With this type of board the organisation may well achieve its purpose in an efficient manner. However, there is a danger that if the trustees become too dependent on staff, or overly respectful of their expert knowledge, the organisation may become inwardly focused and may fail to take advantage of the wider perspective that non-executives can bring. Such organisations can end up meeting the needs and expectations of their staff, rather than of their donors or beneficiaries. In the 'approving board' typology, with the balance of power weighted heavily in favour of staff, the trustees often find it difficult to hold the staff accountable for their actions. Such boards can find it difficult to recruit people of calibre. As pressures on people's time increase, many will only give up time to sit on a board if they feel their presence will make a difference. As John Harvey-Jones wrote in *Making It Happen*: 'Nothing is more frustrating than spending a year of one's time working on a board, and at the end of it, sitting down and racking one's brain to think whether one has had any effect whatsoever' (Harvey-Jones 1988: 218).

Leadership boards take responsibility for determining the organisation's purpose and goals and regard the role of staff as being to implement their vision, policies and plans. They are often found in younger organisations, or those where the trustees have a strong personal commitment to achieving the organisational goals. Leadership boards are the most pro-active in discharging their key responsibilities. The best drive their organisations to focus on achieving their aims, while others fail, because the trustees de-motivate their staff by giving them insufficient responsibility, or frustrate them by getting over-involved in management detail, or the trustees let their own passionate belief in the cause lead them to exploit their staff.

Representational boards are frequently found in membership organisations and umbrella bodies. Accountability and knowledge of the beneficiaries' needs are usually strong, as the board's membership represents the charity's significant stakeholders. However, these boards often face difficulties in agreeing the mission and values and in setting goals. Members may fail to recognise the conflict between their duty to act in the best interest of the charity's beneficiaries and their duty to represent the interests of a particular stakeholder or group of stakeholders. Members are normally elected by a democratic process that frequently fails to produce a board team with the requisite skills, experience or degree of competence necessary to perform its task.

Involved boards are often found in recently formed organisations, where the trustees are often themselves volunteer service providers or fundraisers, and any staff have been recruited for support rather than management roles. They have the advantage of having trustees who are highly committed to the charity, and willing to devote considerable time and energy to it. However, if the trustees fail to recognise that they have duties as governors of the charity, and that these are different from their duties as operational workers, then the pressures of coping with day-to-day matters will, all too often, drive any consideration of the more strategic issues off the agenda, and in the longer term the trustees may fail to develop appropriate roles for themselves and their staff.

Examining how boards change the ways in which they discharge particular responsibilities as their income increases, can shed some light on why some boards remain 'involved' while others develop into approving or leadership boards. Consider grant-making for example. In a small, newly formed organisation it is common practice for the trustees to decide which applications for grants they will fund. In some growing organisations the trustees will continue to do this, even though the amount they have to distribute each year grows to millions of pounds and grant-making begins to take one full day a week. But this can only happen if the organisation has trustees that are willing to give so much time to the charity. In other organisations, the board will recognise that growth brings with it the need for new trustees, with experience of directing large organisations. No matter how committed these people are to the charity's aims, they are unlikely to have the time to spend a day a week grant-making. So the board decides to develop criteria for grant-making and establish a grant-making policy, and then delegates to staff the power to make grants within its criteria and policy guidelines. Depending on the degree to which the trustees or staff take the lead in developing the grant-making policy and criteria, the board will have developed into a 'leadership' or 'approving' model. What many boards overlook is that when they delegate their work to staff in this way, they must establish procedures for monitoring that staff are, in fact, giving grants in accordance with the board's stated policy guidelines and criteria, in order to discharge their responsibilities as trustees.

Budgeting is another area which different types of board handle in different ways. Trustee boards are responsible, in law, for safe-guarding the charity's assets and applying them effectively to meet the needs of the beneficiaries. To do this involves estimating their likely income for the coming year and drawing up costed plans of the work that can be done with that income, and with any reserves that can be drawn upon. Where staff are employed, it is usual for the staff to draw up the budget and present it to the trustees for approval. Trustees frequently question individual items of expenditure – usually the least significant – but they rarely refuse to agree the budget. After all there would be little point in doing this, because if they wanted to add or remove items of expenditure, all the staff would need to do to keep the budget balanced would be to revise their estimate of income. Most boards accept that budgets are tools which managers need to guide expenditure during the year, rather than accurate predictions of future income and expenditure.

Most boards rarely question the degree of detail in which the budget is presented. Over the years, staff develop a feeling for what is acceptable. Listing the cost of pencils, computer disks and soap for the washrooms would be too detailed; just giving total income and expenditure too broad. Boards rarely specify the degree of detail they require. Most just accept the budget that is placed in front of them. But if trustees query items of expenditure, it suggests they have some criteria for deciding what should, and should not, be included. If this is the case, then the trustees should be taking the lead in defining these criteria before the staff start to prepare the budget. It is a waste of time and money to ask staff to prepare a budget and then for the trustees to amend it simply because the budget does not meet the trustees' requirements – these should be specified before the staff start their work. Leadership boards specify the parameters within which they want staff to draw up the budget. Then, when the budget comes to the board for approval, all the trustees need to check is that it meets their parameters.

Many boards are too big to do their job effectively. Once a group gets larger than ten to twelve its ability to debate issues and reach decisions becomes impaired. NCVO's research showed that the average board size of a charity with a turnover of more than £1 million was fifteen, but there were wide variations and many charities have boards of between thirty and fifty trustees (Sargant and Kirkland 1995: 1). The National Federation of Housing Associations' report recommended a maximum board size of fifteen and a minimum size of seven (National Federation of Housing Associations 1995: 27).

Large boards are often the result of attempts to increase accountability or make the organisation user-led. But there are more effective ways of a board holding itself accountable for its actions, or ensuring that services meet the needs of beneficiaries, than placing users, or other stakeholders, on the board solely for this purpose. Good consultation procedures will ensure that the board hears the views of many more of those who will be affected by its decisions, than it would if it relied on the opinions of a few, frequently untypical, representatives.

In many organisations, the chairperson, or the honorary officers, assume too much power, forgetting that it is the full board that should engage in, and bear responsibility for, decision-making. Over-powerful chairpersons usually develop when boards have not delegated day-to-day operational decisions, so the chief executive frequently has to turn to someone to make decisions between meetings; or when boards fail to meet frequently enough to take the necessary decisions. Chairpersons and honorary officers should see themselves as 'first among equals'. If they do not, they run the risk of disempowering and de-motivating the rest of the board.

Over-powerful chairpersons or honorary officers may also blur the chief executive's accountability to the board. For example, a chief executive can be placed in an impossible position if instructed by the chairperson to do something that the chief executive knows does not have the full board's majority support. When interacting with the chief executive between board meetings, the chairperson, or honorary officers, must remember that they should always act on behalf of the board. On those rare occasions when they do have to take decisions on the board's behalf, they should always report them to the full board at the earliest opportunity.

Similarly sub-committees can blur line-management accountability. How can the chief executive hold the director of fundraising accountable for the results of the fundraising department, if the director of fundraising has to take instructions from a fundraising sub-committee? Sub-committees can perform a useful function in helping the board reach decisions, but all too often they disempower the board of trustees. The board may feel uncomfortable about challenging the recommendations of its expert sub-group. It may base its decisions on the recommendations of a sub-group who are considering a matter from one perspective – for example, the impact on the beneficiaries of increasing charges for services – rather than considering the matter from the broader organisational perspective. Or the board may abdicate its responsibility by delegating too much authority to a sub-committee.

Many organisations set up sub-committees not to help the board do its work, but as a way of obtaining free, expert advice for its staff. There is no harm in having advisory committees, provided it is clear that their function is to give advice, either to the trustees or to the staff, and that they are not part of the charity's decision-making process. Many organisations fail to make this distinction, however, and as result it is harder for the board to hold staff accountable, and harder for staff to be clear about the parameters within which they are free to act.

In the early 1990s the debate about trusteeship was couched in terms of training and effectiveness, and the possibility of trustee 'flight' – would trustees resign *en masse* on learning about their responsibilities and the possibility, however remote, of suffering financial loss as a result of their trusteeship? But the debate has now moved on. People are now not only raising questions about the training, effectiveness and supply of trustees, but they are also raising questions about accountability, competence and even whether having a committee of unpaid non-executives is the best model of governance for some of today's larger voluntary organisations.

There is growing public unease about the competence and legitimacy of the governance of many quangos, both among the general public and among those working in them. This is hardly surprising when Baroness Denton was quoted in 1993 as saying that she had been responsible for 804 public appointments and 'I can't remember knowingly appointing a Labour supporter' (*Independent on Sunday*, 28 March 1993). The chairpersons of some NHS trusts were forced to resign in 1995, following allegations that large sums of public money had been wasted, and there have been some well-publicised cases of fraud in housing associations. There is also anecdotal evidence of increasing numbers of school governors resigning now they have realised the complexity of the task they have taken on. This seems to be particularly true of parent governors, many of whom took on the role hoping it would provide them with the means to improve the education of their own children, but who have since found that most meetings concern budgetary matters where they may have little expertise to offer.

This unease has now spread to questions being asked about the governance of charities, particularly now so many charities, both large and small, rely heavily on central or local government funding. The original trust model, in which charity trustees are accountable to the donors for safeguarding the charity's assets and applying them in the best interest of the beneficiaries, seems less and less appropriate for the types of organisations that increasingly make up today's voluntary sector, where the donors are not distant, altruistic philanthropists, but the tax-paying public, or where the charity's staff and volunteers have to raise the money to fund the organisation's services.

Accountability can be defined as the price we pay for being given power. It is part of the system of checks and balances society puts in place to prevent the abuse of power. Charity trustees are not at liberty to do whatever they choose with the charity's assets. They have an obligation to account for their actions and policies. This obligation may be imposed in part by law, for example charities are required to file accounts and a trustees' report with the Charity Commission and must provide the public, on request, with a copy of their accounts. Indeed, the need to demonstrate accountability underpins the charity accounting regulations contained in Part VI of the Charities Act 1993 and the latest Statement of Recommended Practice on Accounting for Charities. Some type of formal accountability may also be demanded as a condition of funding by many funders. Trustees have a duty to ensure that funds are accepted only to fulfil the mission of the organisation, rather than to ensure its survival. But, in part, the obligation to account will be a moral one. Charity trustees should regard themselves as being morally accountable for their actions and policies to a number of other stakeholders including the beneficiaries, potential beneficiaries, staff, volunteers and the wider community in varying degrees.

Accountability is not just about explaining and justifying actions and policy. Accountability is also about taking the views of stakeholders into account when planning service provision or setting policy. This may be a weaker form of accountability, because the stakeholders cannot impose any formal sanctions on the trustees if they fail to consult, though if they do not they run the risk that some stakeholders, volunteers for example, may withdraw their support.

Most boards of trustees discharge their responsibility to hold themselves legally accountable, if only out of fear of the sanctions that might be imposed; but the degree to which they discharge their moral accountability varies considerably. There are many examples of good practice, often in organisations where the governing body has remained close to the organisation's roots, such as community organisations and self-help groups. But this is an area in which improvements can still be made.

In the United States, calls for greater accountability have led to all organisations in receipt of government or federal funding being required to hold their board meetings in public. However, experience shows that holding these types of discussions in public merely moves the real debate into the corridors, and can lead to unnecessary anxiety. For example, if a charity is questioning whether it should continue a particular project or service, the staff involved will naturally become anxious about job security and the users or beneficiaries will worry about how they would cope if the service was discontinued.

In calling for increased accountability, many people are questioning not just how boards hold themselves responsible for the exercise of power, but also the legitimacy with which their actions and policies are validated in the first place. In the 1994 Arnold

Goodman lecture, the Duke of Edinburgh commented on the increasing claims of voluntary organisations to represent the interests of different groups in society and challenged the basis of their authority. NCVO's survey of trustees confirmed that most trustee boards and management committees are self-perpetuating oligarchies. When asked how they recruited new trustees, almost a third cited personal recommendation (Sargant and Kirkland 1995: 30). Even when there is a democratic election procedure, as in the case of most membership organisations, the majority of trustees are elected unopposed.

When people argue that trustee boards should be more accountable, are they really saying that they do not approve of power being in the hands of a self-perpetuating oligarchy and that they believe trustee boards should be democratically elected? While having a trustee board that is a self-perpetuating oligarchy is rarely in the best interest of a voluntary organisation or its potential beneficiaries, having a democratically elected board is rarely in their best interest either. Just like a senior staff team, a trustee board needs to be made up from a number of competent individuals each of whom brings differing skills and experience that together enable the board to carry out its function. Increasingly, organisations are using trustee-person specifications, which implicity suggest a selection procedure in which individuals have to demonstrate that they match given criteria for board membership. No democratic election procedure will guarantee to deliver a board that has the necessary balance and range of skills and experience needed. If calls for democratically elected boards are the result of a belief that government is becoming less democratic and accountable, then society should address that situation by pressing for government to be more accountable and accept that most charities were never intended to be democratic institutions.

It is now common practice for organisations to hold regular reviews of their management structures, procedures and practices, but it is still rare for them to review their governing structures and processes. As a result many boards of trustees have failed to develop apace with the growth of their charity, and many trustees will admit that they no longer feel up to their task. Self-examination should become part of every board's procedures.

Trustees must be competent to carry out the task they have taken on. The necessary degree of competence should be judged in terms of 'fitness for task' and should move apace with the changing size and complexity of the organisation. The degree of financial expertise required by the honorary treasurer of the local church preservation trust is very different from that required by the treasurer of a multi-million-pound charity contracting with social service departments to provide domiciliary and residential care for substance abusers. No organisation would appoint staff they did not believe to be competent. Surely it is even more crucial to their success that they have competent trustees to direct them?

For many organisations, being user-led will be vitally important if they are to succeed. But being a user is not a sufficient qualification for board membership. User trustees must also possess relevant governance skills and experience, or be offered opportunities to develop them. Many people lack the necessary experience, but have the potential for trusteeship if given the chance to develop.

The traditional 'guardianship' model of trusteeship in which trustees must receive and safeguard money or other assets given by one group of people (the donors) and apply it for the benefit of another (the beneficiaries) is based on trust law and was well suited to the grant-making trusts that largely made up the voluntary sector in years gone by. However, it is less appropriate for many of the voluntary organisations operating today, particularly membership organisations that receive funding from a wide variety of sources. As the donor group becomes less cohesive, the guardianship model of trusteeship becomes less effective, as a disparate donor group is less able to hold the trustees accountable and the legitimacy with which the trustees can claim to be acting in accordance with the donors' wishes becomes open to challenge.

In many self-help groups the donors are, by definition, the beneficiaries, and there is considerable overlap between these two groups in many membership organisations. Being user-led, or having a large number of grass-root supporters involved in moulding the organisation's policies, is the key to these charities' successful development and long-term survival. Having to use a model of governance that presupposes distinct groups of donors and beneficiaries presents problems.

The guardianship model is also less appropriate for organisations delivering services previously provided by central or local government, as the contract with the funder usually specifies in considerable detail the service to be provided and the make-up of the client group. Contracting may leave little scope for trustees to play an active role in deciding whether the best way of meeting the beneficiaries' needs is by providing the proposed service, and the trustees' role increasingly looks like that of an agent of the funder.

The senior staff of larger charities play such a key role that they could be judged to be shadow directors. Some argue that, for these charities at least, a corporate model of governance, with a mix of executive and non-executive directors, would be more appropriate. However, this would remove one of the key advantages of the present system, that is, a board that has no self-interest in the outcomes of its decisions. If the real reason for calls for staff to become board members is to improve the effectiveness of the board, there are better ways of achieving this.

If the sector is to thrive in the next century it will need more effective boards. It will need effective boards that ask awkward, even inconvenient, questions; boards that do not unquestioningly accept their staff's recommendations, but want to test their assumptions and conclusions and be convinced of their arguments; boards that represent no one except the long-term interests of the organisation and its beneficiaries. It will need effective boards comprised of people who are interested in the work of the organisation and committed to its goals; competent people, respected in the community, with a capacity to influence others; people who can work as part of a team, with a capacity for growth as board members; and people who are willing to ask challenging questions, make suggestions and who are not afraid to offer constructive criticism. Effective boards do not just happen; developing them takes thought, time and hard work. As Cyril O. Houle wrote in his book on governance (1989: 165): 'A good board is a victory, not a gift.'

REFERENCES

Cadbury, Sir A. (1992) *Report of the Committee on the Financial Aspects of Corporate Governance*, London: Gee.

Chait, R. (1993) *How to Help Your Board Govern More and Manage Less*, Washington, DC: National Center for Nonprofit Boards (available from the National Council for Voluntary Organisations').

Charity Commissioners for England and Wales (1996) *Responsibilities of Charity Trustees*, London: HMSO.

Dayton, K. N. (1985) *Governance is Governance*, Washington, DC: The Independent Sector.

Harvey-Jones, J. (1988) *Making It Happen*, London: Collins.

Houle, C. O. (1989) *Governing Boards: Their Nature and Nurture*, San Francisco: Jossey-Bass.

Nathan, Lord (1990) *Effectiveness and the Voluntary Sector*, London: National Council for Voluntary Organisations.

National Council for Voluntary Organisations (1992a) *On Trust: Increasing the Effectiveness of Charity Trustees and Management Committees*, London: NCVO.

—— (1992b) *On Trust: Trustee Training and Support Needs*, London: NCVO.

National Federation of Housing Associations (1995) *Competence and Accountability: The Report of an Inquiry into Housing Association Governance*, London: NFHA.

Sargant, N. and Kirkland, K. (1995) *Building on Trust: A Study of Charity Trustees*, London: National Council for Voluntary Organisations.

Chapter 8

Giving in trust
The role of the grant-making trust

Nigel Siederer

Grant-making trusts and foundations[1] like to claim that they concentrate their funding on responses to new, recently discovered, or under-recognised needs and problems, including fundamental research and the promotion of ideas and understanding; new and innovative methods of tackling problems, including action research; and disadvantaged and minority groups that have trouble using ordinary services, or which are inadequately served by them. They also fund work which is unpopular, and thus hard to finance through conventional fundraising; as well as work for which the case for government funding has not yet been established or accepted, or for which government funding is inappropriate. Last, they traditionally involve themselves with one-off purchases or projects (for example, capital grants for buildings, and commissions of enquiry); and short- and medium-term work which is likely to bring a long-term benefit and/or attract long-term funding from elsewhere (Association of Charitable Foundations 1994).

Trusts have taken this approach for much of the post-war period. They have been concerned not to be drawn into permanent funding. Even where revenue costs have been funded, grants have tended to be for three years at a time, with a preference for project rather than core funding. Where the pioneering nature of an organisation has made core funding appropriate, trusts have often been reluctant to be the sole funder. The implicit assumption has been that successful innovative work would bring its own reward, in the form of long-term government funding. Trust grants would therefore 'prime the pump'. This supposition has been underpinned by the knowledge that government spending in relevant fields is around a hundred times larger than that of trusts. This is shown, for example, in education, where government spends around £31 billion compared with trusts' £319 million.

In recent years, this approach has come under question for several reasons. The first is that government spending has shrunk relative to other sectors, and there has been a grudging recognition that the 'pump-priming' strategy assumes, unrealistically, that government coffers can expand without limit.

Second, the government has itself started to make 'pump-priming' grants, providing short-term and experimental funding in the expectation that other sources, notably the private sector, will step in. A plethora of government schemes has been established on a match-funding basis, with charities encouraged to rely less on government and to diversify their funding. Government funding has been increasingly biased towards capital costs rather than revenue, with assumptions that match- and revenue funding can be found from elsewhere. Four of the five streams of funding from the National Lottery are subject to government directives based on the same premise.

Third, the arrival of the contract culture, while presenting some organisations with new opportunities for funding, has blurred the boundaries between the state and the voluntary sector, making it more difficult to map out a distinctive role for trusts. Some (mainly larger) charities have sought trust funds to enable them to compete for contracts, presenting trusts with the dilemma of whether to subsidise what should properly be, and in the past often have been, state-funded services.

The fourth reason for this questioning is that because contract funding is often linked to direct services, finance for charities' non-service work can be difficult to find, especially advocacy, research and campaigning – for which trust funding has been sought, sometimes for long periods. In a wider sense, there is an implied threat that the voluntary sector's capacity to undertake such work at all – often seen as essential to its independence – will be lost unless trust funding is forthcoming.

Fifth, many small and medium-sized voluntary organisations, especially in new and poorly established parts of the voluntary sector, are ill-placed to compete in the contract market, bringing a crisis in funding, where long-term and core funding can be difficult to obtain, other than from charitable trusts. Trusts have thus come under pressure to relax their policies, because no other source is likely to help some organisations which may be particularly valuable in disadvantaged and minority communities.

Sixth, infrastructure organisations, such as councils for voluntary service, have also fared badly in the contract culture. Among other functions, such bodies often provide a seed-bed for new ideas and developments. However, the long-term unevenness in their geographical coverage, exacerbated by a spate of recent closures, hampers the voluntary sector's capacity for innovation, and so weakens the supply of the type of grant application that trusts find particularly attractive.

There is also recognition that some ideas and initiatives can take longer than three years to develop. The effect of a normal maximum of three years' funding may be to inhibit the flowering of success from promising beginnings; or time may be wasted through mid-term fundraising or in replacing key personnel who leave because of funding insecurity. Projects may be forced to switch, to no significant advantage, from one 'pump-priming' trust grant to another. 'Why not fund for ten years?' ran one polemic (Cook 1994a, 1994b).

Last, the pressure to fund innovation can bring an unwillingness to replicate genuinely successful initiatives in other geographical areas. It also fails to recognise that genuinely innovative ideas, though not uncommon, represent a relatively small proportion of the average trust's postbag.

All of these factors have brought pressures to moderate the strict view of trusts as providers of short-term, 'pump-priming' grants. Trusts are increasingly asking themselves which of these pressures are legitimate and deserve a positive response, and which must be resisted if the distinctive role of trust funding is to be preserved.

Trusts have begun to recognise that the notions of short-term and pump-priming funding may be of recent origin. Looking back at the earlier history of trusts, many of London's playing fields and parks were started by grants from the City Parochial Foundation (Belcher 1991); while the philanthropy of Andrew Carnegie, through trusts including the Carnegie UK Trust, played a pioneering role in the development of public libraries. Such initiatives arose out of the determination of philanthropists and philanthropic organisations, and were funded initially without concern about whether the state would ever step in. Trusts still have much scope to take a lead on an issue and see it through, as, for example, the Nuffield Foundation's work on medical ethics and the Gulbenkian Foundation's on school bullying.

On the other hand, there is a determined resistance to taking on what is now widely seen as the proper role of the state. Trusts are likely to give short shrift to state schools which approach them for funds for the school roof or a teacher's salary. An NHS (or trust) hospital's request for funding of a bed is likely to be refused. Trusts' view of such requests can fairly be described as that of an unreconstructed proponent of the welfare state. They will not fund mainstream public services, and can be expected to take a robust view of what *ought* to be part of those services. However, again this must be seen in historical context. Present-day views of what ought to be publicly funded differ radically from those of the past, and many contemporary mainstream services were started on a voluntary basis, with or without philanthropic funding.

However, trusts do not automatically refuse requests from statutory organisations. Development of teaching of new and minority subjects and of new teaching methods is often seen as legitimate pioneering. The Nuffield Foundation, for example, has funded work on curriculum development in the fields of language, design and technology. Trusts, such as Wellcome, fund for experimental medical treatments and research. That the applicant body may be a state school or hospital is not important, for charity law directs trust funds towards charitable *purposes*, wherever performed, rather than to charitable *organisations*. There are, however, concerns about high overhead costs in some state institutions, and a trust may have a clause in its deed (or adopt a policy) which limits it to funding registered charities or non-statutory organisations. Some requests are not clear cut. For example, should a school's core budget normally provide computers, so placing requests for charitable funds beyond the bounds of legitimacy?

If the boundaries between the state and voluntary sectors are no longer clear, then it also follows that voluntary organisations *per se* will not be regarded as automatically eligible for trust funding. The trick is to decide when the work that an organisation wants to do ought reasonably to be funded by the state. Even if it is not so funded, should it be? In the 'contract culture' context, is it 'contractable'?

Trusts have become weary of the changing role of government, a feeling that is shared by many of their counterparts among companies with corporate giving programmes. To be more precise, trusts and companies have become frustrated with dealing with requests for support from charities whose work has been damaged or undermined by instability in government funding. There is, of course, a recognition that government has a legitimate right to redirect funding. The frustration has arisen because, too often, changes have taken place over-hurriedly (sometimes without prior notice or consultation), and have been driven by short-term policy, coupled with unrealistic expectations of the capacity of trusts and companies to replace what the government has withdrawn.

An attempt, in 1993, to improve relations through a series of joint seminars led to a better understanding of each other's perspectives, but no meeting of minds as to respective roles (*Resourcing the Voluntary Sector* 1993). Comparison of the different reasons why government, companies and trusts fund the voluntary sector is however instructive. Where government departments and statutory agencies work with the voluntary sector mainly to pursue their own policy objectives, and companies give out of a sense of community responsibility and enlightened self-interest, trusts fund the voluntary sector for philanthropic reasons. Philanthropy is indeed trusts' essential purpose; they give money to a good cause on the merits of the cause, and are given tax relief as an incentive to do so. This does not mean that trusts give their money away blithely; but it *does* mean that trusts are often willing to take more risks.

The exchange of views between government, trusts and companies *did* bring common recognition that there are issues of good and poor practice in grant-making, and that grant-seekers and recipients have legitimate expectations of funders. This produced initial agreement to prepare a code of practice for funders of the voluntary sector. Further discussion threw up problems of enforceability, but generated much goodwill, leading in 1995 to the publication of *Draft Guidelines for Funders of Voluntary Organisations*. Issued jointly by the Association of Charitable Foundations, Charities Aid Foundation, the Corporate Responsibility Group, the Home Office Voluntary Services Unit on behalf of central government, and the English local authority associations, the draft guidelines are the first documents of their kind. They recognise the need for funders to provide adequate information about their grants, to process applications in a reasonably open way, and to deal fairly with applicants in making decisions and over monitoring and evaluation. They emphasise the problems that are caused by late decisions to award, renew or terminate grants, and recognise that special steps may be needed to reach potential applicants from disadvantaged groups. They recognise the differences between core, project and service or contract funding. After a period of consultation, the intention is to rework the guidelines into a permanent statement of good practice, which individual funders will be encouraged to follow.

The discussions between funders also brought recognition of the need to improve statistical information about the voluntary sector. At present, there is no common understanding of what the voluntary sector *is*, still less of who funds it and in what shares. It is therefore difficult to quantify trusts' importance in the wider panoply of funders.

The sector's total income is unknown, and extrapolation from estimates of the total income of registered charities in England and Wales presents the problem that these estimates have varied considerably between different surveys. It fell, for example, from £16 billion in 1992 to £12.8 billion in 1994 (Charity Commission 1992, 1994). Quite apart from the omission of charities in Scotland and Northern Ireland, it is unclear whether this change represented a real fall or simply a change in survey methods. Attempts to reconcile such estimates with the aggregate expenditure of the various types of funder produces further bafflement. About half of charities' income appears to come from fees and sales, but includes large blocks of activity not normally associated with the voluntary sector, such as fees to independent schools, private hospitals and nursing homes. Of the other sources of funds, personal charitable giving has been estimated at around £4 billion, but with wide margins of error. Figures for total central government grants are frequently cited as being in the range of £3.5 billion to £3.6 billion. This however includes government funding to housing associations, which in 1993–4 was 83 per cent of the total (*Dimensions of the Voluntary Sector* 1996, drawing on figures in *Hansard*, 19 July 1995, 1445–8). Outside the housing field, government grant aid was around £600 million a year, rather less (though of the same order) than that of trusts, at around £800 million. For 1994–5, local government grants and fees have been estimated at £1.27 billion (*Dimensions of the Voluntary Sector*

1996). Depending on what is counted, trust grant aid – at around £800 million per year – therefore represents between 6 and 10 per cent of the voluntary sector's income. It is thus a highly significant contribution, albeit a very diverse one.

Attempts to compile statistics about trusts themselves are bedevilled by similar problems: confusion about definitions, and the lack of a generally accepted typology of trusts or method of categorising their grants. Each of the compilers of information about trusts takes a different approach to these questions. The *Directory of Grant-Making Trusts* (1995) includes several very large operating charities and government fringe bodies that between them account for £220 million of the £1,030 million spending of the 3,147 trusts listed. Adjustment produces a lower total spending figure of £810 million from 3,133 trusts. *Dimensions of the Voluntary Sector* (1996: 55) calculates the total grant expenditure of the top 500 grant-making trusts at £705.1 million in 1995 (a figure which shows an unexplained fall of over £100 million from the figures reported a year previously) (*Dimensions of the Voluntary Sector* 1995: 158). The two volumes of the *Guide to the Major Trusts* (1995–6) give a figure of £700 million for the spending of the top 1,000 trusts. The inconsistencies between these major sources of information suggest that all compilations of statistics about trusts should be treated with caution. The *Directory* provides an estimate of the total value of trust assets used for investment purposes: £8.1 billion, excluding the assets of the Wellcome Trust, which alone are valued at £5 billion. This is consistent with an estimate of £12.4 billion for the top 500 trusts (including Wellcome), in *Dimensions of the Voluntary Sector* (1996).

There *is* agreement that trusts are very diverse in size. As Table 8.1 shows, the richest 36 trusts, 1.1 per cent of the numerical total, account for over half the total spending; the vast majority are much smaller – the smallest two-thirds providing only 6 per cent of the grant aid by value.

The fields of education and research (Table 8.2) thus receive the largest sums of money, while the health and social services sectors receive the largest number of grants. Trusts have significant interests in the arts and the environment (where the figure includes grants for the preservation of historic buildings). Another survey (*Dimensions of the Voluntary Sector* 1995: 65) suggests that grants to individuals comprise 14.4 per cent of trust spending; and that local organisations receive over half (52.7 per

Table 8.1 Sizes of trusts

Income range	No. of trusts	Value of grants (£ million)	Proportion (%)
£10 million plus	14	311	39.7
£5 – £10 million	22	103	13.2
£1 – £5 million	110	169	21.6
£500,000 – £1 million	91	46	5.9
£100,000 – £500,000	518	88	11.2
Less than £100,000	2195	48	6.1
Others	183	18	2.3
Total	3133	783	100.0

Source: *Directory of Grant-Making Trusts* 1995: viii

Table 8.2 Subject interests of trusts

	Proportion of grants (number)	Proportion of grants by value (%)	Median value of grants (£'000)
Culture & recreation	17.8	9.8	23.0
Education & research	16.7	40.7	69.5
Health	9.5	12.1	37.0
Social services	32.3	15.3	46.8
Environment	6.6	5.1	12.5
Development & housing	3.4	2.2	15.7
Law, advocacy & politics	0.3	0.4	9.5
Philanthropic inter- mediaries & volunteerism promotion	0.3	0.5	3.6
International	2.2	1.6	30.0
Religion	8.8	8.9	26.5
Business, professional associations, unions	0.1	<0.1	2.5
Other	1.8	3.5	25.4

Source: Based on a survey in *Dimensions of the Voluntary Sector* 1995: 66
Note: The survey is of approximately 10,000 grants, made by at least 162 trusts, in *Dimensions of the Voluntary Sector* (1995). The exact method by which trusts' grants are placed in a given category begs a number of questions, mainly about the methodology used to allocate grants that might fall into more than one category, e.g. art education. The categories are derived from the 'International Classification of Non-Profit Organisations', explained in Salamon and Anheier 1994: Appendix B.

cent), with national organisations at 25.2 per cent, and international or overseas bodies at 7.6 per cent.

Despite trusts' image as venerable institutions, the *Directory's* (1995) records of dates of formation show that 95 per cent are of twentieth-century creation, and 85 per cent were formed in the post-war period. The boom in formation of new trusts in the 1960s and 1970s probably reflects the unfavourable tax regime for personal wealth in those decades, and hence the relatively high value of charity tax exemption. A later fall, in the 1980s and 1990s, may also reflect the more recessionary times, and, more recently, the advent of alternative tax-efficient methods of giving to charity, such as Gift Aid. The capacity to engage in philanthropic giving is very often the consequence of the building of a successful business. Some of the business entrepreneurs of the 1980s have indeed created personal charitable trusts, though not yet on the scale of earlier times[1] (Zealley 1994).

The following categorisations develop work done in 1989 by Norton:

Trusts with a geographical focus Many trusts have a geographical restriction, and can only make grants for the benefit of the population in a particular area. There are large local charities, for example in areas as diverse as Burton-upon-Trent, Sutton Coldfield, and the Shetland Islands, as well as the large City Parochial Foundation in London. Other trusts, though having no strict limits, none the less have a preference for a particular region or locality (for example, some of the Cadbury group, with their non-exclusive bias towards the West Midlands). One emerging type of local trust are *community trusts and foundations*, formed to act as a focus for local giving by companies and individuals, and to build local permanent endowment funds. Though the idea of the community trust is relatively new to the United Kingdom, successful trusts have been built in Northern Ireland, Tyne and Wear, Greater Bristol, Wiltshire, Milton Keynes, and elsewhere.

Trusts with restricted objects and policies Some trusts are unrestricted in the type of work they can fund. Others have quite narrow restrictions in their deeds. For example, the Wellcome Trust, the United Kingdom's largest, funds only medical research and the history of medicine. A third type has intermediate limits, which allow them to fund a wide range of work in a given field (for example, the Prince's Trust, which funds young people, and BBC Children in Need). Some trusts adopt policies of funding in one or more fields for a few years at a time, thus temporarily excluding themselves from other fields. There are 'relief in need' charities, which help individuals in poverty, rather than organisations; and 'benevolent funds', which are linked to particular professions, or are established to help students.

Trusts with a religious basis Many trust deeds reflect the religion of their settlor, though relatively few are established for religious purposes *per se*. More typical are trusts that assist communities with a particular religious affiliation, or which make grants consistent with the ethical basis of a religion. A large number of trusts reflect the rich Jewish philanthropic tradition; some of these are secular, some assist Jewish causes in the United Kingdom, and some help causes in Israel. The Quaker trusts, including those associated with the Cadbury and Rowntree families, are well known. Many others have an affiliation with a branch of Christianity, for example the association of the Sir Halley Stewart Trust with Non-conformism, or the Church Urban Fund, the Church of England's initiative to help deprived urban areas. The Aga Khan Foundation is one of the few with a link to Islam, notwithstanding the Islamic community's strong tradition of personal charitable giving.

Non-charitable trusts Although most trusts are themselves registered charities, a few have foregone the tax concessions associated with charitable status, and can fund work which is not charitable in law, including explicitly political campaigns and parties. The best known are the Joseph Rowntree Reform Trust and the Barrow Cadbury Fund. The Charity Commission's acceptance of the legitimacy of political work by charities has enabled the non-charitable trusts to focus their work more narrowly.

Trusts can also be categorised according to their sources of funds:

Endowed trusts The vast majority of trusts are founded by a transfer (or endowment) of funds or land, either during the settlor's lifetime or through their will at death. The funds are invested and the proceeds used to make charitable grants. (Modern investment policies of larger trusts normally allow the trustees to invest for capital growth as well as income, provided that they protect the underlying value of the capital.) The link with the settlor and his or her family often weakens over time, giving such trusts virtually complete independence.

Personal and family trusts Many endowed trusts were originally established as a vehicle for tax-effective personal giving by an individual or a family, and tend to support only causes for which the trustees have a personal affinity. They may be endowed or funded by *ad hoc* or regular gifts, or by a mix. A trust's charitable status creates obligations of openness and transparency, which may be unwelcome to family trustees. Their disquiet may increase as the Charities Act 1993 comes into force, bringing requirements to publish an annual report, a policy statement and a list of the main grants.

Livery companies The City of London's 'Great 12' livery companies (and many smaller ones) represent a particular type of independent endowed trust. Each company administers substantial charitable funds; their names – for example, Mercers', Drapers', Clothworkers', Goldsmiths' – reflect their centuries-old origins in gifts and subscriptions from members of the eponymous trades, for which some of their funds are still reserved, though most are now available for more general charitable purposes.

Company trusts Many trusts have a close link with a company, being endowed with company shares or fully funded from current company profits, and having trustees nominated by the company. In the long term, the relationship will become more distant, as the trustees are bound to invest for the wisest financial return and may sell part or all of any shareholding – on the general principle that investments should be diversified, or occasionally because of a lucrative takeover bid. Many well-known trusts end up sharing the name of a famous company, but nothing else; some, indeed, outlive the company on whose success they were founded.

Public subscription and appeal trusts Many well-known trusts are, or were, funded by public donations. For example, the endowments of the Royal Jubilee Trusts and King Edward's Hospital Fund for London (King's Fund) comprise funds originally subscribed by the public. Contemporary counterparts are the broadcasting appeals, notably Comic Relief, BBC Children in Need (actually now more than 60 years old), and the Heart of Variety Appeal, which is supported through a range of fundraising activities. The national broadcasting appeals typically raise between £10 million and £20 million through each event, and are thus among the United Kingdom's more substantial grant-making trusts. Their regional counterparts, such as Capital Radio's Help a London Child, may raise up to £1 million a year. In a similar vein is the National Lottery, which will provide an incidental, but very substantial, benefit for good causes, with distribution machinery that is similar to charitable trusts (see below).

Intermediary trusts These trusts are formed to raise funds and make grants in a special field, developing expertise that is useful to other grant-makers – including trusts and government – who are normally the main source of funds. Some intermediary trusts also have substantial public fund-raising programmes, and may try to achieve independence by building their own endowment. Examples are the Mental Health Foundation, the Housing Associations' Charitable Trust and the National AIDS Trust. Community trusts also fall into this category, adding value through their knowledge of needs of the local area.

Leat (1992) has devised a description of styles of trust giving:

Gift-givers Gift-giving trusts (the vast majority) make grants in response to requests. They do not have very clear priorities, and tend to make smaller grants – without funding projects or organisations as a whole, and without extensive investigation before choosing who to give to. Gift-givers do however need to know that the recipient is reliable, and grants are often given to enable something specific to be bought.

Investors Investors usually spend time deciding the areas and organisations that they want to support. They research the proposed field of activity and the applicant organisation. They will want to achieve the maximum effect with their grants, but are likely to invest over several areas as a means of diversifying the risks that they take. Investors are likely to be interested in the results of projects they fund, but are still highly dependent on proposals and ideas put to them.

Collaborative entrepreneurs This style of trust work is similar to the 'investor' style, but the trust itself is likely to choose the work that it wishes to fund. It will seek out, or even create, the organisation that can act as its partner in executing the work. It is likely to make long-term grants, or award commissions or contracts, and to be represented on project steering committees, as distinct from the 'arm's-length' approach of 'investors'.

Though distributing their funds responsibly and carefully, and increasingly forced to choose priorities, trusts are not constrained to play an entirely safe role. They like to fund innovation, and to support work which does not attract funds from conventional sources. This necessarily involves an element of risk, which is at the heart of successful grant-making. A recent gathering of trusts discussed a typology of risk (Hazell and Elizabeth 1995):

Person risk Trusts may back a maverick, a person with a brilliant idea, and find that real innovative work results. The risk is that, despite the promise of the idea, the key person may not have the skills to carry it through.

Organisation risk Organisations which appear weak and inexperienced, or which present an unfamiliar style of work or come from a minority culture, may be the very ones that can be successful in meeting previously unmet needs in a pioneering way. On the other hand, they may be too inexperienced to deliver, and providing money may not be enough to ensure success. Extra support in the form of appropriate consultancy may be useful, provided that this is not seen as an imposition.

Political risk A project may produce a result that is a challenge to established thinking, and expose a trust to unwelcome publicity or draw it into controversy. Some trusts may however welcome this, and see it as entirely proper that their funding should be used to provoke debate about unpopular issues that might not otherwise take place.

Project risk Projects may fail because of external factors, such as a change of government or of government policy in the field concerned. This may lead to funds being wasted, although through no fault of the trust or the project itself.

Trusts' interests in good practice have led to much discussion of issues of fairness in access to trust funds (Doven and Ellis 1995; Hedley and Rochester 1993). The issue of 'fairness' is a delicate one, in which individual trusts may feel that their autonomy and individuality are under threat, in the cause of a 'political correctness' of which many are suspicious. But there is a growing recognition that a trust has a duty to look carefully, not just at individual applications, but at where and how its funds are distributed overall. Increasingly, trusts are recognising the need to monitor their own work, to check that the spread of grants reflects their intentions, that they address the greatest needs in the fields in which they operate, and that they do not inadvertently exclude groups with which trustees and staff may be unfamiliar. Trusts are also seeing the importance of making information widely available to grant-seekers, and of looking at how they can attract applications from disadvantaged groups who may not be on the usual information grapevines. The larger trusts are becoming more determined about their policies, often identifying five-year priorities for subject and geographical areas in which they wish to make a special impact. The need to set priorities is partly driven by an increase in the sheer volume of applications, reflecting the desperation of many applicants. A means of attracting and assessing applications on a fair and rational basis is increasingly essential if trusts are to do, and be seen to do, their job competently.

The National Lottery's impact on trusts will be very significant, and very different from its impact on the rest of the charitable sector. Trusts are aware of, but not participating in, the raging debates: how far do lottery funds represent a *de facto* tax on poor communities where lottery participation is most common? To what extent are lottery tickets bought with funds that would otherwise be given to charity? And how far will the lottery funds be given to things which would otherwise be funded by the government? For trusts, it is the sheer volume of funds that will have the most impact. Each of the five objects of lottery funding – arts, sports, heritage, charities and the Millennium Fund – will bring about £300 million per year on to the philanthropic scene; all but one will be providing far more than is given by charitable trusts in the same field. The exception, and the largest area of overlap with trusts, is the distribution run by the National Lottery Charities Board – whose emergence will add about 35 per cent to current philanthropic giving to charitable causes within its purview. The board, with far more freedom than the other lottery distributors, is not restricted to capital-only grants or to requirements that recipients must raise substantial funding from other sources. The board, in fact, has most of the characteristics of a generalist independent charitable trust. (At the end of 1995, agreement was reached for the board to join the Association of Charitable Foundations, which acknowledged that the board, alone among the lottery distributors, has sufficient *de facto* independence to meet the Association's membership criteria.) Where the other lottery distributors will bring pressures on trusts to provide match funding and revenue grants, the Charities Board may actually ease trusts' burden, at least initially. It will however cause administrative problems by recruiting trust staff and advisers for its own operations. In the longer run, the Charities Board is likely to fund much mainstream charitable work – and may well be able to make a decisive impact on neglected fields such as the voluntary sector's infrastructure – leaving trusts freer to focus their own priorities on concerns which are more narrowly defined.

It is both true and a truism that trusts are very diverse. As the above analyses show, they vary greatly in size, style, geographical remit, origins, sources of funding, purposes and policies. Even quite similar trusts may have very different practices, on such matters as whether they make a large number of small grants or a small number of large ones. Trusts are jealously independent, not only of government, but of each other. All this makes generalisation difficult.

Moreover, precisely because of their independence and diversity, and contrary to common supposition, trusts do not spend a great deal of time exchanging views with each other about individual applications. However, they do meet together both nationally, and increasingly in regional and local groups. Since the formation of the Association of Charitable Foundations in 1989, there has been considerable growth in trusts' capacity to discuss policy issues in particular fields and across the voluntary sector as a whole, and to share in developing good practice in administration and decision-making techniques.

Perhaps this is why common attributes and concerns are more readily observable than in the past. Many of these are responses to changes in the external funding environment, which only the very largest trusts can aspire to influence. The effects of changes in the patterns of government spending at central and local level, and in voluntary sector funding, are widely felt by trusts in the form of increased demand for grants. The arrival of the National Lottery will ease this by providing extra funds, while bringing administrative disorder, together with demand that trusts provide matching money for partial lottery grants. Not all trusts will be affected. Some will choose not to be, and will continue to make a range of small grants to a similar range of organisations every year, providing a backdrop of core funding that underpins much valuable voluntary activity. But most trusts will evince a wish to respond to the changing circumstances, if only to find ways of reasserting their traditional role.

NOTE

1 The words 'trust' and 'foundation' are virtually synonymous, and other words like 'settlement' or 'charity' are in common use. All charitable foundations are trusts, i.e. they are managed by trustees, who may or may not be supported by paid staff. A 'foundation' is a trust whose income derives from an endowment of land or invested capital. Not all foundations make grants; some use their income to finance charitable work of their own. Not all grant-making charities have an endowment. In this chapter, the word 'trust' has been used throughout to mean grant-making charities of any sort.

REFERENCES

Association of Charitable Foundations (1994) *Applying to a Charitable Trust or Foundation*, London: Association of Charitable Foundations.
Belcher, V. (1991) *The City Parochial Foundation 1891–1991 – A Trust for the Poor of London*, Aldershot: Scolar Press.
Charity Commission (1992) *Report of the Charity Commissioners for England and Wales*, London: HMSO.
—— (1994) *Report of the Charity Commissioners for England and Wales*, London: HMSO.
Cook, T. (1994a) 'Ten year funding', *Trust Monitor*, June–July: 20–1.
—— (1994b) 'Why not fund for ten years?', *Trust & Foundation News*, January–February: 7–8.
Dimensions of the Voluntary Sector (1995) ed. S. Saxon-Harrold and J. Kendall, London: Charities Aid Foundation.
—— (1996) ed. C. Pharoah, London: Charities Aid Foundation.
Directory of Grant-Making Trusts (1995) ed. A. Villemur, London: Charities Aid Foundation.
Doven, R. and Ellis, F. (1995) *Fairness in Funding: An Equal Opportunities Guide for Grant-Makers*, London: Association of Charitable Foundations.
Draft Guidelines for Funders of Voluntary Organisations (1995), pamphlet issued by the Association of Charitable Foundations, Charities Aid Foundation, the Corporate Responsibility Group, the Home Office Voluntary Services Unit, and the English local authority associations, London: Association of Charitable Foundations.
Guide to the Major Trusts (1995–6) Volume 1, ed. L. Fitzherbert, S. Forrester and J. Grau; Volume 2, ed. P. Brown and D. Casson, London: Directory of Social Change.

Hazell, R. and Elizabeth, S. (1995) 'Taking risks with grants', *Trust & Foundation News*, June/July: 11–12 (notes taken by Carlton Younger of a seminar led by Susan Elizabeth of King's Fund and Robert Hazell of the Nuffield Foundation).

Hedley, R. and Rochester, C. (1993) *Good Grant-Making: A Practical Guide*, London: Association of Charitable Foundations.

Leat, D. (1992) *Grant-Giving: A Guide to Policy Making* and *Trusts in Transition: The Policy and Practice of Grant-giving Trusts*, York: Joseph Rowntree Foundation.

Norton, M. (1989) *Raising Money from Trusts*, London: Directory of Social Change.

Resourcing the Voluntary Sector (1993), ed. R. Hazell and T. Whybrew, London: Association of Charitable Foundations, Charities Aid Foundation and Corporate Responsibility Group.

Salamon, L. M. and Anheier, H. K. (1994) *The Emerging Sector: An Overview*, Baltimore: Johns Hopkins Nonprofit Sector Project Studies.

Zealley, C. (1994) *Creating a Charitable Trust*, London: Directory of Social Change and Association of Charitable Foundations.

Chapter 9

A lawful endeavour
Charities and the law

Roger Winfield

Running a charity used to be so much easier. Charities were, of course, bound to comply with the general law of the land, but there was little law dedicated specifically to charities. The limited attention the legislators gave to charity law can be illustrated by the relatively few books there were, until recently, on the topic, compared with, say, company law.

A major law library in London keeps a record, not only of the books and other texts currently on its shelves, but also of those which have been removed because they are out of date. In the latter category there are more than six times as many books under the heading of 'companies' as those under the heading of 'charities'. In the former category – current texts – the gap has narrowed significantly to only twice as many in favour of companies.

Until Parliament passed, in quick succession, the 1992 and 1993 Charities Acts the law relating to charities in England and Wales had never received such intensive scrutiny. The basis of present-day charity law was contained in the preamble to an Act of Parliament of 1601 (Statute of Charitable Uses). 'Charitable' was redefined in 1891 by Lord Macnaghten under the four categories we know today: the relief of poverty, the advancement of education, the advancement of religion, and other purposes beneficial to the community (*Income Tax Special Purposes Comrs* v *Pemsel* [1891] AC 531 at p583, HL).

When the last major piece of charity legislation, prior to 1992, was enacted, Harold Macmillan was prime minister, 56 black South Africans were shot at Sharpeville and 'Cathy's clown' by the Everly Brothers was the pop hit of the year. The year was 1960. That Charities Act was both a sweeper, gathering in and replacing various old Acts, and an innovator of a more regulated system for charities. It was, however, fairly mild compared with the 'tough-guy' Acts of the early 1990s.

Why are charities increasingly having to involve lawyers – solicitors and barristers – in their affairs? Why do more charitable funds have to be used for legal advice? The answer can be found in the ideological changes of the 1980s.

It is ironic that the drives to reduce the cost of running the welfare state, and increase the ability of business to create bigger profits, each brought with them more rules. The government felt it had to be seen to be putting in place protections for those who might fall victim to some of the worst excesses of the free market.

The burden of over-regulation of both companies and charities was subsequently recognised and a number of task forces were set up to advise on the problem. Charities were, by then, having to operate within the regime created by the Charities Act 1992, so the sector was given its own task force. The Deregulation Task Force on Charities made many recommendations in its report, published in July 1994, some of which have been implemented, by the Charity Commission and under the Deregulation and Contracting Out Act 1994. Nevertheless, charities now have many more rules and regulations to follow than they could have imagined in their worst nightmares before 1992.

The charity sector is growing rapidly. In 1995a the Charity Commission added to its register 8,752 new charities, bringing the total to 184,467 (Charity Commission 1996). According to the Charity Commissioners, the estimated gross income of the 154,500 main registered charities in 1995 was approximately £16,000 million.

The biggest charities have grown even bigger as they have taken on many of the responsibilities which used to belong to central or local government. It was a requirement of the National Health Service and Community Care Act 1990 that local authorities must spend 85 per cent of their social security transfer funds on services provided by the private and voluntary sectors. Daycare for elderly people and running homes for people with learning difficulties are two examples of areas in which charities are now delivering services as a consequence of the provisions of the Act.

Inevitably, a government contracting work out to an ever-increasing number of charities felt it wanted more stringent rules

governing their administration. After the 1992 and 1993 Acts
and the accompanying regulations, charities, their trustees, chief
executives, employees and volunteers have had much to exercise
them.

Running a charity is a complex task. They are non-profit organisations but are expected, increasingly, to behave like businesses.
Like businesses they must not stray outside their registered
objects. But in 1994 the Charity Commissioners decided to relax
the previously rigid rules relating to amending the governing
document of a charity in which its objects are spelled out (Charity
Commission 1995a). The commissioners gave, as the main reason
for this change, that charity trustees are responsible for the proper
administration of their charity and should have the necessary
powers to do this. Is it conceivable, however, that the decision
might also have been influenced by the need to better equip
charities to operate in an increasingly commercial environment?

Inevitably, the cost of legal advice takes up an increasing
amount of charitable funds. When in 1995 the Corporation of
London announced that it was making available £10 million a
year for London charities, it included legal and financial advice
for small charities as one of its five priority areas (*NCVO News*
1995c).

Those running charities are now being asked to perform heroic
feats, running their charities like commercial concerns while
retaining the ethos of voluntary service. The problem was
expressed succinctly by Karen Irving, director of Parents for
Children, a charity which finds families for damaged and dis-
turbed children, when she wrote:

> The Government says voluntary organisations should grow and
> plug the welfare gap by providing social services that used to
> be provided by local authorities and the NHS. But meanwhile
> the seed money from the state which used to help them is
> drying up because the Government says charities must now be
> commercially viable.
>
> (Irving 1995)

Something might have to give but not too soon it is hoped.
While many cherished British institutions – the Church, the mon-
archy, the judiciary and Parliament – have come under increasingly hostile scrutiny both by the media and users and found
wanting, the not-for-profit sector has been making a mighty effort

to preserve a system which has worked well for nearly 400 years. However, as Westminster, as regulator, becomes increasingly a local side-show, the British charity sector is having to fight its corner in the European ring.

When starting a new charity, a number of basic, early decisions have to be made. We shall see later in this chapter which factors make charitable status useful – they are mainly financial – but we shall assume, for present purposes, that the organisers have already decided that it is a charity which they want to form.

To see some of the decisions that face a new charity, let us look briefly at Public Concern at Work (PCAW), a free legal advice centre for employees concerned about malpractice at work, which also provides training for employers.

Registered as a charity in 1993, PCAW discovered that the route to charitable status can be more like a winding mountain road than a fast, straight motorway. The detail of negotiations between the promoters of PCAW and the Charity Commission, and the reasons for the chief commissioner's decision, are contained in *Decisions of the Charity Commissioners*, Volume 2 (Charity Commission 1994). Like other fledgling organisations PCAW had to ask itself a number of questions. What legal structure will best suit us? What should the objects be and will they be acceptable to the Charity Commission? Do we need a solicitor? What sort of premises would be appropriate? When can we start operating?

One of the most important questions is: does the charity become either a trust or association with trustees or does it incorporate and become a limited company? Essentially, according to the Charity Commission in its model constitutions, a trust is appropriate where the charity will be administered by a small number of people or the charity will not employ many staff or carry on any kind of business (Charity Commission 1995b). An unincorporated association is appropriate where the people who will control the organisation are democratically elected from time to time, or the organisation will have a membership (Charity Commission 1995b). A company is appropriate where the organisation is expected to control substantial assets, or to employ a large staff, or is likely to engage in charitable purposes which involve risks of a commercial nature, which may lead to large potential financial liabilities (Charity Commission 1995b).

In the case of trusts and unincorporated associations, the

trustees are personally liable for all the activities of the charities including any financial default. With a company the trustees' liability is limited, but the administrative burden is greater. A charity which is incorporated as a limited company has to comply with four main Acts covering charitable companies – the Charities Acts of 1992 and 1993 and the Companies Acts of 1985 and 1989.

A company has a legal existence independent of its members. It therefore enters into contracts, for example, in its own name. Where the charity is unincorporated it is the trustees, personally, who contract. (The number necessary will be found in its governing instrument.) Apart from the legal implications of this, the administrative inconvenience can be considerable. Any change of trustee might require the transfer of a contract, including a lease, from the retiring trustee into the name of the new one.

PCAW knew that it would have substantial funds at the beginning and its staff numbers were likely to grow. A company was the obvious structure.

Why did PCAW want charitable status? Traditionally, charitable status has given the assurance of reliability, honesty and selflessness to those dealing with the organisation. Charitable status is the basis for fundraising. It carries tax relief. Local authorities have discretion to waive business rates by up to 100 per cent. Stamp duty is not charged on property transactions. PCAW knew that it had to raise money and that it would need to lease premises from which to operate. Charitable status was seen as being essential to the success of the new venture.

The chief charity commissioner stated his faith in the old definition of charity when he said:

> This framework remains broad enough to embrace what is important today. It enables the Charity Commission, answerable to the courts, to develop the scope of charity to meet the changing needs of the modern world. The hospice movement is a good example of the renewal of an old tradition. So is the new charity, PCAW, to promote business ethics. The Charity Commission's decision that gun clubs do not meet the requirements of charitable status in the modern world is a further example.
>
> (*Guardian*, 22 June 1994)

As long as the organisers can show that the objects fall within at least one of the four traditional headings for charitable status, they will have a good chance of obtaining charitable status from the Charity Commission.

The major charity legislation of 1960, 1992 and 1993 has been essentially regulatory in nature and not defining. Parliament has not thought it necessary to alter the unbroken common law development from the Elizabethan statute of 1601 through the conventional definition of charity deriving from Victorian philanthropy.

The Nuffield Foundation sponsored a study of the way in which businesses heard and addressed the serious ethical concerns of their employees. In the foreword to the research report, the director-general of the Confederation of British Industry wrote: 'Business does not operate in a vacuum: it is part of the community and is expected to provide the lead in an increasingly complex world' (Winfield 1990).

We have already seen that the fourth charitable object comprises purposes beneficial to the community. The benefit need not extend to the whole community. Provided that the class to be benefited is large enough to produce a public character it will be charitable. If, in the case of PCAW, it had been limited to the employees of one company or even one industry, it might not have been considered public enough to justify the benefits of charitable status. The concept of public benefit, therefore, already existed when the Charity Commission was asked to approve PCAW as a charity. There were, however, no precedents for the acceptance, as charitable, of the object of promoting ethical standards of conduct and compliance with the law. PCAW had, therefore, to be shown to be charitable by analogy to some purpose or purposes set out in the preamble to the statute of 1601, or to purposes which the courts had held to be charitable.

In 1985 the Charity Commissioners had considered the extent to which any novel purpose for the public benefit could be charitable (Charity Commission 1985). 'We are clear', the commissioners stated, 'that we should take a constructive approach in adapting the concept of charity to meet the constantly evolving needs of society.' Nine years later the commissioners were able to apply those principles to decide that the objects of PCAW were of public benefit. But the decision took nearly a year to make. What happened in the interim?

Before approaching the Charity Commission those behind the creation of PCAW engaged solicitors to express, in legal form, the purposes for which the organisation was being created –

to draft its objects. When difficulties were encountered in the negotiations with the Charity Commission, counsel wrote an opinion which was helpful in getting the objects registered in the form wanted by PCAW. When it was time to look for premises, the advice of a solicitor was taken not only on the actual lease, but also on what to look out for in the preliminary negotiations with landlords and their letting agents.

As charities will increasingly need to consult solicitors, this is a convenient point at which to look at the working relationship between the client charity and its solicitor. Again, the case of PCAW illustrates important aspects of that relationship.

In many ways a solicitor is only as good as his or her client. The less the client contributes to the thinking about the problem, the less the result is likely to be satisfactory to the client. Even after the problem has been given to the solicitor the client too has to worry it into shape. That the organisers of PCAW instructed an experienced firm of solicitors to handle their application to the Charity Commission did not mean that they stopped thinking. The solicitors were, and always are, there to advise on what is possible and to carry out the client's instructions. PCAW's organisers knew what sort of organisation they – not the solicitors or even the Charity Commission – wanted. Both lawyers and client played major parts in securing charitable status and premises on terms which were acceptable to the client. Working relationships were established which would prove useful to the charity in the future.

It took the Charity Commission a year to agree to register PCAW as a charity. While some might say, unkindly, that this is not a long wait for a solicitor, it is certainly a very long and worrying wait for people anxious to get on with putting their ideas into practice. Failure to get charitable status does not stop an organisation from operating. PCAW was ready to open its doors long before the Charity Commission gave its green light. It decided, however, to wait for the Charity Commission's decision to avoid committing itself to arrangements which might have to be changed because of requirements of the Charity Commission.

A company seeking charitable status is particularly vulnerable to wasting money by starting to operate before it obtains the final decision of the Charity Commissioners. A company's objects are contained in its memorandum of association, whether or not it is a charity. The rest of its constitution can be found in its articles of association which, with the memorandum of association, must be registered at Companies House (Companies Act 1985 section 12). Only after registration is it a legal body. Its bank, for example, will not open an account until it has seen the company's certificate of incorporation as a company and its memorandum and articles of association. PCAW would have thrown money away if it had registered its objects at Companies House before the Charity Commission made its decision. Its objects were redrafted a number of times to meet objections by the commission. Amendments to the memorandum of association had therefore to be made. It was wise to leave the memorandum of association in draft form until final approval was received from the commission.

Something to bear in mind when preparing articles of association, indeed any constitution, is the procedure for signing and sealing documents. Getting documents signed is often an administrative nightmare for a charity. Trustees might not spend much time at the organisation. Often the document has to be signed at short notice. The message is, therefore, keep the signing requirements simple – not more than two or three signatories. The Charities Act 1993 contains extensive provisions for the signing of documents for charitable companies. These provisions apply if nothing specific is mentioned in the charity's articles of association.

In relation to all the affairs of their charity, trustees must act as a prudent person would in looking after his or her own business affairs (*Halsbury's Laws of England* 1987: paragraph 831). PCAW needed premises from which to operate. Dealing with land – this is the charity law expression which covers land with or without buildings, freeholds or leases – is fraught with danger for trustees. It could amount to a breach of trust, making the trustees personally liable if they committed their charity to an expensive land transaction without taking proper advice. Land law in England and Wales is both extensive and complicated.

What should charity trustees look at when they are thinking about acquiring land? While the cost of taking professional advice can be met from the charity's income, some preliminary work by the charity might help to keep the cost down. In PCAW's case, taking a lease was the only realistic option. It wanted to be based in Central London where buying property would have been too expensive. The chances are that the majority of land transactions by charities involve taking leases. Can the premises be used for the purpose of the charity? This is an important early question. While the lease itself might allow the required use, the planning law might not. The planning registers are open to public inspection, at the local authority, and planning departments will often give information over the telephone. PCAW knew it needed offices rather than, for example, a shop, and directed its efforts accordingly. Do the premises need work doing before they can be used? It would be wise to get a preliminary estimate of the likely cost, as this will have a direct bearing on the charity's ability to take those premises. It will also affect the level of rent and the date rent should start to be paid. A rent-free period should be negotiated, if possible, to cover at least some of the cost of the works necessary to allow the charity to use the premises.

In the hurry to secure premises, with pressure from a landlord, it is easy to forget that a land transaction is a bargain between two parties. Negotiating the best deal should be the objective of each side. Charities are no different from businesses in this respect, except that there may be a greater obligation on charity trustees to negotiate as hard as is prudent in the circumstances of the case. The charity trustees will often need the help of their professional advisers, solicitors and surveyors, in these negotiations. PCAW prepared a budget for its property costs at an early stage. This helped it to negotiate on the level of rent and service charge.

The responsibility for repairing the premises is a crucial area to decide at the outset. Will the charity be liable directly, or through a service charge, for major works to the fabric of the building or the roof or foundations? The trustees will need to budget accordingly.

Because of the importance which has been attached to the ownership of land in Britain since the Domesday Book, there is a vast and sophisticated body of law relating to property. It contains expensive pitfalls for the unwary. Due to post-war changes in business, the Landlord and Tenant Act 1954 led to new regulated tenancies of business premises. These give business people protection at the end of their lease against being evicted except in certain defined circumstances when they get compensation instead (Landlord and Tenant Act 1954 Part 2 sections 23–46). Increasingly, however, landlords try to persuade tenants to agree to give up this security of tenure. Charity tenants would do well to resist this line, except in special circumstances, and unless a compensating benefit is offered in return. The Charities Acts of 1992 and 1993 did not pass up the opportunity to add to the collection of property legislation. Sections 36 to 40 of the 1993 Act set out, in great detail, quite complicated steps trustees must take when dealing with land. They need to be familiar with the basic principles, even if their charity is only taking a short lease.

Like it or not, the present climate is such that only the fittest will survive. Charities now have to look more carefully at all their overhead costs, and property expenses often take a high percentage of a charity's income.

Whether property is a good investment will depend on the needs and resources of a charity. It will be an appropriate way for some charities to invest their funds, but totally unsuitable for others. There is a duty on trustees to consider the need for diversification of their charity's investments. What this means is investing in a number of separate investments to reduce the risk of substantial loss to the charity, should one investment fail (Trustee Investments Act 1961). Trustees also have a duty to ensure that funds are properly protected; in other words that the capital is not put at risk and will be protected against inflation.

Henry Smith's Charity did not think property a good investment in 1995. Henry Smith died in 1628 having bequeathed to his trustees £1,000, the income from which was to be used 'for the relief and ransom of poor captives being slaves under Turkish pirates' and a further £1,000, the income from which was to be applied 'for the use and relief of the poorest of my kindred'. He also directed that the sums be laid out in the purchase of land to yield an income of at least £60 a year. For much of its 300-year history, Smith's Charity's only asset was the South Kensington Estate, 58 acres of prime London residential property near Harrods. By 1995, the South Kensington Estate still accounted for 50 per cent of the charity's assets. The chairperson of the trustees of Henry Smith's Charity, explaining why they had decided to sell the South Kensington Estate in 1995, said that they 'felt pretty vulnerable having so many of our eggs in one basket. We realised the political risk was high' (Bar-Hillel and McGowan 1995). The sale price was £280 million and the purchaser another charity, the Wellcome Trust. The latter's chairperson was not so concerned. Wellcome only had 3 per cent of its £7.3 billion assets in property.

It is the duty of charity trustees to manage land in the interests of their charity. However, there are dangers, as the following example illustrates. A landlord charity granted a three-year lease to another charity. The lease contained a tenant's break clause; the right for the new tenant to get out of the lease early on by giving 6 months' notice to the landlord.

The new tenant fell behind with its rent. It then gave notice to end the lease before the 6 months which had been previously agreed. Remembering their duty as charity trustees, the landlord trustees realised that they could not just accept the position and write off a substantial amount of rental income.

The tenant charity claimed that it had no more funds. The landlord charity knew, however, that the premises contained valuable equipment worth at least as much as the rent which was owed, and which the tenant intended to remove. If the landlord did not move quickly it would be too late. The equipment would be removed, possibly at night, and, after moving out of the premises, the tenant would continue to claim that it had no money.

Getting heavy with a defaulting tenant has not normally been part of the voluntary sector ethos. Sympathy was more likely to be the approach. A harsher regime has been ushered in by the new Charities Acts and action was called for on the part of the landlord in this example. The bailiffs were called in. They went to the premises with a van big enough to hold the tenant's equipment, if that became necessary. When the tenant turned up to remove its equipment, the bailiffs were able to stop it doing so. The tenant was given the choice of allowing its equipment to be taken away for sale to meet the rent, or of finding the money to pay the rent. The tenant trustees found the rent – that day! Not only was the landlord charity acting within its powers, freely negotiated with the tenant when the lease was signed, but it was carrying out its general duty to look after the interests of the charity and its beneficiaries.

The problem of charities being asked to release confidential information was mentioned by Dyer (1994):

In a growing number of rape and sexual abuse cases, lawyers for the defence are seeking disclosure of confidential files from doctors and social workers. The British Medical Association is worried that 'fishing expeditions' by defence lawyers are forcing

doctors to reveal confidential patient information, at the risk
of being fined or imprisoned for contempt of court.

(Dyer 1994)

It is Friday afternoon. As the chief executive of a counselling
charity, you are told that one of your employees has been sum-
moned to appear at the Old Bailey on Monday morning with the
files relating to one of your clients. What do you do? Do you say
that as the summons is a court document it must be obeyed
without question? Do you reluctantly take the line of least resistance and authorise the employee to attend court with the file,
because it will not be possible to get advice before Monday? Or
do you reflect a little and say that you need legal help in making
the decision? You are, after all, the chief executive so the buck
stops with you.

This dilemma had to be faced by Brook Advisory Centres in
October 1994. It raised some interesting and relevant questions
which are of general application to charities.

Brook Advisory Centres is a well-respected national charity
which gives pregnancy and contraceptive advice to young people
at its clinics and through its publications and talks. Many of those
seeking advice at Brook are under age. The belief, by the young
person, that what she or he tells the Brook counsellor, nurse or
doctor is in confidence is essential to the maintenance of Brook's
reputation.

In the case quoted, Brook decided to consult its solicitor, who
advised that the summons should be resisted. Working over the
weekend, Brook and the solicitor prepared a preliminary case for
Monday morning, and the solicitor arranged for a barrister to
present Brook's case to an Old Bailey judge.

After two and a half days in court, the judge ruled in Brook's
favour. He said that organisations like Brook should not be com-
pelled to break confidentiality, and in some cases betray their
clients, unless obliged to do so by law. The judge found that in
Brook's case there was no such obligation.

Many charities are in relationships where confidentiality is
important. It is not for this chapter to explore in detail this
complex area of the law. It is, however, right to emphasise that
to breach confidence can lead to legal action against the charity.
Its trustees are ultimately responsible for the charity. It might be

a breach of trust if confidentiality was deliberately and voluntarily breached, resulting in the trustees being held personally liable.

The Brook Advisory Centres' case demonstrated the value of an established relationship between charity and solicitor. When the crisis broke, valuable time was not lost in finding a solicitor or in getting-to-know-you sessions. However, Brook had always used solicitors regularly for a wide variety of work, which meant that such a contact was not a new experience for either side at that important time. Also, Brook had funds with which to pay for legal representation.

Not all charities have a tradition of working closely with solicitors or have seen the necessity for it. The nature of the charity's work, as well as the availability of funds to pay for a solicitor, will determine whether the charity trustees develop a relationship with a solicitor. Family Service Units (FSU) is a charity which has needed in recent years to develop a policy towards legal advice. Formed in 1948, FSU is a national charity which provides independent social work services for some of England and Scotland's most deprived families, through inner-city units. It works in partnership with local authorities, other organisations and the individuals concerned, to prevent families breaking down. Combating discrimination and responding creatively to the needs of the multi-racial communities where it works are declared aims of FSU.

FSU's legal structure is that of an incorporated charity with a single registration with the Charity Commission. It operates through local units, each with their own management committees. The charity trustees are therefore the trustees of the national organisation, with each local unit providing at least one national trustee.

Solicitors had been used by FSU on a case-by-case basis, particularly for employment matters. However, the director felt that with the introduction of care in the community, the contract culture and the new charity legislation, she needed access to legal advice particularly on policy matters. FSU decided to meet this need by appointing an honorary legal adviser who was a solicitor. Solicitors also continued to be instructed on individual cases where necessary.

As FSU had long provided specialist services for local authorities in return for substantial grants, totalling £3.7 million in 1994, it was immediately faced with the problem of having to negotiate contracts with those same authorities. The twenty or so local authorities, for whom FSU provides services, had the advantage of legal departments to draft these new contracts. There was, however, no consistency of approach by the local authorities in the form of the document: one local authority's contract was different from another's. The consequences of the contracts would be crucial to the charity. Fixed-term contracts would affect employment and premises arrangements. It was essential for minimum requirements to be developed, so that the honorary legal adviser could prepare guidelines and checklists for FSU to follow when negotiating the contracts. Checklists were prepared to help reduce the potential cost of professional legal advice if it was decided that solicitors should be used to complete individual contracts.

Other problems on which FSU consulted its honorary legal adviser included employment issues, payment of trustees, trustee indemnity insurance, and an analysis of the role of its trustees in the new, more regulated, charity world.

The use of an honorary legal adviser, who understands the culture and workings of a charity, can help particularly on broader policy issues. Specific individual cases are more appropriately handled by a solicitor acting in a professional capacity, with the protection of professional indemnity insurance and a complaints procedure should things go badly wrong.

The law is, that in the absence of evidence to the contrary, trustees are presumed to have faithfully discharged their duty (*Taylor* v *Millington* (1858) 4 Jur NS 204 at 205 per Wood V-C). We have seen that, for charity trustees, one of the attractions of incorporation as a company is that their liability for defaults, including financial losses, is limited. This protection can, however, be lost.

If a charity becomes insolvent, the trustees will be at personal risk if they have behaved recklessly or dishonestly. If it appears that the charity trustees knew – or ought to have known – that there was no reasonable prospect that the charity would avoid becoming insolvent, as opposed to going into voluntary liquidation, then the court has power to order the trustees to contribute personally to the charity's assets for the benefit of its creditors. These provisions are contained in the Insolvency Act 1986 section 214 and apply to directors of all insolvent companies, whether or not they are charitable.

There are other circumstances in which charity trustees will be personally liable. Whether they are directors of a company or individuals, charity trustees using the charity's money for improper purposes – for example, to pay themselves a salary, or to fund purposes outside the charity's registered objects, or negligently to allow other people to misappropriate funds – are strictly liable, personally, to repay the money and make good any losses (*Halsbury's Laws of England* 1987: paragraph 960).

Will our current structures for charities – trust, association or limited company – be with us unchanged in a few years' time? Two areas of study suggest that they might not.

Increasingly the question is being asked: should there be a separate incorporated structure for charities to reduce the burden of having to comply with both charity and company legislation? Australia and New Zealand, for example, already have a distinct incorporated structure for charities. A comparative study of the legal structures in different jurisdictions, followed by a survey of the difficulties experienced by charities arising from their legal structure, is being conducted in England by the National Council for Voluntary Organisations (NCVO), the Association of Charity Lawyers and the University of Liverpool supported by the Charity Law Association. This might provide evidence that charities would benefit from a separate system (*NCVO News* 1995a).

Inevitably Europe plays an increasingly influential role in the development of the modern voluntary organisation. Article 23 of the Maastricht Treaty recognises the role of the voluntary sector as a partner to governments in the delivery of social welfare services. The number of UK community and voluntary organisations that include a European element to their work has increased in the last few years.

NCVO is carrying out a study in conjunction with the European Council for Voluntary Organisations, with funding from the European Commission, to address the needs of cross-national voluntary organisations. Issues covered include the legal formalities and costs involved in setting up an association operating in several different countries; the fiscal position, regulation, any restrictions as to nationality or residence imposed on members of the governing council; and questions of liability (*NCVO News* 1995b). It seems likely that British charities will soon have a Euro-structure and a new set of requirements to add to their shopping list of legal needs.

REFERENCES

Bar-Hillel, M. and McGowan, P. (1995) 'Ambush in high summer', *The Standard*, 7 August.

Charities and Voluntary Organisations Task Force Proposals for Reform (1994) Volume 2, *Full Report*, London.

Charity Commission for England and Wales (1985) *Report of the Charity Commissioners for England and Wales for the Year 1985*, London: HMSO.

—— (1994) *Decisions of the Charity Commissioners*, Volume 2, London: HMSO.

—— (1995a) *Report of the Charity Commissioners for England and Wales for the Year 1994*, London: HMSO.

—— (1995b) *Decisions of the Charity Commissioners*, Volume 3, London: HMSO.

—— (1996) *Report of the Charity Commissions of England and Wales for the Year 1995*, London: HMSO.

Dyer, C. (1994) 'Fishing for real abuses', *Guardian*, 15 November.

Halsbury's Laws of England (1987), vol. 48, 4th edn, London: Butterworths.

Irving, K. (1995) 'Big charity business', *The Times*, 13 April.

NCVO News (1995a) 'Legal structures survey', February.

—— (1995b) 'New study to prompt cross-national work in Europe', July.

—— (1995c) 'New money for London charities', July.

Winfield, M. (1990) *Minding Your Own Business*, London: Social Audit.

Chapter 10

Balancing the books
Charitable finance

Pesh Framjee

With over 170,000 charities accounting for over £17 billion of income it is somewhat surprising that there has been no mandatory audit and accounting regime for charities. This will all change now. In February 1995 the Home Office published draft regulations on the new accounting, auditing and reporting regime under the Charities Act 1993. The consultation period ended on 17 May 1995 and new regulations were published in October 1995 to come into force for accounting periods beginning on or after 1 March 1996. To facilitate a better understanding of the regulations they have been published along with the revised Statement of Recommended Practice (SORP) on accounting by charities.

The draft regulations set out the detailed statutory framework for the maintenance of accounting records and introduce the Statement of Financial Activities (SOFA) as the basis of a charity's accounts. There is also a requirement to prepare a trustees' report and charities which breach certain financial thresholds will have to be independently examined or audited.

Charities exceeding £100,000 of gross income will have to prepare full accounts in accordance with the SORP. If their gross income is under £100,000 they can prepare a simple receipts and payments account. Those charities exceeding £250,000 of gross income or total expenditure in the current or the preceding two years will have to have a full audit. If they fall under this band but exceed £10,000 of gross income they will require an independent examination. The regulations do not apply to charities which are incorporated under the Companies Act and these charities have further hurdles before they are entitled to the audit exemption. In addition to income having to be under £250,000 they are not entitled to the audit exemption if they are a parent or subsidiary company or if their net assets exceed £1.4 million. There is no requirement for independent examination and Companies Act charities with income above £90,000 but under £250,000 will require an accountant's report.

This chapter discusses the best practice recommendations for charity financial reporting and explains the principles and focuses on areas where interpretation may be contentious, so that those involved with charity financial reporting can understand the rationales and ensure compliance.

Although the objectives of charity accounting have remained unchanged, experience has shown that the original guidelines needed to be strengthened and clarified in certain areas. The thrust of the changes stems from the desire for greater account-ability of all the resources entrusted to a charity.

Many of these concepts mirror important aspects of trust law and to comply with that law charities are expected to maintain records that should allow much of the information required by the SORP to be obtained easily. In many areas the requirements are virtually identical to the original SORP 2 but additional clarification and refinements have been made so that the account-ing treatment and public presentation reflect the legal require-ment and the needs of users of charity accounts.

The regulations stipulate the minimum accounting requirement for charities which are not also companies; in effect the statutory framework. The revised SORP will, as best practice for all chari-ties, provide the flesh on the bones. The accounting regulations and the SORP have been drafted to ensure that compliance with the SORP will ensure full compliance with the accounting regulations. Although the SORP, being recommended practice, is not mandatory the Charity Commissioners have explained that they would expect charities to comply with the requirements unless another SORP, which is more specific to them, is published. Charity accounts should specifically note compliance with the SORP as part of the accounting policies. It is important to recog-nise that the SORP only applies to material items.

It preparing accounts on a receipts and payment basis charities with income under £100,000 can adopt a simplified approach. Furthermore, in certain cases a departure from the principles of the SORP may be necessary to give a true and fair view and in such cases the departure should be explained, stating the reasons for such departure. When considering the principles expressed in the SORP, there is a need to understand the underlying reasons for the recommendations and a common-sense approach to their application should be adopted. Narrow and rigid interpretations are often made on certain aspects when clearly this is not the rationale behind those aspects. Above all, a charity's accounts should be transparent and the accounting policies and the notes should explain what has been done. In addition to the Charity SORP there are other SORPs which are applicable to specific classes of charities. There are SORPs for universities, housing associations and unit trusts (the last should be followed by common investment funds).

Statements of Standard Accounting Practice and more recently issued Financial Reporting Standards are together seen as being authoritative statements on accounting practice. They aim to narrow the areas of difference and variety in the accounting treatments of the matters with which they deal, to ensure that accounts are prepared on a broadly similar basis. They are applicable to all financial statements which are intended to give a true and fair view of the organisation's state of affairs at the balance sheet date and of income and expenditure for the financial period ending on that date. Compliance with accounting standards will normally be required if financial statements are to give a true and fair view.

It is important to recognise that many charities are already following the principles of the revised SORP as indication of best practice, since nothing in the new SORP conflicts with existing accounting principles. In fact the SORP has received the 'negative franking' from the Accounting Standards Board. The SORP specifically does not reiterate all the principles of generally accepted accounting practice. Therefore charities preparing accounts to give a true and fair view must also consider Accounting Standards.

The SORP has been written to ensure that it is in line with the accounting requirements of the Charities Act 1993. In fact, charities preparing accounts under the SORP will automatically meet the Charities Act accounting requirements. In addition, there is nothing in the SORP that would be unacceptable for charitable companies. In certain cases a summary income and expenditure account may be required.

Many charity accountants have long complained that the traditional income and expenditure account did not reflect or explain fully all the financial activities of the charity. They consider that the very nature of raising and using of charity resources requires a different approach from that of commercial profit-orientated companies.

Charities do not usually have shareholders with an equity interest, so matters such as distributable profit and dividends do not feature. A charity's resource providers do not usually expect a direct return on their donations. The users of charity financial statements need to assess the services that the charity is providing and its ability to continue providing them. The accounts should also show how the trustees have discharged their stewardship responsibilities during the year and while it may be that the bottom-line surplus or deficit provides some of this information, any presentation that focuses on such a bottom line tends to ignore some fundamental differences between accounting for charities and commercial organisations.

With most commercial organisations, the bottom-line profit for the year is vitally significant. To some extent it measures performance, and users of accounts justifiably turn to it to ascertain the results for the period. Revenue and costs are matched because there is a strong relationship between them: for example, sales in a period are matched with the cost of those sales, as they are interdependent.

Charities, unless they are receiving fees or funding for specific work, are not usually in the business of directly matching income and expenditure. They do not generally work towards a particular result for the year-end date. For example, a charity which receives income in the last few months of the accounting period would rightly include the income in that period's accounts notwithstanding that the expenditure funded by this money may not be incurred until later accounting periods. Therefore, to emphasise a bottom line at a particular point in time could be misleading, as income and expenditure in a given period are often not directly linked and may bear little or no resemblance to each other. There are certain charities where matching of their activities may be appropriate. For example, fee income from residential care may be matched with costs of residential care. However, even with these, the inclusion of voluntary income or expenditure which is not related to the fee income can often skew the bottom line.

Furthermore, the traditional income and expenditure account with the historical distinction between revenue and capital does not always adequately explain a charity's activities. The motive of capital expenditure may be different from that of commercial companies which usually invest in fixed assets to generate income, whereas a charity may invest in fixed assets as part of its primary purpose, for example, building hospices, purchasing wetlands, and so on. This difference may be quite important to certain charities whose *raison d'être* requires them to incur significant capital expenditure on a recurring basis.

In certain years a charity may use income to purchase fixed assets and since this expenditure, being of a capital nature, will not be shown in the income and expenditure account, it might appear that it has a surplus. In fact the charity might have spent large amounts on fixed assets which may be as important to its mission as is the other revenue expenditure shown in the income and expenditure account. Therefore judging the charity on the bottom-line criteria can often be misleading.

In recognition that charities do not generally have any one single indicator of performance comparable to a business enterprise bottom line, it is perhaps more important to consider changes in the *nature* as well as the *amounts* of the net resources of a charity. This coupled with other information about the charity's efforts and accomplishments will assist in assessing performance. Accordingly, the SORP and the Regulations under the Charities Act recommend a primary statement that records all the resources entrusted to the charity and reflects all the financial activities in the period under review. The proposals are that this statement will be called the Statement of Financial Activities.

In producing the SORP this departure from an 'operating' statement format had to be carefully weighed up and certain options were considered: for example, that the reporting statement should be divided into two parts: a statement of 'operations' and a statement of other changes in net assets. The suggestion was that the first statement would report operating income and expenses and would be followed by another statement that would report all other income, expenses, gains and losses. There is, however, no consensus on how to define an operating measure and on which income and expenses should be included or excluded from 'operations'. For example, some would include in 'operations' only donations and resources available for current period use, whether restricted or not. Others suggested the exclusion of restricted income if the restrictions were not met in the current period. Some would exclude from 'operations', revenues, gains or losses from non-recurring, unexpected or unusual events such as a very large legacy.

Many example accounts produced by charities show that distinctions based on operations tend to be arbitrary and are dependent on the impossible task of trying to match a charity's total income and total expenditure when, in most cases, no such matching is possible or even desirable. Hence the SOFA tries to move away from giving undue emphasis to the bottom line based on matching, and focuses instead on the periodic measurement of the changes in both the nature and amounts of all the net resources of a charity.

Some charities, usually those providing services, do try and match income and expenditure, such as costs of and revenues from housing services or costs and fees from education. However, the format of a traditional income and expenditure account that lists separately the income and the expenditure did not really assist those charities, since it merely listed all revenue such as donations and also fee income and then deducted all revenue expenditure. Consequently, no direct matching was possible and inevitably, these charities linked by way of notes the revenue and costs where they are directly attributable. This practice, which shows whether there has been a surplus or deficit on a particular activity where matching is appropriate and useful, should continue where it is applicable.

The exposure draft format which highlighted capital expenditure on the face of the SOFA has been altered. Charities with significant capital expenditure on fixed assets should present a statement of capital expenditure to highlight the importance and relevance of such expenditure. In many cases capital expenditure and a statement of such expenditure should be given due prominence. It does not imply that capital expenditure is a reduction in resources but rather that it is a change in the nature of those resources. This statement would be important to see how the charity expends its liquid resources and how its capital spend may affect its liquidity and ability to provide services.

The distinction between income and capital permeates trust law. Income includes all resources which become available to the charity and which the trustees are legally required to apply in furtherance of the charitable purposes within a reasonable time. Capital, on the other hand, must be invested or retained. In addition, due to the constraints of trust law and the important matter of donor-imposed restrictions, it is vital that users of the accounts can see what the increase or decrease in net resources represents. A charity may, for example, have maintained the level of its net assets only because it received restricted income earmarked for a particular purpose which compensated for a significant decrease in general income. This would not be obvious in the traditional single-column format which usually does not distinguish between the types of funds. It is important that to ensure compliance with the terms of the special trusts and funds, the accounts assist this understanding.

Many charities receive significant amounts of restricted resources and these restrictions often affect types and levels of services. Consequently, information about the change in the nature of net assets is vitally useful in assessing a charity's ability to respond to short-term needs or higher levels of service. Therefore, the recommendations are that the resources of a charity should be grouped according to the restrictions on their use. These are *unrestricted funds*, which are funds available for general use and include those that have been designated for particular purposes by the trustees of a charity. Second are *restricted income funds* which are funds which are restricted for particular purposes, either by the wishes of the donor or by the nature of the appeal. Therefore, those preparing and auditing charity accounts will have to consider carefully appeal literature, direct mail and other forms of solicitation to ascertain whether income received as a result of the solicitation should be restricted. Third are *capital funds* or funds which are not for direct application. Where the trustees have no power to apply capital as income it will be permanent endowment. Where the trustees have a power to expend it if necessary, this will be expendable endowment. Expendable endowment should be treated as capital until the right to expend it is exercised, in which case it should be transferred to income prior to application.

Appendix 3 to the SORP provides a useful explanation on the principles of Fund Accounting and the definition of income and capital are covered in the Glossary.

An analysis and visible segregation on the face of the SOFA and in the Balance Sheet is vital to be able to identify what services and activities a charity could continue to carry out. For example, if an international aid charity has received income specifically for Kurdish refugees, this will be shown as a restricted fund and will highlight that the money is unavailable for other purposes. This information would be far more important than a composite surplus or deficit on revenue income and revenue expenditure.

Since charities have to account separately for all their funds, the assets and liabilities representing the various funds should be clearly analysed. This is important so as to provide an indication as to whether sufficient resources are held in an appropriate form to enable the funds concerned to be applied in accordance with any restrictions. Therefore, restricted funds for short-term application should be matched with short-term assets and investments. The SORP therefore requires an analysis of the assets and liabilities that are included within the three principal categories of funds stated above. Some charities achieve this by preparing a columnar balance sheet.

To maintain the sanctity of funds, all gains and losses on assets held in a particular fund form part of that fund, as does income received or expenditure incurred on account of that fund. Generally, income generated from assets held in a restricted-income fund will be restricted income unless the donor has specified otherwise. Conversely, income generated on capital funds such as permanent endowment will be available for general application unless the donor specifies otherwise.

It is stressed that the concept of fund accounting is not a new requirement but the SORP merely clarifies the position under trust law, and the accounting records should be structured so as to achieve the required separation between funds. This means that it is vital to analyse correctly and allocate both income and expenditure.

Having recognised that income received for a particular purpose must be used only for that purpose, it is necessary to allocate expenditure against special funds. Therefore, expenditure needs to be analysed in a way that enables a proper calculation of what has been expended and what needs to be carried forward as a balance on the restricted funds.

When a charity's trustees propose to use general funds for a particular purpose they can set aside amounts for future expenditure. In these circumstances such amounts should be treated as designated funds. These transfers to or from designated funds are an allocation of the general-fund balance carried forward and not a reduction of unrestricted funds. There will, therefore, be no change to total net assets. However, it will highlight that some of these are designated for a particular purpose. Designated funds should not be confused with restricted funds. The former are usually a result of an internal decision (which can be altered) while the latter arise from donor-imposed restrictions or the terms of a specific appeal.

It is also possible to use designated funds to create a distinction between funds. For example, a charity with significant amounts of mission critical fixed assets, such as care homes or hospices, may decide to set up a property or fixed-asset fund which will equate to the net book value of the assets. This fund will then segregate from the general fund the amount which has already been 'utilised' and is represented by fixed assets.

The original SORP 2 established that whether income is restricted should not affect the manner in which it is accounted for or the timing of its recognition as income. The original SORP explicitly stated that restricted income and unrestricted income received at the same time should be accounted for at the same time. This is, in part, based on the principle that restrictions, although limiting or, indeed, even directing the use of the income, are similar to the understanding that all income should be used to support the charitable objectives. The difference is that with restricted income the donor's wish is explicit and usually more prescriptive, but this alone does not alter the fact that income has been received which results in the transfer of economic benefit from the donor to the charity.

The new SORP follows this theme and states that all income and resources entrusted to the charity in the period under review should be recognised in the Statement of Financial Activities. It emphasises that restricted income imposes special responsibilities and that restrictions can affect the charity's services. Accordingly, all restricted income, although recognised at the same time as unrestricted income, should be clearly identified. Restricted incoming resources which have not been spent by the accounting reference date should be carried forward in the appropriate restricted fund.

The new SORP does, however, highlight the important difference between restrictions and conditions. Restrictions on income simply limit the type of expenditure or the use of the donated income or asset. On the other hand, conditions usually create a barrier that must be overcome before the income is recognised. This concept is clear, in theory, but sometimes obscure in practice. In essence, if resources are received with restrictions on how they can be used for the charity's particular objectives this is not fundamentally different from the requirement that even unrestricted income must be used for the charity's specific objectives. In both cases resources have been received which enhance the charity's capacity to provide services and there has been a measurable transfer of economic benefit which has given rise to new assets which should be recognised.

On the other hand, with a conditional donation, the charity is not entitled to the income and cannot use the resources until the condition has been met. There is an obligation to perform or in some other way overcome the barrier which prevents the charity from entitlement to the resources. Hence the principle is that income should not be recognised until the conditions for its receipt have been met.

Charity law requires trustees to account for all funds entrusted to them for their use. The accounts that they are required to prepare must show the 'gross income' which is defined in Section 97 of the Charities Act 1993 as *'gross recorded income from all sources including special trusts'*, special trusts are also defined in the section as *'property which is held or administered by or on behalf of a charity for any special purpose of the charity'*.

Accordingly, restricted income as defined by the SORP would be income received under special trust and must, like unrestricted income, be included in gross recorded income. For a charity, the receipt and acceptance of restricted income involves a fiduciary responsibility to use the resources to fulfil the specified charitable objectives. The donor's direction as to its use merely focuses the fiduciary responsibility on a specific use. This is earmarked income and should be recognised as such without attempting to set up a liability or defer the income, since the receipt of restricted income does not really affect the liabilities any further than if the trustees themselves designated a specific use for assets.

The SORP recognises that the fiduciary responsibility imposed by restricted income is fundamentally different from the responsibility imposed by incurring a liability such as a creditor's claim and consequently, to comply with charity law, restricted income should be recognised as part of 'gross income'.

The size of charities is often measured by their income. Perhaps this is due to the fact that with commercial companies size is often measured through turnover. There is however a fundamental difference. The sales of a commercial company are its *raison d'être*, with a charity it is its expenditure and not its income which fulfils its objectives. For this reason it is vital that the analysis and presentation of expenditure in the accounts is given particular importance. The aim should be to reflect fairly the activities of a charity so that readers of the accounts can understand how the charity's expenditure fulfils its objectives.

The new SORP expands on the recommendations which, although expressed in the original SORP, were not clearly explained and hence not always followed. The original SORP required that expenditure was split between charitable and non-charitable expenditure. It suggested further that non-charitable expenditure should be divided between fundraising, publicity and administration.

A number of charities have ignored this, and many income and expenditure accounts merely list expenditure by their natural expense classification, such as rent, salaries and wages, printing and stationery, and so on. This information does not convey very much about the activities of the charity to the reader. In fact, when looking at these accounts, it is often not clear how the charity is spending money on its objectives. Expenditure information by natural classification has its uses but it is more important to identify the costs incurred on each of the different activities of the charity. Charities should continue to disclose certain expenses such as salaries by natural classification, but this could be done in the notes to the accounts.

The new SORP therefore recommends that expenditure should be listed by functional classification. This is the aggregation of costs incurred in pursuit of a defined purpose, for example, provision of services to the elderly or counselling. It is achieved by adding together all the costs (salaries, rent, depreciation, and so on) relating to that specific activity. It is likely, therefore, to include an allocation exercise as well as aggregation, since it summarises expenditure according to the purpose for which costs are incurred. The SORP recommends a twofold functional classification that reports expenditure on major projects or services and the costs of supporting those charitable activities (charitable expenditure) distinguishing them from expenditure on fundraising, publicity and administration (other expenditure).

The regulations under the Charities Act 1993 endorse this classification and require resources expended to be divided into: expenditure directly relating to the objects of the charity; expenditure on fundraising and publicity; and expenditure on the cost of managing and administrating the charity. (Charities with income under £100,000 do not have to provide this analysis.) Recognising that the administration expenditure figure was often an account into which everything that could not be directly charged was dumped, the new SORP has introduced a new heading of 'support costs'. These are costs which comprise all services supplied centrally, be they at headquarters or through a regional network, which are identifiable as being wholly or mainly in support of the charity's charitable expenditure. They would include an appropriate proportion of overheads such as finance-staff time and office accommodation. Support costs would be shown as charitable expenditure.

Tabulating information in this way will move towards the user being able to see information that may assist in linking a charity's expenses with its accomplishments. Charities should attempt to select appropriate headings for functional costs which best explain the areas of their work. A good start is to review the annual report to see what it says about how the charity has expended its resources. The headings on the SOFA should then tie in with the narrative comment.

Any discussion on charity expenditure would be incomplete without reference to the ubiquitous cost ratios. The charity world and the giving public have an obsession with questions such as: 'How much is spent on administration?', 'How much is going directly to the beneficiaries?', and people turn to the accounts or to published statistics to try to measure a charity's efficiency.

Some believe that there should be regulations as to how much a charity can spend on its overheads. To dispel the fears of inefficiency and wastefulness there must be accountability. Accountability demands honesty, and old prejudices and misconceptions have to be dispelled. The public are often led to believe that a charity's effectiveness can be measured by how much of the income is spent on charitable objectives. Minimal overheads are meant to mean that the charity is effective. Due to a lack of performance information, inputs are used to evaluate performance.

The relative lack of performance accountability highlights a pressing need in the sector. Annual accounts and management information reports are very successful at measuring inputs such as wages and salaries, heat and lighting, printing and stationery, and so on. They say very little about outputs and, more importantly, outcomes and the effect of an organisation's performance on its stakeholders. Very often the information is not comparable. Some charities allocate the costs of their finance departments and others do not. Even if all charities were using a similar method it would be wrong to compare different charities on this basis.

It is time more charities provided different measures of effectiveness and also educated the public that charities cannot be run on a shoe-string and that there is nothing wrong in incurring expenditure to ensure that there is a proper infrastructure. At the same time there is a need to ensure that we are seen to be fair in allocating costs. Recently there has been concern in the United States that charities are masking their true fundraising costs by allocating large elements of their costs such as direct-mail costs to headings such as 'public awareness' and 'information dissemination'. It is important that charities do not abuse the flexibility offered by the new recommendations and do not misallocate costs purely to 'window dress' the accounts. Above all, whatever method is used the accounting policies should provide a clear explanation.

A chapter of this length can but scratch the surface of charity finance and there are many other important issues which must be addressed. The new regime stresses that there is no such thing as a private charity and that there is a need for greater accountability. Accountability means transparency. If a charity cannot demonstrate its stewardship over funds entrusted to it, then it brings into question its financial-management abilities and leads to accusations of inefficiency and/or maladministration. Charities should be positive about facing the challenge of new times. Greater accountability will lead to greater public confidence and more recognition of the important role that charities play in our society.

Chapter 11

At the top
The role of the chief executive

Mike Whitlam

The role of a professional management chief executive is a relatively new phenomenon in the voluntary sector. Indeed, it was only in 1986 that a number of chief executives felt it necessary to establish an Association for Chief Executives of National Voluntary Organisations, commonly known as ACENVO. The brief of this body was threefold. It was established to provide a network for chief executives to support each other because there was a strong feeling at that time that the position of chief executive was a very lonely one. Second, ACENVO was intended to provide a network for the exchange of information. Finally, it represented the views of chief executives on important issues affecting the voluntary sector. The establishment of ACENVO was perhaps a reflection of how rapidly the voluntary sector was changing during the late 1980s and early 1990s.

The chief executive's role varies according to his or her relationship with the board of trustees and the age, development and structure of the organisation. In the commercial sector the chief executive plays a significant role in managing the company to profitability and is often charged with the function of expanding the organisation and improving the quality of its activities. The role is very similar in the voluntary sector in that the chief executive is expected to manage the organisation and the people and resources on a day-to-day basis. He or she is responsible for ensuring effective financial management, the quality of activities and development of the organisation. However, performance indicators other than profit must be used by the voluntary sector chief executive.

One other important difference between the roles of the chief executive in the voluntary sector as compared to the commercial sector is the relationship with the board. In the commercial sector, the chief executive is often a board member; in a voluntary organisation the chief executive would be accountable to a board of trustees but not be a member of the board. The main task of the board of trustees should be to set the overall direction for the organisation. However, in many organisations the trustees are also involved in the day-to-day running of the organisation. The extent of this involvement depends on a number of factors, not least of which is the stage to which the organisation has developed. For example, if the organisation is at a very early stage in its development, described by some as stage 1, 'kitchen table crusading' (Straw 1987), then it is likely that the trustees would be using their professional skills daily to help run the organisation. However, if the organisation has further developed to stage 4, where there is a fully competent professional team to manage the organisation on a day-to-day basis, then the trustees will play much more of a non-executive role, involved with addressing overall strategic issues.

John Carver (1995) has said that the board's responsibility was to address broad top-level strategic issues and set parameters for the chief executives and staff. The board should determine not what the chief executive could do but what was inappropriate for them to do. This has proved to be, for some, a rather controversial concept.

Although the chief executive's role varies from organisation to organisation there are some elements of the role that are constant. ACENVO, in 1991, established a model job description for chief executives, the key features of which were:

1 Reports to:
The board of trustees
2 Main purpose of the job:
   (a) To give direction to the formulation and leadership to the achievement of the organisation's philosophy, objectives and strategies and to its annual targets.
   (b) To be responsible for the management and administration of the organisation in the execution of the board of trustees' policies.
   (c) Together with the chairperson, to enable the board of trustees to fulfil its functions and to ensure that the board receives appropriate advice and information on all relevant matters.

3 Principal accountability
   (a) Serving the board of trustees
       For example: seeking trustees' approval of a schedule of
       meetings, ensuring items requiring the consideration of the
       board are placed on appropriate agenda, reporting period-
       ically on the organisation's progress to the board, helping
       the chairperson involve the members of the board,
       formulating policy proposals for the approval of the
       board.
   (b) Leading and managing the organisation
       For example: ensuring the organisation has a long-term
       strategy to enable it to achieve its objectives; monitor and
       review progress; lead the senior management team; manage
       staff reporting directly to the chief executive; establish an
       effective system of recruitment; where an equal opportuni-
       ties policy is in place, work towards its implementation and
       preparation of the annual budget for submission to the
       board of trustees.

It was once said that in the voluntary sector the chief executive
must be prepared to undertake almost any task, and there are
many anecdotes of chief executives who, for example, in the space
of one hour, have had to unblock a drain before shaking the
hand of a member of the royal family. However, in an increasingly
more management-orientated sector, chief executives are having
to give more attention to their role as people managers, strategic
planners, financial managers – both in terms of income and expenditure – as well as marketing the business and being the media
spokesperson for the organisation.

The role of managing a voluntary organisation in the 1990s,
particularly one that is heavily dependent upon volunteers, is
not easy. Although many of the principles are the same as the
commercial and public sector, managing an unpaid (volunteer),
as well as a paid, work force with an increased expectation of
high-quality performance, service specifications and time-focused
targets, means that there is a real need for additional skills. The
voluntary sector really is the place for 'super-manager'.

The Committee on the Financial Aspects of Corporate Governance, chaired by Sir Adrian Cadbury, reported on a code of best
practice for company boards (Cadbury 1992a, 1992b). This code
said that 'there should be a clearly accepted division of responsi-

bilities at the head of a company, which will ensure a balance of power and authority such that no one individual has unfettered powers of decision'. In other words, the board should work as a board. This has implications for the chief executive.

Diana Leat (1993) suggests that differences between the managing boards of a for-profit and not-for-profit organisation are not as different as one might think. She says: 'The organisational structure of charities, which requires volunteer trustees/a board directing professional managers who are paid to manage but have no legal power to determine policy, creates an inherent problem in the management of such organisations.' Could this be part of what makes a chief executive's job in a voluntary organisation problematic?

Given the ACENVO model job description and the tasks that are necessarily undertaken by a chief executive, it is important that a chief executive in the voluntary sector is respected for his or her skills in management and policy-making just as they would be in the commercial sector. A group of chief executives from the voluntary sector, asked what would be the characteristics that they expected of other chief executives, offered, among other examples, that he or she should be calm; able to cope under pressure; able to keep 'many balls in the air'; computer literate; and comfortable with a very wide range of people from those who live on the streets to those who own them. The chief executive, they also believed, should be a decision-maker and not a procrastinator; assertive but not aggressive; and determined not stubborn. Thus, the voluntary sector chief executive has to be a professionally competent manager, but also be able to apply business skills, taking a very clear and firm account of the principles, ethics and values of the organisation which he or she runs.

For most business organisations the bottom line is profit. For the voluntary organisation, the ability to provide specific services or campaign on behalf of a client or user group is what matters. Commercial chief executives will argue that they value the caring side of their organisations as much as charities and that to be sensitive to the work force and the needs of their customers is good for them and good for business. Nevertheless, charities frequently need to go further because profit-making is not the limit of their activities.

One of the most important roles of the chief executive is the strategic management of the organisation, including monitoring the implementation of strategic plans. It is vital for a successful organisation to have a mission statement and vision for the future. The chief executive must develop and follow through strategic plans with measurable objectives and outcomes. It should not be just a theoretical plan, but one that relates very clearly to the needs of the organisation and its customs. Measures of success will require close and careful monitoring.

The model which I have found most useful is shown in Figure 11.1. It is the key to not only understand one's own organisation but the environment in which the organisation operates. It is also important for the organisation to be clear as to its future and to be proud of its success. It is one way the chief executive can lead and motivate his or her staff and volunteers.

Charities form a widely varying part of the voluntary sector. There are currently approximately 180,000 registered charities. The smaller ones may have no chief executive and be totally managed by volunteers, whereas the larger ones have thousands of staff. For example, in 1994, the British Red Cross employed in total 2,751 paid staff, was supported by approximately 87,150 volunteers, and had an annual turnover of £91.8 million. This is similar to other leading charities in the top 500 fundraising charities. The top ten charities have tens of millions of pounds worth of turnover, and hundreds, if not thousands, of paid staff and volunteers.

The size of the charity will have an impact on the role of the chief executive. In the larger charities the chief executive will tend to have a management team of around five or six directors, whereas in the smaller organisations the chief executive might have to undertake senior management tasks him- or herself, while at the same time directly managing staff at a departmental level. This makes the task of fulfilling a strategic and operational role even more difficult for the chief executive of a small charity.

There really is no established pattern for the structure of charities, but there is now within the sector an increasing level of information about the shape and feel of organisations. For example, the 1995 edition of *Dimensions of the Voluntary Sector* covered charity fundraising patterns; reviewed the behaviour of corporate funders and grant-making trusts; reviewed the income and expenditure of charities; compared the size of various parts of the voluntary sector; and reviewed the voluntary sector as a whole. This and other sources of information support strategic planning and are extremely important to the chief executive.

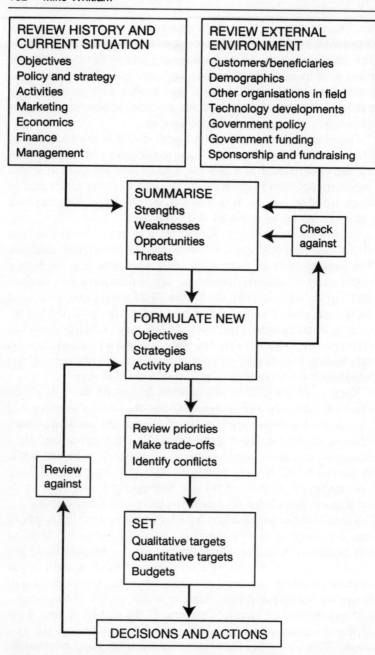

Figure 11.1 Conceptual model for planning processes

The chief executive is the buffer between staff and the board. The board is often made up of people both from within the charity and outside and members of the board will have differing views of their role and responsibilities (Kramer 1985; Carver 1990; National Council for Voluntary Organisations/Charity Commission 1992; NCVO 1994; Whitlam 1986). Kramer's view of the relationship between the chief executive and the board is that it is more complex than a partnership. The relationship is influenced by the distribution of power and the impact of conflicts. The power referred to here relates to the balance of the differing resources the chief executive and board bring to their relationship and the dependency of the chief executive and board on one another: for example, their levels of executive influence, status, professionalism and skills.

The board and chief executive relationship is influenced by their situation. The greater the size, degree of complexity, bureaucratisation, professionalism and decentralisation of the organisation, the greater the dependence of the board members on the chief executive for information and assistance.

Often the smaller the organisation the greater the power struggle. The larger and more bureaucratic the organisation the greater the management authority and autonomy of the chief executive. However, likelihood of conflict is greater due to longer lines of communication in a larger organisation and more tenuous control between levels of authority. The larger the board the more nominal the involvement of trustees leaving the chief executive in control. The stage of development of an organisation also affects the power of the board and chief executive. The board is more powerful at the early rather than late stage of an organisation's development.

Kramer proposes a contingency model for the board and chief executive relationship where the relationship is a continuum of three types of relationship which vary as appropriate. These types of relationship are consensus, clash of opinion, and no agreement possible. Thankfully, the third stage is rare. How the relationship varies will reflect the strategy used by the chief executive and the board to achieve desired goals.

Carver (1990), on the other hand, summarises his 'policy governance model' by saying that it was created 'to enable strategic leadership by governing boards. It addresses board job design and board–management partnership. The board governs on behalf of some identifiable "ownership" deciding the broad values of the organisation.' Carver writes:

> Written values and perspectives are called policies and occur in four categories: 'Ends' policies prescribe what benefits will occur for which people at what cost; mission and priorities are included. 'Executive Limitations' policies describe the prudence and ethical boundaries on acceptable staff action and practice. 'Governance Process' policies clarify the board's own job and rules, including how it connects to its 'ownership'. 'Board–staff Linkage' policies describe the delegation and accountability linkage through the chief executive officer. The last three are relatively stable, enabling virtually all board time to be spent on 'Ends'.

He adds: 'The chief executive officer is empowered by the board towards "ends" and within "executive limitations".' This 'enables the board to stay out of internal operation, yet control the bounds of acceptability'.

The *On Trust* report (NCVO/Charity Commission 1992), on the other hand, was very clear about its view on the role of trustees. It states that 'the people responsible for the general control and management of the administration of the charity are defined as charity trustees by the Charities Act 1960'. *On Trust* then reviews the legal, financial and management responsibilities of trustees and the role of the honorary officers. The trustees' responsibilities are clearly wide-ranging.

It is the chief executive's role to work with the board and individual trustees to enable them to perform their roles and responsibilities effectively. The relationship between the trustees and chief executive is a complex one. Sadly, in recent years the turnover of chief executives in some organisations has been both rapid and unfortunate, very often because neither the chief executive nor the trustees have clarified their respective roles.

Given the rapidly changing environment in which chief executives operate there are strategies which they must adopt to enable themselves to keep on top of the job and survive. Concern regarding the rapid change in the voluntary sector led to the launch of a national commission by the National Council for Voluntary Organisations to look at the future of the voluntary sector. The commission looked at how the sector is changing and reached conclusions about the key issues for the voluntary sector such as

the governance of charities; the different problems of organisations at different stages of their development and their varying
ability to cope with change; the professionalisation of charity
management; and the effect of government policy. The commission was launched in January 1995, and produced its final
report in July 1996. It is expected that the results of this work
will have a major impact on the strategic planning and decision-
making of chief executives.

There are a number of strategies chief executives can adopt to
manage change. Many chief executives claim that they are not
understood by their board, and in particular, by its chairperson.
While this may well be the case, clarification of the role of the
board and chief executive respectively will help their relationship.
Very often, however, the problem is more fundamental than that.
Conflict may arise because trustees and/or the chief executive do
not understand that their roles and responsibilities must change
with their organisation's development. If the board and the management group understand the stage their particular organisation
has reached, they are better able to adopt the most appropriate
strategies and structures for their organisation's current stage of
development.

It is equally important that the organisation is managed through
the stages of development and does not drift from one stage of
its development to another. Instead it should move through the
stages by virtue of conscious decisions.

What are these stages? They have been variously described,
but the one which I prefer, referred to earlier, was developed by
Straw (1987). He describes four life-cycle stages: kitchen table
crusading; kitchen table with bells (offices, materials, paid help,
etc.); national staff structure; and looks like any other public- or
private-sector organisation except the head office is in the back
street.

Stage 1 is when a number of people come together with a
passionate commitment to change or create something. At some
point, the organisation will move into stage 2 and require office
space, maybe some secretarial help, computers and other administrative 'whistles and bells'. This stage is highly volunteer-led with
some professional staff support. The organisation, though, often
drifts into stage 3 when there is a tension between board members
and the growing number of professional staff. If there is no clear
strategy or clear agreement as to respective responsibilities, an

organisation can become inward-looking and may lose its sense of direction. This is not a comfortable stage and not one in which the organisation should remain for very long. The leadership of the organisation can manage these changes and, for example, can make a conscious decision to go back to being a stage-2 organisation or to move on to stage 4 where the professional staff undertake much of the work with volunteer management acting exclusively as a strategic non-executive board. The real problem arises when the board membership of a stage-4 organisation includes people who still believe that the organisation is at stage 1 and they expect to be involved in day-to-day management issues. It is very important that the chief executive and the board have a good understanding of the stage of their organisation's development so that fundamental mistakes like this are avoided.

Having understood the organisation's development, it is also extremely important for the board and the chief executive to understand the environment in which they are working. Some board members have been known to criticise their chief executives for 'wasting time looking at other organisations' activities'. Indeed, competitor analysis, in the voluntary sector, is thought by some to be an anathema. But how can an organisation ensure that its mission is being implemented in the most efficient and effective way to meet the real needs of its users and clients, if the organisation does not understand what clients and users really want and who else may be providing the same or similar services? There needs to be thorough research carried out on the organisation's environment and this must be given full consideration by both the management group and the board.

If the area of the organisation's interest is one which is rapidly changing (for example, international disaster relief after the cold war) then it becomes even more important that time and energy are given to analysing and understanding the external environment. There are many ways in which this can be done, and for a small organisation it is often the responsibility of the chief executive to keep abreast the external environment.

There are various environments that the chief executive must understand. This will depend on the activities of the organisation but could, for example, include understanding the voluntary sector, the fundraising world, the environmental or health and social services fields, charity and company law, financial accounting in the charity sector, the media, and changes to the needs of clients or customers. Keeping up to date with such issues is not an easy task and for larger organisations there are staff, and sometimes volunteers, employed to research and understand the various environments in which the organisation must operate. The chief executive who does not have these support systems within the organisation should develop alternative methods to obtain information. A chief executive could obtain information by purchasing from services monitoring legislation, charity law development, finance development, and so on.

The chief executive will also need to give additional time to networking, attending meetings and conferences outside of the organisation, and to reading. This is a perfectly legitimate part of a chief executive's role and must not be assumed by the board to be carried out after working hours.

Giving time to competitor analysis is often something that is frowned upon by volunteers and indeed some paid staff working within a voluntary organisation, particularly where the funds have been hard earned. However, it is interesting just how often the chief executive is questioned about competitors by trustees and users. For example, a chief executive could be asked: 'Why is X organisation getting more media coverage than we are?', 'Why did X organisation manage to secure funds from Y trust?'; or 'Why has X organisation been successful in developing Z services?' Analysing the activities of competitors is a very common aspect of securing business success. We can learn from other organisations and avoid duplication or reinvention of the wheel.

Understanding the external environment is difficult enough, but it is extremely important for the chief executive also to understand the internal environment of the organisation. In some voluntary organisations this is relatively easy to achieve because of the single nature of the organisation or its small size. In other larger organisations special systems need to be developed.

No matter what the size of the organisation, however, it is important to understand its dynamics; for example, the power bases, and the respective expectations of the various stakeholders. Some chief executives do not give enough time to thinking about who in their organisation are the stakeholders and then suddenly find that they have been caught out.

Some managers instil the virtues of the philosophy of 'management by walking about'. It is also important for the chief executive to give some time to meeting and talking with those who support the organisation such as volunteers, paid staff, supporters or donors. The chief executive can also obtain valuable information from listening directly to non-managerial staff while maintaining line management accountability for people on the shop floor. It is amazing how one can hear different stories when listening to people in less formal settings.

Board members may be faced with the position of trying to identify a new chief executive for their organisation. The growth and rapid expansion of the voluntary sector in recent years has meant that it has been necessary to bring many chief executives into the sector. For some people, coming from the more enlightened voluntary organisations, it has been possible for them to receive internal training and external management training enabling them to become chief executives in their own or other agencies. Recent developments such as career-development groups and management-development programmes will almost certainly lead to 'home-grown' chief executives. The British Red Cross, for example, in the last three years has established two management-development programmes for potential managers. Although it is early days, the benefits to the staff in these programmes are already showing.

However, the speed of the growth of the sector has meant that many staff have had to come into voluntary organisations from other sectors. A large number, for example, have come from the commercial sector and not, as one might have imagined, from other related social and health care fields. Leat (1993) looks at managers coming into the sector from outside and gives some disquieting evidence.

Another phenomenon which has resulted from this movement into the voluntary sector is the increased use of recruitment agencies. Three specialist recruitment agencies which recruit chief executives for the sector have come into being and, perhaps more interestingly, many of the major recruitment companies now recognise the size and importance of the sector and have started to recruit for the sector. Given such a development, these recruitment agencies should ensure that they are fully conversant with the needs of the sector, and work with ACENVO to ensure that new chief executives in the sector are supported in their early days.

Chief executives' backgrounds are as diverse and rich as one might imagine given the characteristics of the commercial, social services, health care and military sectors, and so on, from which they come. There is, though, no obvious training course for chief executives, although ACENVO has developed action learning sets and other training. Action learning sets are an opportunity for eight or so chief executives to meet together with a facilitator and develop their thinking using the group's resources as well as those of the facilitator. This has proved to be an extremely useful training tool for chief executives.

A number of chief executives are increasingly turning to standard MBA courses which have an option for the voluntary sector. The Open University Business School, London Business School, Warwick University, Birmingham University and Cranfield Institute run courses which have a relevance to the voluntary sector. Additionally, there are also many alternative master's degrees which pursue a combination of social policy and management. One of the newer innovations is a course at the London School of Economics for people coming to the United Kingdom from the developing world who wish to manage non-government organisations. This course, in addition to having tailor-made modules, makes a great deal of use of the current London School of Economics' programmes.

The idea that training is important for budding chief executives and, indeed, for those once appointed, is now being recognised, but many are slow to make use of the opportunities. There is almost a sense with some chief executives that having acquired the post they are questioning whether there is anything else to learn. The position of chief executive can be quite isolated and it is very important that training opportunities are created within the sector and in conjunction with other sectors to ensure that the quality of management shown by voluntary sector chief executives is as good as any sector in the United Kingdom.

Reference has been made to the loneliness and isolation of the position of chief executive. Although not the main role of the chief executive, in many organisations he or she is the buffer between the staff and the trustees. The chief executive is often able to receive strong support from a good management team, but if the organisation is of a size whereby the chief executive does not have a good management team, he or she must turn to the trustees or externally for support.

Many chief executives have found it difficult to obtain real support from their trustees given that they are accountable to the trustee board. Also, it is not easy for chief executives to show their inadequacies to a board which has appointed them to lead the organisation. It is for these reasons that the use of mentoring, shadowing and an external support person are often valuable alternatives. Trustees should give very serious thought to enabling their chief executive to pay for training sessions with an external facilitator or mentor who has no line-management accountability in the organisation.

ACENVO was developed in recognition of the need for peer group support. It has grown to a body with over 500 members developing many opportunities for chief executive support. One such area is informal social support. As Bruce (1995) says:

> Support is a collective term which covers myriad attitudes and behaviours including encouragement, backing, advice, being a sounding board, being a confidante, being a listening post, responding to proposed options, providing a second opinion, providing a shoulder to cry on, praise, criticism acceptably put, etc.
>
> Support in the form of positive backing from the chair is massively empowering; continuing neutrality of the chair is debilitating; and regular opposition from the chair makes the chief executive's role virtually untenable – one or the other will have to go! Positive backing from your management team is also a sheer delight; backing from your management team in the form of a majority being positive and the minority giving grudging acceptance is quite manageable; grudging acceptance from the team is quite tenable provided there is chair/board backing; continuing non-acceptance from an individual in the management team means he or she will have to go; non-acceptance by the whole management team and neutrality/opposition from the chair/board means the chief executive will have to go!

The chief executive is often regarded as the face of the voluntary organisation. When the organisation is held to account publicly, it is often the chief executive and not the trustees who has to face the press and explain the difficulty. Similarly, when the agency is promoting a particular campaign, it is the chief executive who leads the campaign publicly. There is no clear rule, however, as to whether it should be the chief executive or a trustee who takes this role, but what is important is that the organisation must be clear about the image it wishes to project and ensure that whoever leads, projects that image.

The public-relations role does not come naturally and increasingly chief executives and trustees are seeking media training to ensure that they project well and are seen to be as professional as their colleagues and competitors. A bad media performance can do untold damage to the organisation and cost it dearly. A bad performance on high profile television programmes such as *Newsnight* or the evening news can ensure that volunteers and supporters no longer give their time or their money to that organisation. On the other hand, it is unhelpful to organisations if their chief executives have become such 'stars' in the media that it has become the driving force behind many of their decisions. The chief executive's media activities should be managed with care. The positive use of the media can be a powerful tool but in the wrong hands it can destroy an organisation.

The chief executive, the leader, the manager – these are all terms which describe the person who has day-to-day responsibility for ensuring that a voluntary organisation achieves its primary objectives. It will be against these objectives that the success of the chief executive is judged. The role of the chief executive is important and often lonely, but the value to an organisation of effective leadership cannot be underestimated. As Watson (1983) claimed: 'Outstanding companies are distinguished by the way leadership is practised to make the work of individuals both meaningful and effective.'

REFERENCES

Bruce, I. (1995) Personal communication.

Cadbury, Sir A. (1992a) *Report of the Committee on the Financial Aspects of Corporate Governance*, London: Gee.

—— (1992b) *The Code of Best Practice*, London: Gee.

Carver, J. (1990) *Boards that Make a Difference*, San Francisco: Jossey-Bass.

Dimensions of the Voluntary Sector (1995) ed. S. Saxon-Harrold and J. Kendall, London: Charities Aid Foundation.

Kramer, R. M. (1985) 'Towards a contingency model of board–executive relations', *Administration in Social Work* 9(3): 15–33.

Leat, D. (1993) *Managing across Sectors: Similarities and Differences between For-Profit and Voluntary Non-Profit Organisations*, London: VOLPROF, Centre for Voluntary Sector and Not-For-Profit Management, City University Business School.

National Council for Voluntary Organisations (1994) *The Good Trustee Guide*, London: NCVO.

National Council for Voluntary Organisations and Charity Commission (1992) *On Trust: Increasing the Effectiveness of Charity Trustees and Management Committees*, London: NCVO.

Straw, E. (1987) A paper on organisation life cycles, source unknown.

Watson, C. M. (1983) 'Leadership, management and the seven keys', *Business Horizon* March–April: 8–13.

Whitlam, M. (1986) 'Who manages the charity?', unpublished thesis, Cranfield.

Chapter 12

Beyond the rattling tin
Funding and fundraising

Jeremy Hughes

Public donations have, historically, supported everything from monmental buildings, schools and hospitals, the Crusades and the emergence of modern charities for 'the relief of suffering'. Fundraising is not an optional extra, but is fundamental to the existence of many voluntary bodies. It is about the possible, always looking at new ways to persuade your fellow citizen to give. Fundraising practice is constantly changing and developing, and has its external influences, basic principles that underlie its practice; and different techniques.

Key controls on fundraising practice are policies on the use of donated funds; the competition for funds; legislative controls and public attitudes. For many charities, fundraising must be set in the context of overall funding requirements. Annual expenditure must be met by income which may come from one of three areas: voluntary income ('fundraising'); statutory income ('funding'); and income from the charity's investments and reserves. While the purpose of this chapter is to explore fundraising, the other two areas of funding can and do have a major impact on voluntary income generation. The Charity Commission is clear that voluntary income should not be used to meet costs that should properly be met by statutory bodies, even where those bodies contract with a voluntary organisation to undertake the work. But while the commission may be clear, others are not. Whether by choice, or through government pressure, local authorities sometimes expect voluntary income to help pay for services. Indeed, one director of social services told me that we should expect to 'pay for the privilege' of working for disabled people in her area. This reality is in stark contrast to the policy position adopted by the Association of Directors of Social Services that charities should not be expected to provide voluntary funds (NCVO/ADSS 1995). Whatever the relationship between statutory body and voluntary organisation, potential donors will have their own often strongly held views. If it is perceived that a charity's work should be paid for by government, then donations will be harder to come by. The Leonard Cheshire Foundation has found that there are some who precisely for this reason will contribute to the work of the charity in the developing world but not its services for disabled people in the United Kingdom. To counter this, care is taken to highlight to donors those areas of work that are not supported by central or local government funding. Equally, if a charity is seen to have large investments and reserves this may affect donations. Guide Dogs for the Blind often work hard to defend their fundraising activities against media criticism of an annual expenditure of £32.8 million when they have over £200 million in reserves (*The Henderson Top 2000 Charities* 1995: 273). The Charity Commissioners have suggested that a norm might be for a charity to hold no more than two years' operating costs in reserves, a suggestion that has led to considerable debate.

The demand for voluntary income has never been greater. Each year, several thousand new charities are registered. This growth has not just arisen from new causes, championed by concerned individuals. Over the past fifteen years schools, colleges, hospitals, theatres and museums have come to depend on voluntary income as the belt has been tightened on government funding. The managers of NHS trusts meet to discuss voluntary income generation over and above that of the long-established leagues of hospital friends. Former pupils of state schools are being asked to contribute to the cost of the cake, not just the icing. And being on a theatre's mailing list means being asked to give as well as to buy tickets. But against this background of increasing demand, there has been no matching increase in giving. The individual giving survey undertaken by the Charities Aid Foundation has shown the typical (median) amount given by those individuals that do donate to charity is around £2 to £3 per month (*Directory of Grant-Making Trusts* 1995: 12). Even some of the largest, best-established charities have seen their income fall, for example leading to the Imperial Cancer Research Fund announcing in September 1994 that its research budget for 1995–6 would be £6.5 million less than originally planned. A concerted drive for improved efficiency and productivity in many charities has still left a shortfall of funds, with many who have reserves slipping into deficit budgets, while others who have no cushioning are being forced to cut services.

Aside from the efforts of individual charities, little has been done to encourage giving. Despite pressure from prominent figures, such as Lord Whitelaw and his Council for Charitable Support, little progress has been made in reforming the taxation system to benefit charities. Individual and corporate giving, while attracting some tax relief, enjoys nothing like the tax advantages offered in the United States. (Nevertheless fundraisers should take care to encourage as much tax relief giving as possible, for example by sending a Gift-Aid form to recover tax on all gifts over a threshold, currently £250.) Meanwhile charities are uniquely unable to recover VAT expenditure. Even where there has been a new way of tax-efficient giving, this has not taken off. Payroll giving (whereby a charity donation is deducted from the pay packet) has foundered on inadequate promotion and an operating system that distances donors from the charities they support (Institute of Charity Fundraising Managers 1995a). Meanwhile, attempts to mount generic promotional campaigns to encourage public giving, such as that advanced in the late 1980s by The Windsor Group of the top thirty charities' chief executives, have failed to get off the ground for lack of government or private funding.

So, in a situation where the same sized cake is being divided into more slices, not surprisingly charity fundraising has become increasingly competitive. Take children's charities. While the top five childcare charities work more closely together on providing services through jointly run projects, fundraisers seek to promote their agency as superior to that of the others. In this case there was some talk of merger in the 1980s, but research showed that there is 'brand loyalty' among donors. Each charity has its own character or stance that attracts donations. Marketing techniques have been adopted from the commercial world. But, importantly, they have been adapted to allow collaboration in ways that do not undermine each charity's quest for competitive advantage. Swapping names and addresses of donors ('reciprocal mailings') is one clear example, as is the development and servicing of trading, through charity consortia, with traditional goods such as Christmas cards now supplemented by professional services, such as insurance or investment plans.

The increasing use of sophisticated marketing techniques in fundraising has been one of the justifications for increased regulation of fundraising practice. Some areas of fundraising, such as street collections, have long been covered by legislation. The Charity Act 1992 has extended this regulation, particularly through the provisions of Part 2 which came into force in 1995. Key provisions within Part 2 ensure, first, that commercial partners of charities do not misrepresent how much money will go to the charity in any promotion, and second, control the use of professional fundraising companies. Further controls are set out in the ill-thought-out provisions of Part 3 which has yet to be implemented. Part 3 seeks to update the controls on public collections without recognising that collections depend on volunteers who often have very limited involvement with the charity they support. Other regulatory changes have also included the clearer statement of accounts by local volunteer groups of a charity as part of the SORP 2 accountancy rules. Separate legislation controls fundraising practice in Scotland and ICFM Scotland has published *The Scottish Guide to Fundraising Practice* (ICFM 1995b).

Increasingly fundraising has regulated its own practice. The professional body of fundraisers, the Institute of Charity Fundraising Managers (ICFM), requires members and affiliated charities to abide by its policies which include codes of practice to cover all the main areas of fundraising. In many cases these go well beyond the legal requirements as the institute seeks to ensure that the goodwill of donors, essential to successful fundraising, is protected for the future. It is all too aware of the damage done by publicity such as that around 'Lady' Aberdour and her expropriation of £2.7 million of funds raised for the National Hospital, Bloomsbury, between 1989 and 1991. Not surprisingly the media were less interested in the hospital's successful recovery of these funds. (Current codes of fundraising practice are listed in the ICFM's monthly bulletin *Update*.)

One further legislative change has had a major impact on fundraising: the National Lottery which started in November 1994. Initial indications suggested that charities will be net losers, and the ICFM took action over launch advertising that portrayed the National Lottery as a way of supporting 'good causes'. Concern persists that the public remain unaware that only 5.6 pence in the pound goes to the National Lottery Charities Board. Opinion research commissioned by the National Council for Voluntary Organisations (NCVO) suggested that most people thought the figure was 20 per cent (NCVO 1995). While in some cases charities can apply to the other National Lottery distributive bodies (sport, arts, heritage and Millennium funds) who with the National Lottery Charities Board share a total 28 per cent of the lottery income, most charities have to apply to the board. It is also the only board that will support revenue as well as capital expenditure. The board received 15,000 applications requesting £2.4 billion from their first grants programme in summer 1995, but is estimated by NCVO to have only £248 million a year to distribute.

The National Lottery initially adversely affected some charities' own lottery activity, notably the cancer charity Tenovus in South Wales which had to close down its scratch-card lottery at the end of March 1995 as sales had dropped by a quarter since the National Lottery launch. The NCVO research has suggested that even after allowing for grants made by the board, the damage done to direct giving will leave charities some £41 million a year worse off. The way in which the board dispenses its funds could also skew fundraising results. Well-publicised large grants to particular charities, while boosting those charities' income, might lead individuals to feel that their gifts of a few pounds are no longer needed. However, some commentators suggest that the relaxation of regulation on charity lotteries that accompanied the establishment of the National Lottery, plus the surge of interest in scratch-card games that followed the launch of National Lottery Instants, will actually promote giving through charities' own raffles and lotteries. Research by the Centre for Inter-Firm Comparisons into income from lotteries for 63 leading charities showed this increasing by 70 per cent in April–June 1995 over the same period a year earlier. A national survey in June 1996 of professional fundraisers found 59 per cent had seen an increase in income from lottery scratch cards in the past year, while 57 per cent had seen a drop in income from street collections. Overall, 25 per cent felt their clients had lost income because of the National Lottery (Batten and Atherton 1996).

The way fundraisers can work is also influenced by the way in which they are perceived. As will be seen later in this chapter, today's fundraising demands many skills and makes the role of a professional, paid fundraiser invaluable to any charity that wishes to raise significant income. That fundraiser is in many ways a facilitator, identifying and supporting volunteers who are the backbone of so much fundraising. As yet, this role of the paid fundraiser, and the importance of salaries that attract and retain trained, experienced professionals, are not sufficiently understood by charity trustees or by the public. Much of the work of the ICFM, including its training programmes, seeks to redress this situation.

Fundraising practice is ever changing, responding to a changing world and to regulatory control. Nevertheless, some basic principles remain and with these understood fundraising techniques can be developed for any particular situation. The principle behind all successful fundraising is responding to the donors' wishes. But behind this also lies the need for thorough research and good liaison with charity colleagues and, for many charities, with users of services as well.

Donors need to be given what *they* want. By definition, donors want to give, but that does not mean they are uninterested in a return. Grandparents want to give a Christmas present to their grandchildren but will feel disappointed if they don't receive a thank-you letter or call. That thank-you also encourages another gift at the next birthday or Christmas. Fundraisers need to find out why the donor wants to give and should reward that gift appropriately. In recent years much has been talked of 'relationship fundraising' (Burnett 1992). Increasingly, charities have recognised that donors need to be treated better if they are to give again. The regular giver has a 'relationship' with his or her chosen charity and this must be acknowledged and fostered. In particular, efforts have been made to soften and customise direct-marketing techniques for the charity sector. But real relationship fundraising is much more than the 'personalisation' of mailings that some have interpreted it to be. The *Reader's Digest* is expert at personalising its mailshots to encourage the purchase of a book or magazine. Charities need to work harder at understanding and responding to donors as the 'product' purchased is less tangible.

Aside from commercial associations whereby charity endorsement promotes a product (such as the Worldwide Fund for Nature's successful marketing of their panda logo), the only return the charity donor gets back is that the original motivation to give has been satisfied. The trick for the charity is to ensure that this return of satisfaction is coupled with a motivation to give again. This is well illustrated by donor discussion groups held by NCH Action For Children when it launched an appeal to raise £5 million to set up projects to help sexually abused children. The donors felt the results of the charity's projects were their achievement. Part of this was an expectation that they would be asked to help again as the work developed. They certainly did not want to be told: 'Thank you very much, your role is now complete.'

Research is key to the development of successful relationships with donors. General views about the charity need to be regularly monitored as well as any new fundraising approaches being tested. It is a relatively small number of individual donors who give the largest amounts of money – notably those who are committed to giving regularly and those who leave a legacy. The importance of these select individuals is summarised by the 'donor pyramid' which has gained universal recognition as a fundraising principle (see Figure 12.1). It applies Pareto's principle, that 80 per cent of funds raised will come from 20 per cent of donors. Over time, fewer donors stay with a charity but the size of their donations increases. They also sign up for more tax-efficient giving through covenants and, ultimately, a legacy. Research to identify and cultivate these key donors thus becomes crucial to the charity's fundraising success.

Satisfied donors need to have a good understanding of how their money is being spent. The charity can simply be seen as the custodian of the donor's social responsibility. A principal concern of fundraisers is therefore to maintain close liaison with operational colleagues. The potential for raising voluntary income must be included when developing a charity's strategic plan. Not only does this ensure good donor communication. It also commonly spells disaster to turn to the fundraiser after the expenditure decision has been made. This is simply illustrated by trying to raise funds for a new building after it has been built with loaned money. Given the choice between the charity that wants to repay a loan and the one that cannot build a needed facility without their donation, most donors will go for the latter.

Different aspects of a charity's work offer different fundraising opportunities, giving rise to the final fundraising principle. Fundraisers must be mindful of what fundraising presentations are acceptable, particularly in care-providing causes. Some areas

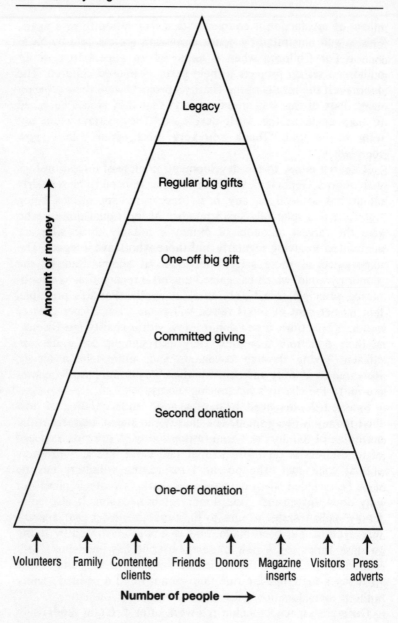

Figure 12.1 Donor development pyramid
Source: Fundraising HQ, 'Getting started in fundraising'

might not lend themselves to an emotional fundraising appeal: for example, a children's charity's work with young offenders. But concentrating on the softer fundraising message can distort public perceptions of the charity and of the users of its services. Many charities acknowledge their advocacy role on behalf of users, promoting the rights, including the right to be heard and listened to, of those in society traditionally seen as 'disadvantaged' or an 'underclass'. Fundraisers have therefore had to accept, sometimes reluctantly, that the stereotype image should no longer be used. Save the Children took a lead with its guidelines on the use of photography and was determined to move away from a starving, helpless, hopeless developing world image (Save the Children Fund 1991). NCH Action For Children formally changed its name from The National Children's Home to avoid over-association with residential care. The direct action of the disability movement over the portrayal of disabled people on the ITV Telethon in 1992 led to many charities for disabled people reviewing how they portray service users. There will undoubtedly be a continuing debate about whether a volunteer collecting in the high street, who happens to be a wheelchair user (and who will collect many times that of ambulant colleagues), is encouraging images of dependency. So long as that person is genuinely a volunteer, and not a service user 'encouraged' to take part, then I don't believe any greater dependency is implied than is inherent in charitable or indeed state-funded welfare provision.

With fundraising principles acknowledged and adhered to, a charity can maximise its fundraising potential. In the short term, this may not raise as much as might be possible if the principles were ignored. But the longer-term benefit is a committed body of supporters and operational colleagues happy to see fundraisers working alongside them.

Professional fundraisers and the professional press get excited about new techniques in fundraising that promise fantastic returns for moderate investment. Generally, fundraisers aspire to a 4:1 return on investment but what can actually be achieved varies greatly from charity to charity. In particular, the mix of different fundraising techniques becomes all important. I have highlighted below the three key areas of fundraising application. First, community fundraising led by volunteers at the local level. Second, direct marketing that cultivates individual donors face to face, by post and by phone. Third, raising money from companies and trusts. Some of the techniques may only be open to the large charity. A sales-promotion link with a company that seeks to promote their product only really works with a well-known name that also tackles a 'soft' fundraising need (such as children, animals or the environment). Prisoners Abroad or The Medical Centre for the Victims of Torture would find it much harder to develop such a partnership. Many smaller charities would also not be able to invest in recruiting donors by direct mail where each donor recruited may cost £50 or more and might not be expected to yield a 'profit' for three or more years. It is the smaller, locally based charities that are often best placed to develop street collections and coffee mornings that can raise thousands of pounds with minimum expense.

The bulk of fundraising activity (as opposed to the 'big money') remains at the collecting-tin level – community fundraising. It is dependent on a vast army of volunteers and on local branches or support groups. As such it must be responsive to changes in society which have generally reduced the willingness of people to serve on committees. While few would agree with Margaret Thatcher's view that 'there is no such thing as society', people do have less time to give to society than they did 20 years ago. There is a greater expectation of, and reliance on, state provision for many social needs. And those that are giving to charity are increasingly selective about whom they support, though commonly giving more generously to those with whom they identify.

Community fundraising is responding to these challenges. Often, with the guidance of a paid fundraiser, the dedicated volunteers are making better use of a scarce resource – themselves! One of the surest ways of doing this is to get other organisations to do the work. Rotary, Lions, Women's Institute, Round Table are just some of the local bodies that commonly adopt a charity for a year or more; often the personal choice of the chairperson. The local mayor also often selects one or more charities to support during his or her term of office.

Even where a local group is not successful in being 'adopted', the support of leading (i.e. wealthy) figures in the community is essential to the success of much fundraising. Increasingly, there are competing charitable demands on a relatively small section of the population leading to a reassessment of community fundraising activities. For example, today events, particularly those aimed at that relatively small group of people, are high-risk ventures and often raise much less than expected. A profit might only arise after 70 per cent or more of the tickets have been sold. I once had to dissuade a fundraiser from mounting a charity medieval banquet at a local stately home. When I asked her why people should pay £15 extra for the charity event when they could attend a similar event, without charity endorsement, the week before, she had no answer. Too few people were known to be willing to pay the premium charity price to make the event viable. Even the traditional and well-established summer fête, when looked at closely, may only raise a few hundred pounds despite months of voluntary effort. Fundraisers need to be honest about events. If they are 'friend-raising' rather than 'fundraising' then that should be admitted from the start and a fundraising programme established to follow up the 'friends'.

A particular type of event fundraising is sponsored activities. These have often involved schools, though this becomes more difficult as schools increasingly raise funds for themselves. Some are simple and small scale, such as sponsored swims and walks. As such they can produce a high return on investment. The leader in this field is undoubtedly the London Marathon where, for over 30,000 runners, it is more the norm than exception to be raising money for charity. And large sums result. In 1995, the Leonard Cheshire Foundation, as one of the two official charities of the Marathon, raised £250,000 from 300 runners.

Some charities have entered into commercial partnerships with outdoor-event organisers (such as abseiling, parachute and bungee jumps) with an offer of free participation if a certain amount is raised for charity. Often this has led to the participant being more interested in the event than in the charity and so having limited motivation to maximise fundraising. Greater fundraising success per participant can be expected where the charity organises its own event. For example, in 1993 the Muscular Dystrophy Group raised almost £4,000 from abseilers off the Tyne Bridge sponsored by their colleagues at Findus Foods. Such events can also help fuel future fundraising by attracting local media coverage.

The other mainstay of community fundraising is collections. Better targeting of street collections (for example, by application to the local superstore or shopping mall) can increase returns. Over the past decade there has also been a major increase in house-to-house collections, with collectors commonly recruited by telephone and asked to collect from 40 to 50 houses in their own street. Geo-demographic mapping and use of electoral registers help to target areas and individuals with impressive results. In 1994, Oxfam professionalised their collector management leading to 25,000 volunteers participating and an increase in the amount raised per collector.

However, fundraising techniques lose their effectiveness as they become too commonplace and less attractive to donors. A current example is the collection envelope dropped through your letter-box. I have a neighbour who has been recruited to collect by four charities and he is increasingly embarrassed at knocking on our door. Others complain about the frequency with which envelopes drop through the letterbox. But they can rest assured. Like all fundraising techniques, house-to-house collections will be dropped when they no longer work. Charities cannot afford to run fundraising programmes that are not cost effective. The truth is that, at present, despite some complaints, most still do find house-to-house a good fundraiser. Good management is the key. One charity calculated to lose 30 per cent of monies collected through pilfering by collectors recruited by phone and not properly vetted and supported! Better selection and supervision could have avoided this. And while house-to-house does continue, new approaches such as 'desk-to-desk' collections at workplaces are always being tested.

While community fundraising remains the biggest area of volunteer involvement and local activity, it is in direct marketing that the greatest investment has taken place and some of the largest sums are raised. Charities are reported to be second only to the financial-services sector in the volume of direct mail generated. Investment in recruiting new supporters is justified by the donor pyramid which shows that it is not just their initial gifts (commonly between £10 and £20) that are important. The prudent charity disregards the first gift. It is when a donor gives again in response to subsequent mailings that they demonstrate a real identification with the cause. It is here that 'relationship fundraising' techniques come into play. Every effort is made to ensure donors are given what they want; are encouraged to give again; to take out a covenant; to increase the size of that covenant; and ultimately to include the charity in their will. The 'relationship' is developed not just through the appeal mailings (focusing on aspects of the charity's work known to be supported by that donor) but also through trading offers (such as Christmas cards, flowers, and affinity credit cards), by telephone and by face-to-face contact.

Direct-marketing techniques always need to be kept under review and new approaches tested. The NSPCC has revised its programme of mailings. Instead of receiving an appeal almost monthly, the charity is now asking supporters how often they wish to hear from it. The 'intelligent donor' has been recognised – the person with whom the 'relationship' is strengthened (and amount given increased) by not 'over-appealing'. Other charities have withdrawn from reciprocal mailings knowing that their donors are annoyed by unsolicited mail. A number of charities rushed into television and radio advertising when this first became available in the early 1990s, only to find this to be a very costly way to recruit new donors, unless their charity is well known and the appeal 'topical' (such as international disasters, or the plight of children and the homeless at Christmas). New techniques in the second half of the 1990s involve the more sophisticated use of the telephone (researching donor wishes as well as asking for their money) and the development of interactive fundraising on the Internet.

Whatever the technique, it is the quality of the communication that is important. In the 1980s, formula direct mail developed. Donors have been subjected to four-page typed letters with key phrases underlined 'by hand' in a different ink, a 'handwritten' postscript stressing the value of the gift and an enclosed note, photograph or other item 'from the charity's front line' – the aid worker, child carer or animal protector's 'personal' account of their important work. Thankfully, as response levels drop, particularly for recruitment mailings, this formula approach is being questioned. One Christmas I rejected the direct-mail company's well-crafted Christmas mailing pack and replaced it with a three-paragraph letter accompanied only by a reply coupon. The response level was higher than on the previous packs sent out!

It is at the top of the donor pyramid that technique becomes most important. What can a charity do to encourage supporters to leave it the residue of their estates, or at least a sizeable pecuniary legacy? As with direct mail, there is increasing sophistication and treatment of the donor as intelligent. Most large charities have a 'make a will' pack which encourages the supporter to do just that. But people frequently change their wills, particularly later in life, as their circumstances change. Typically, the last revision is within four years of death. The successful charity seeks to identify those who have written them into the will or who might do so. These may be people who have ticked the appropriate box on a reply coupon. But more often, the charity may identify the potential legator by detective work such as through the shaky handwriting and the note that accompanies a donation – 'I'm sorry not to be able to send more but since my husband died I have tried to be careful with money'; or by contacting the trustee or committee member who retired from office ten years ago at the charity's compulsory age of 75. By responding personally to these supporters, the charity can secure a future legacy. This can be done by post and on the telephone. But most charities find nothing is as successful as regularly visiting the potential legator. Some charities recruit volunteers specifically for this purpose. But be warned. I have heard of a volunteer being left the money personally, rather than the charity benefiting, because the elderly person visited so enjoyed the companionship!

Overall there is some evidence that the amount left to charities in legacies is declining, with increased personal expenditure on nursing care being one reason for a drop in the value of estates.

Professional technique is also essential to maximise the funds raised from what is the least personal form of fund-raising – donations from companies and trusts. Just like the individual donor, corporate donors are also looking for some 'return on their investment'. In a decreasing number of cases, the parallel with the individual may be very close as it is the chairperson or other board member who personally selects the recipient of a charitable gift. More often, a policy for charitable giving has been established, often tying in with the company's own business. For example, one of Britain's top corporate donors, National Westminister Bank, has prioritised giving that enhances financial management and money-awareness skills. The link with a company's business priorities is even stronger where the giving is directly seen as marketing promotion. The decision in 1995 of Flora to sponsor the London Marathon demonstrates that synergy of interests. More controversial is the marketing association between the Worldwide Fund for Nature and Pampers nappies as many felt that disposable nappies were incompatible with promoting environmentalism.

Considerable funds can be raised from trusts where research

shows that a charity's activities meet the trusts' criteria for eligibility. Indeed, three of the five top charities judged by their investment income are grant-makers: the Wellcome Trust, Leverhulme Trust, and Gatsby Charitable Foundation. The top trust donors give out considerable sums with the National Lottery Charities Board now joining their ranks as the largest grant-maker. The *Directory of Grant-Making Trusts* and *A Guide to the Major Trusts* are published annually and help steer fundraisers in England and Wales to the best trust prospects for their charity, while in Scotland the number of trusts is smaller and covered in the *Scottish Trusts Guide*.

In all corporate and trust fundraising, detailed research and well-timed and well-presented funding applications are key to success. It is the area of fundraising most dependent on the paid professional fundraiser although, particularly for major capital appeals, that fundraiser will depend on the influence of a lay appeal committee to open doors for him or her. The fundraising case is immeasurably strengthened when the request for support is made by someone close to the potential donor. Those askers in turn must themselves have given to the appeal if their request for support is to have credibility.

In a world of fierce competition for donations, the professionalism with which a charity seeks funds will in large measure determine the outcome. That professionalism is enshrined in employed fundraisers. But they, in turn, must share their skills and techniques with the thousands of volunteers who remain fundamental to much fundraising activity. All must abide by some principles of fundraising and recognise the external factors, including legislative controls that affect their work. At the same time, trustees, politicians and the public generally should be encouraged to welcome technical proficiency and high standards in fundraising. That way, the greatest amount can be raised at the lowest cost to support charitable activity.

REFERENCES

Batten, L. and Atherton, N. (1996) Presentation of research into ICFM members' perceptions of the effects of the National Lottery, Epsom: Crossbow Research.

Burnett, K. (1992) *Relationship Fundraising: A Donor-Based Approach to the Business of Raising Money*, London: White Lion Press.

Charity Commissioners for England and Wales (1995) *Charities and Fund-Raising*, London: HMSO.

Directory of Grant-Making Trusts (1995) ed. A. Villemur, London: Charities Aid Foundation.

Fundraising HQ 'Getting started in fundraising', unpublished workbook, Edinburgh

Guide to the Major Trusts (1995) Volume 1 ed. L. Fitzherbert, S. Forrester and J. Grau; Volume 2 ed. P. Brown and D. Casson, London: Directory of Social Change.

The Henderson Top 2000 Charities 1995 (1995), London: Hemmington Scott.

Institute of Charity Fundraising Managers (1995a) *A Review of Tax-Free Payroll Giving to Charity*, London: ICFM.

—— (1995b) *The Scottish Guide to Fundraising Practice*, London: ICFM.

National Council for Voluntary Organisations (1995) *The Impact of the National Lottery on Charitable Donations from the General Public*, London: NCVO.

National Council for Voluntary Organisations/Association of Directors of Social Services (1995) *Community Care and Voluntary Organisations Joint Policy Statement*, London: NCVO.

Save the Children Fund (1991) *Image Guidelines*, London: Save the Children Fund.

Chapter 13

Marketing force
Meeting true need

Ian Bruce

Running a large or small voluntary organisation is very difficult, and arguably more so than running a commercial organisation (Drucker 1990). Effective working needs a philosophy and practical framework for action which is followed by virtually everyone in the organisation. As someone who started out in the commercial world, spent time in local government, but has always felt most at home in the voluntary sector, I take my inspiration from an unlikely and non-politically correct source – marketing in the commercial sector.

A marketing approach is useful if you believe passionately that the needs of the people for whom the organisation was established should be paramount. Marketing is a highly effective method of managing the work output of a voluntary organisation which wants to meet, for example, the needs and wishes of older people, children, adults with learning difficulties, theatre goers, bird lovers, and so on.

The philosophy of marketing is to put the customer, not the organisation, first. It also gives a very practical work-management methodology which has millions of person years invested in it, giving us terms and techniques such as targeting, customer segmentation, pricing, and other-player (competitor) analysis. These techniques can help ensure that we meet the true needs of the clients of today, rather than out-of-date objectives or simply the needs of staff and trustees.

A marketing approach can be applied not only to service provision, but also to public campaigning, pressure-group work, public relations and fundraising. Each of these areas of work have 'customers' who have needs and desires which must be met if the voluntary organisation activity is to be effective.

If marketing is so useful to voluntary organisations, why is it so underutilised? It first came in during the late 1960s and early 1970s via the advertising agencies working with charities on publicity and fundraising campaigns. A marketing approach is now the dominant working method in the more professional fundraising and public relations arms of larger charities. However, this has only served to reinforce the suspicions of service providers already in tension with their fundraising colleagues who they fear will exploit unfortunate images of clients in order to turn a fast buck. Further, there is a widespread feeling among many voluntary organisation workers that marketing is selling people things they do not need at prices they cannot afford. At best they think that marketing is advertising and selling. Neither could be further from the truth.

However, there might be a set of far more fundamental and serious underlying reasons why service-providing staff and trustees are uncomfortable with a marketing approach (Bruce 1994, 1995). These include the fact that many voluntary organisation beneficiaries are economically, politically and socially weak and are not easily able to make their voice heard; in this situation it is difficult to prevent the 'haves' who run the organisation from developing patronising attitudes towards the 'haves-not' on the basis that the organisation rather than the customer is always right. This can be further enhanced in those charities where professionals (e.g. social workers, teachers, architects, lawyers, etc.) predominate on the staff and/or the trustee board. (Professionals find the dictum 'The customer knows best' hard to take!) Voluntary organisations that have been set up on the basis of belief – those, for example, that have been founded or based on religion or those which are particularly cause-orientated, like vegetarianism, or opposition to blood sports – can be particularly antipathetic to customer needs (Blois 1987). Perhaps the most important factor making voluntary organisations disinterested in marketing is because demand often exceeds supply; our products get snapped up and we become careless about customer needs.

There are many definitions of marketing, but perhaps the simplest formulation is 'meeting customer need within the objectives of the organisation'. This establishes the primacy of customer need, but recognises the organisational framework within which need is being met. (More sophisticated definitions of not-for-profit marketing can be found in Kotler and Fox 1985; Lovelock and Weinberg 1989; and Bruce 1994.)

At first sight, to some charity managers, it seems an unnecessary question to ask 'Whose needs are we meeting? Who are our customers?' To them it is obvious whom they are serving – older people, cancer sufferers, physically disabled people, music lovers, people concerned with pollution. If charity managers regard these questions as largely unnecessary, what it probably means is that they are either saying that the people they currently serve are the people they ought to serve; or that they can hardly cope with the customers they have got, let alone taking on a whole lot more.

However, the situation is clearly a lot more complicated than this. Purely for the sake of example, let us consider deaf people. Is the charity here to help today's deaf people (i.e. amelioration through welfare services etc.)? or tomorrow's deaf people (i.e. cure implying funding medical research), or helping to ensure there are no deaf people in the future (i.e. prevention through immunisation, public education, etc.)? There are obviously many sub-choices, and, more importantly, different needs within these choices.

Take, for example, amelioration through welfare services. Is the organisation going to aim its services at all hearing-impaired people, or only deaf people, and where is the line drawn? Is it serving all deaf people or primarily children, or adults or older people? Is it differentiating between age of onset of hearing impairment?

These questions are absolutely fundamental for two reasons. First, the voluntary organisation will almost certainly not have enough resources to serve all the potential target groups. Second, and arguably more important, these different target groups will in many instances have very different needs. Services aimed at one group will be of very little use to another; or services aimed generally at the whole population will be of only limited use to any one sub-group.

So understanding who a voluntary organisation's customers are and who they might be is a crucial issue right at the heart of voluntary sector marketing, providing the fundamental benchmark of how well the organisation is doing now, and helping it to decide what its future actions might be.

In the voluntary sector, we have a bewildering variety of customers – students, clients, patients, audience, pupils, members, patrons, donors, volunteers, advocates, corporate employees, central government, local government, inspectors and many more. Any voluntary organisation will only use a few of these terms, but we have no language to help us generalise and analyse the different approaches required for different groupings. The following terms help to develop and discuss a customer-orientated approach.

Just about the only word that encompasses all the bewildering array of the targets of voluntary organisation attention is the term 'customer'. 'Customer' can be used to cover a range of targets such as student, patron, client, donor, and others. However, in terms of discussing and developing a voluntary sector marketing orientation, we need more refined generic terms, and the ones used here are *beneficiaries, supporters, stakeholders* and *regulators* (Bruce 1994).

Beneficiaries are the fundamental group of customers for whom the voluntary organisation was set up. The term encompasses the clients of social welfare organisations, the students of educational bodies, the audience of arts organisations, the members of tenants' and residents' associations, and others.

Supporter customers encompass all those people who bring resources to the voluntary organisation but are not paid staff or part of governance. Examples of supporter customers are donors, volunteer fundraisers, voluntary service workers, service purchasers where they are not beneficiaries (e.g. local authorities), and so on.

Stakeholder customers are primarily those people on the paid staff or involved in governance (e.g. trustees, committee members). The latter category may include beneficiary representatives, supporter representatives, and other people identified as having a special stake in the activities of the voluntary body.

Regulators can usefully be regarded as a separate target group. While they remain 'hidden' for quite lengthy periods of time, their 'needs' need to be addressed continuously, and at times of inspection their needs and wishes are addressed with an alacrity and intensity which could well be applied to all the voluntary organisations' customer groups! Examples of regulator customers are the Charity Commission; the inspection arms of various government departments covering education, social services, training; the inspection arms of local government, VAT inspectors, the local communities, and so on.

The local community is an interesting, albeit informal, regulatory group. It can, for example, oppose or support the building of a voluntary organisation service outpost. Most voluntary organisations have come across the syndrome of 'What you are doing is a very good thing, but it's not right to put it/do it in our street'!

Table 13.1 shows the four major customer groups of not-for-profit organisations with examples in each category.

Table 13.1 Not-for-profit/voluntary organisation customers

Beneficiaries	Supporters	Stakeholders	Regulators
Clients	Donors	Staff	Charity Commission
Students	Volunteer fund-raisers	Representatives of beneficiaries	Government inspectors
Patients	Volunteer workers	Board members	Tax authority
Users	Purchasers		Local community
General public	Advocates		
Members			
Audience			
Patrons			
Beneficiary intermediaries	*Supporter intermediaries*	*Stakeholder intermediaries*	*Regulator intermediaries*
Government referrers	Church leaders	Staff managers	MPs
Government purchasers	Company chief executives	Union representatives	Local councillors
Community providers	Purchasing cartels	Board leaders	
Family purchasers and referrers	Advocate leaders and influencers		
Not-for-profit referrers			
Policy-makers			
Decision-makers			

Source: Bruce 1994

Table 13.1 introduces another important theoretical and practical consideration – that of intermediary customers, that is, the

people and organisations through whom the voluntary organisation may have to work in order to reach the end customer, that
is, the beneficiary, supporter, stakeholder or regulator customer.
Intermediary customers are absolutely crucial to voluntary organisations if they are to be successful in reaching their end customers. However, it is important to note that intermediary
customers have needs and desires which may be, in certain
important respects, different from and in tension with the needs
and desires of end customers.

So it can be seen that the target markets of charities are
various. Multiple constituencies, says Drucker (1990: 83), make
managing a voluntary organisation very difficult. Further, he
argues that greater dependency on multiple constituencies or
target groups is a distinguishing feature between voluntary organisations and businesses who have fewer. Similarities between businesses and charities are reviewed by Leat (1993).

Voluntary organisations have a vast range of activities which
they direct at their various customer groups, and in marketing
parlance these are called *products* and they can be either *physical
goods, services* or *ideas*. So a physical-goods product aimed at a
beneficiary customer might be a wheelchair sold to a physically
disabled person; an example of a physical-goods product to a
supporter customer might be Christmas cards.

An idea product might be a pressure-group campaign aimed at
government to improve social security benefits for older people.
A service product, certainly the most numerous category in the
voluntary sector, might be a school, residential home, theatre or
home-visiting service.

The voluntary-organisation product (good, service or idea) has
a number of features, and has to go through a number of processes all of which are highly relevant to customer take-up (or
not). This mixture of the product and its associated features and
processes is called the *marketing mix* (Borden 1964: 4–7), so
called because the various elements can be varied between and
among themselves to make them more attractive to the customer.

For physical goods the marketing mix has been popularised
into the four Ps of product, price, promotion and place. For
service and idea products this is insufficient and Booms and
Bitner (1981) add people, physical evidence and process. For the
voluntary organisation marketing mix an eighth *P* is essential,
which is that of philosophy (Bruce 1994: 63–4).

The marketing mix is crucial to successful take-up behaviour by customers and the features and processes which constitute it are discussed below.

By reframing the classical model, voluntary-organisation marketing may be represented as in Figure 13.1. (It should be emphasised that Figure 13.1 is a gross simplification, but it does introduce someone relatively new to marketing to the various

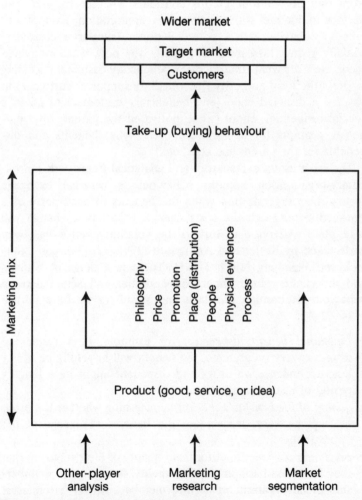

Figure 13.1 Voluntary organisation marketing

elements and analytical tools of a marketing approach in voluntary organisations.)

Each element outlined above is now considered briefly in turn. For more detailed consideration see Bruce (1994).

In the commercial literature, customer take-up behaviour would be called buying behaviour, but the term *take-up* seems more helpful in the world of the voluntary organisation. Take-up behaviour simply tags all the things going on when a customer from one of the four groups considers whether to, and then decides to, interact with the voluntary organisation. Examples of take-up behaviour are a potential donor (supporter customer) actually giving (how much, for what, why now, what motivated them, etc.); a parent (intermediary beneficiary customer) deciding to press the local authority (intermediary supporter customer) to pay for a disabled child (end beneficiary customer) to go to a special residential school (what motivated the parent, what particular prompts for action were there, what benefits and disbenefits for the parent and child etc.).

The most useful explanatory and analytical framework for voluntary-organisation take-up behaviour is classical exchange theory. This suggests that when the benefits to each party of a transaction outweigh the costs, then a voluntary exchange will take place. Adaption of this to the voluntary sector has been undertaken by Kotler and Andreasen (1991: 121–34), and Lovelock and Weinberg (1989: 37–43). There is a range of benefits and disbenefits which impact on potential and actual take-up behaviour. Reframing Lovelock and Weinberg we have (Bruce 1994: 42–4):

- *functional benefits/disbenefits*: for example, in a residential drug-recovery programme, the benefit will hopefully be no, or less, dependence on drugs and disbenefit might be a lengthy period of institutionalisation
- *quality of life benefits/disbenefits*: concerning whether the product will increase or decrease the beneficiary's range of life opportunities
- *psychological benefits*: differ from quality of life benefits in that they have less basis in physical reality, for example, membership of an organisation entitles members to put letters after their name or wear badges publicly on their lapels (as do

professional associations or Rotary) (Lovelock and Weinberg 1984)

- *access benefits and disbenefits*: concerning the physical accessibility of the product (for example, for disabled people); or how psychologically accessible it is (for example, membership of Alcoholics Anonymous requires that one admits to being an alcoholic before joining, which is not a requirement for membership of other organisations)
- *time benefits/disbenefits*: for example, the amount of time a supporter must devote; the length of a beneficiary's rehabilitation course (Lovelock and Weinberg 1984)
- *monetary benefits/disbenefits*: concerning its costs; whether it is worth that cost; and whether beneficiaries can afford the cost (Lovelock and Weinberg 1984)
- *sensory benefits/disbenefits*: for example, the disbenefits of an old people's home that smells of urine; the sensory benefits of good food at a charity dinner.

This is a useful checklist for designing and assessing new goods, services and ideas and in re-evaluating continuing ones which may have problems. For example, using this checklist could help prevent a residential rehabilitation service from running in such a way to produce psychological overdependency of beneficiaries; or a centrally located facility being underused because of transport difficulties; or a pressure-group proposal being rejected because too expensive in its first year which could have been phased in over five years.

Marketing research is sometimes called market research or consumer research. By whatever name, it is one of the most fundamentally useful tools for a voluntary organisation, both in its own right and as a process by which one can sensitise the organisation (its managers, staff and committees) to a marketing approach. This is because the very act of undertaking consumer research requires the identification of a sample which forces an understanding of market segmentation. It quite often requires exploration of the different elements of the marketing mix, and almost certainly needs an exploration of customer take-up behaviour; and will require the identification of the pros and cons of the voluntary organisation's products both in themselves, and in comparison with others (other-player analysis).

Marketing research is essentially gathering information about our actual and potential end customers and actual and potential intermediary customers, and reflecting these findings and conclusions in the design and delivery of the voluntary organisation's physical, service and idea products. Research needs to be undertaken among all the different customer groups (except perhaps regulators), but research among beneficiary customers is fundamental and paramount even where representatives of beneficiary customers (e.g. disabled people, members, and others) are the dominant force in the governance of the organisation.

There are a number of methods of gathering information. Personal marketing research and experience is one of the most used and favoured in voluntary organisations but has the enormous danger of confirming 'the way we do it round here' and of underestimating the numbers and needs of customers not being served. Information gained from representation and experience of customers can be particularly useful for those voluntary organisations that can achieve formal representation of their various customer groups.

Desk marketing research is a relatively cheap and underused activity. There is almost always more market information available on an organisation's target group than conventional wisdom suggests. If there is no appropriately qualified member of staff to do the work, modest outlays of money to post-graduate students will gain the organisation an invaluable annotated bibliography of virtually everything published that is relevant. Similarly the students can do desk research among useful but unlikely places such as the payment section (when such questions as: Who are the largest paying customer groups?' can be asked).

Qualitative marketing research enables voluntary organisations to gain insights into its customer group, in some depth, but does not enable us to be sure how widely applicable these conclusions and insights might be. For example, if a service charity is aware that the majority of its target group are older women, but it is not successfully reaching this group, then a dozen depth interviews with individuals, of both users and non-users, is likely to be very instructive.

Quantitative marketing research can transform a voluntary organisation's service and pressure-group work, provided it is preceded by qualitative work to understand the issues, and providing there is sufficient budget for a robust random or representative sample. For example, marketing research by Cancer Relief

Macmillan revealed that professional support and advice was only reaching those who had cancer, and very little advice and support was reaching carers (Scott 1993). As a result the organisation's services were modified in a significant way.

For the majority of voluntary organisations, and unlike most commercial organisations, actual demand, and certainly potential demand, outstrips the amount of service they can supply, which gives charity managers and workers the impression of 'just coping'. This can have a number of effects such as enhanced job satisfaction because of the obvious demand; debilitation through constantly being unable to do enough; most insidiously, not really wanting to know about further unmet need in the form of potential beneficiary customers. It is this last point which discourages many voluntary organisations from looking at exactly whom it does serve and whom it does not. However, *market segmentation* and *targeting* are crucial activities. There are two fundamental reasons which should persuade a voluntary organisation to segment its market into relatively homogeneous groups of customers, and then consciously decide which ones to target.

The first is that the organisation simply cannot serve every need of its whole market because there almost certainly are not enough resources in the form of money and expertise. If the organisation does attempt to serve the whole market, it will fail and at the very best will provide a low-quality service which is appreciated by very few customers because it is so generalised. The second reason for segmentation and targeting is that it allows, and indeed encourages, the development of products that are much more likely to be appreciated by the customers.

There is one important exception to the general lack of interest in market segmentation and targeting. Customer segmentation and targeting has long been practised to a very high professional level in fundraising generally, and direct marketing in particular.

The traditional criteria for segmenting the markets are geographic (e.g. region, density, climate, etc.); sociographic (e.g. age, sex, family size, income, occupation, social class, etc.); psychographic (e.g. lifestyle, personality, attitudes, etc.); and behaviouristic (e.g. benefits being sought, purchasing rate, usage rate etc.). (For a discussion of the stages of segmentation and targeting, see Bruce 1994: 51–4.)

Successful commercial organisations spend a great deal of time logging what their competitors do, particularly with their leading products. However, in the main, they use one primary tactic, that is, competition. Voluntary organisations have that option but they can also co-operate. Many voluntary organisations invite other players in their field on to their boards which, in process terms, should be helpful. However, effective co-operation or competition requires a great deal of pre-analysis and positioning.

In essence, *other-player analysis and positioning* is examining your own organisation's products (be they physical goods, services and ideas) against the changing political, economic, social and technological environment and the consequent impact on actual and potential customer demand, and comparing all of this with products supplied by other organisations. It is important to note here that these 'other organisations' should not only include voluntary bodies, but also statutory and commercial ones. Other-player analysis and positioning is the bridge from marketing into the voluntary sector's strategic planning, for which there is a rich literature (see, for example, Hudson 1995).

Having now looked at the major tools of marketing, namely marketing research, market segmentation and targeting, and other-player analysis, we can now return to the voluntary organisation marketing mix with its eight Ps of philosophy, product, price, promotion, place, people, physical evidence and process.

The voluntary organisation *marketing mix* lists the ingredients which need to be borne in mind for every voluntary organisation service, physical good or idea product, at the planning stage, at launch and through regular monitoring of established activities. Most managers are dealing with established products, rather than launching new ones and so the ingredients are ones which need to be checked out against the needs and wishes of actual, and, very importantly, potential customers, be they beneficiaries, supporters, stakeholders or regulators. The voluntary organisation marketing mix consists of eight Ps: philosophy, product, price, promotion, place, people, physical evidence and process.

For a voluntary organisation its *philosophy*, and the philosophy of its various products – that is, the answers to such questions as: Why are we here? What is this particular product contributing to our *raison d'être*? – are fundamental. Unless it is to accommodate different customer needs and wishes, varying philosophies across a product range will confuse customers. In extreme circumstances, contrasting philosophies can debilitate voluntary organisations very significantly.

Philosophical choices can be made in the design of products going to a similar customer group such as beneficiaries. For example, in residential homes, a voluntary organisation with empowerment high up on its list of objectives will offer more service choices, and choices involving some risk, than would a voluntary organisation putting a higher priority on care and benevolence.

Philosophical tensions can arise particularly between products aimed at the different customer groupings of beneficiaries, supporters, stakeholders and regulators. The most familiar tension is that between fundraising products and beneficiary products. Fundraisers may find it easier to raise money by presenting pathetic images of beneficiary customers to potential supporters, but they would not wish to do so if the charity philosophy is one of empowerment of beneficiaries, because the supporter (fundraising) product would be undermining the empowerment philosophy of the charity towards its fundamental beneficiary customer group.

The voluntary organisation *product* will tend to be predominantly a physical good, a service or an idea. Examples of physical goods provided by voluntary organisations are technical aids for disabled people, equipment for members of youth organisations, Christmas cards and other fundraising items for the general public and, perhaps pre-eminently, publications for various voluntary organisation target groups.

The most frequent product in voluntary organisations is the service product. To beneficiary customers this might be a school or college, and within that the range of courses available; a theatre, and within that the different performances put on during the season; a residential home, and within that the range of different services provided to the residents; a bird sanctuary, and within that the different services provided to visitors; a sports club and its various facilities; or a home-visiting service.

Idea products are vastly important in the voluntary sector and proportionately more in evidence than in the world of commercial marketing. Idea products are quite often associated with service products but can stand alone. Idea-product ranges include conservation proposals of the environmental charities; legislative proposals of disability charities; and public-education messages from arts organisations. Idea products are most often associated with the public education, public relations, and pressure-group arms of voluntary organisations.

However, it is also interesting to note that fundraising products aimed at donors are also essentially idea products. This is because, however tangible the object of the fundraising is (e.g. a school, a residential centre, or a nursing service), to the vast majority of potential donors it is simply an idea in their minds. Few donors will ever visit what they are being asked to support, especially in advance of the donation.

The *pricing* of voluntary organisation products is frequently given too little attention, and sometimes none at all. Many products are superficially free, but this ignores the 'impact price'. Voluntary organisations which ignore, or think insufficiently about, the impact price of their products will suffer a major detrimental effect on take-up. For example, a charity offering residential rehabilitation to beneficiary customers which does not take account of most rehabilitees' dislike of being away from home, will lose a lot of custom. A pressure group promoting an idea to civil servants, which it is very excited about but which goes against the policies of the government, has a huge impact price. First, there is the personal price a civil servant may feel he or she has to pay in promoting an 'unpopular' idea. Second, it is surprising how often pressure groups put up proposals which have not been properly costed and which, once they are costed, become hopelessly unacceptable.

Perhaps the most sophisticated area of voluntary organisation pricing is that of fundraising products. All good fundraising products are carefully priced, and perhaps the most sophisticated area within fund raising is that of direct mail.

Charities monitor closely the take-up behaviour of their different donor sub-groups and present them with the range of possibilities, nearly always aiming to edge them up into a higher purchasing bracket: for example, £250 will purchase a talking-book machine for one blind person, but £500 will pay for a talking book which will be borrowed by fifty different blind people. However, with the exception of the fundraising area, voluntary organisations are too inattentive to the pricing of their products. With increasing income shortages, increasing contracting out of statutory services under competitive tendering, and increasing donor fatigue, pricing is an area which voluntary organisations ignore at their peril.

Promotion is what most voluntary organisations mean when they talk about 'marketing their services'. However, this narrow definition of marketing, more properly called 'promotion', is a very small part of the marketing mix. Promotion is an umbrella term for advertising, public relations, personal selling and sales promotion.

It is probably fair to say that voluntary organisations are as good as, if not better than, their commercial counterparts in achieving successful advertising and public relations. Advertising and public relations professionals have existed in the voluntary sector for over 30 years and a marketing approach is second nature. However, it is a different story with sales promotion and personal selling. Sales promotion (for example, loss leaders, where one sells in at a lower price in order to gain take-up and subsequently raise prices to more realistic levels) is seldom thought about, probably because it is so closely associated with pricing. Personal selling is undervalued (except in the fundraising area) probably because it does not sit easily with the professional, sometimes pseudo-professional, ethic of service provision to beneficiaries.

Two other key areas of promotion in the voluntary sector found less frequently in the commercial sector are 'coalition building' and 'intermediary and customer referral'. Particularly with idea products, coalitions between voluntary organisations can greatly enhance acceptability to recipients. As far as the take-up of products by beneficiaries and supporters, word-of-mouth referrals (as from one disabled person to another, one donor to another, one volunteer to another) can be very powerful and need to be encouraged.

Place or distribution is the activity that ensures that products get to customers when and where they want to take them up. It is another grossly unattended area of voluntary organisation activity. Distributing physical goods and idea products of voluntary organisations is particularly problematic.

For physical goods, voluntary organisations, in the main, rely on direct-mail methods which can be costly; or volunteer outlets, which can be patchy geographically and relatively uncommitted. Many national voluntary organisations do not give their local network outlets any financial incentive to distribute products. This may keep the end price down but gives the local group less of an incentive. Other means of encouraging distribution at the local level can be through 'overbranding' of the local group's name on the product (for example, a nationally produced leaflet being over-printed with the local group's name and address), be it a good, service or idea.

Generally, distribution in the voluntary sector is problematic. Many voluntary organisations are distributing to minority groups who are relatively inaccessible which makes the challenge very significant.

While in theory the product going to the customer is quite separate and discrete, in practice it is heavily associated in the customer's mind with *people* bringing the product to them, especially in the case of services and ideas. This means that the behaviour of voluntary-organisation personnel is quite crucial in encouraging take-up. That is, take-up is affected by how well trained the personnel are; how much discretion they are given to vary the product according to individual customer needs; how committed they are to the charity and which particular incentives encourage them; and at the simplest level, how polite and sympathetic they are, that is, customer care.

Other customers are often a key part of the people element of the marketing mix. For example, if one of the twelve tables at a fundraising dinner aimed at older, richer supporters is taken by a drunken bunch of Hooray Henrys, then the majority of the supporter customers attending will not be happy and may not come again! If a promotional drive to get younger disabled people to attend a holiday hotel draws in a few younger disabled people who are then in the minority among retired disabled people, then the young people are less likely to enjoy the holiday, because what they were looking for was to be with people of their own age.

For two of the product categories, services and ideas, *physical evidence* of the product is a fundamental success factor. Ideas, by their very nature, are intangible. Services are intangible until they are taken up. So the more tangible physical evidence which can be given to customers, so much the better: leaflets describing a rehabilitation programme, for example, give added confidence to an oral description; a descriptive leaflet in colour with photographs gives a better impression than a black-and-white one; sampling a rehabilitation session is best of all.

An idea product, be it a pressure-group idea or a fundraising idea, will inspire a lot more confidence if physical evidence can be produced: for example, a model of the school for which money is being sought; detailed architectural drawings of the new day centre; or flow charts of how the proposed service might operate, including where the government funding might come from.

The last element of the marketing mix is *process*, that is, how customer-friendly and encouraging the process is through which the beneficiary, supporter, stakeholder or regulator has to go in order to take up the voluntary organisation product (physical good, service or idea). This may seem too obvious an element in the design of voluntary organisation activity to need mentioning. However, let me give just one example: computerised invoicing systems. These were introduced in the 1980s to make services more 'efficient'. Even now, as much as 15 years later, many of these systems are very unfriendly: beneficiary customers cannot understand them and are put off by them; referring agents such as social workers find them difficult.

What is often crucially difficult is that the processes through which the customer goes are often not under the full control of the product manager. Even worse, voluntary organisation service managers may be simply unaware of the problems their customers are experiencing.

So the full charity marketing mix has to be attended to if a product is to be taken up widely. In my experience managers pay insufficient attention to this full list, especially those that are outside their immediate control.

Too many managers in too many voluntary organisations use what in the commercial world is called a production rather than a marketing orientation. In other words, through the very best of intentions, they think they, rather than the customer, know best. In my view this is seldom the case, especially where beneficiary customers are involved. However, even in those relatively few situations in which the voluntary organisation does know best, the various customers have a powerful sanction – to reject the offering! So close attention to the attitudes and behaviour of actual, and, more importantly, potential customers is essential.

Rejecting marketing as being 'too commercial', or treating it as superficial 'promotion', means missing an enormous opportunity to make our important goods, services and ideas more relevant and widespread. Despite the antipathetic language, the fundamentals of a marketing approach – meeting customer needs within the objectives of the organisation – sit comfortably with both voluntary organisation philosophy and practice. They offer us management tools to help chart our way through the changing boundaries between the commercial, statutory, voluntary and informal sectors while staying true to our principles.

REFERENCES

Blois, K. J. (1987) 'Marketing for non-profit organisations', in M. J. Baker (ed.), *The Marketing Book*, London: Heinemann, p. 408.

Booms, B. H. and Bitner, M. J. (1981) 'Marketing strategies and organisation structures for service firms', in J. Donnelly and W. R. George (eds), *Marketing of Services*, Chicago: American Marketing Association, pp. 47–51.

Borden, N. H. (1964) 'The concept of the marketing mix', *Journal of Advertising Research* 4(2): 2–7.

Bruce, I. (1994) *Meeting Need: Successful Charity Marketing*, Hemel Hempstead: Institute of Chartered Secretaries Association/Prentice-Hall.

—— (1995) 'Do Not-for-profits value their customers and their needs?' *International Marketing Review* 12(4).

Drucker, P. (1990) *Managing the Non-Profit Organisation*, Oxford: Butterworth Heinemann.

Hudson, M. (1995) *Managing Without Profit*, Harmondsworth: Penguin.

Kotler, P. and Andreasen, A. (1991) *Strategic Marketing for Non-Profit Organisations*, 4th edn, Englewood Cliffs, NJ: Prentice-Hall.

Kotler, P. and Fox, K. F. A. (1985) *Strategic Marketing for Educational Institutions*, New York: The Free Press/Macmillan.

Leat, D. (1993) *Managing Across Sectors*, London: VOLPROF, Centre for Voluntary Sector and Not-for-Profit Management, City University Business School.

Lovelock, C. H. and Weinberg, C. B. (1984) *Marketing for Public and Non-Profit Managers*, New York: John Wiley.

—— (1989) *Public and Non-profit Marketing*, 2nd edn, Redwood City, Calif.: The Scientific Press.

Scott, D. (1993) 'Fighting cancer with more than medicine', in Cancer Relief Macmillan Fund, *Annual Review*, London: Cancer Relief Macmillan Fund.

Chapter 14

Light at the end of the tunnel?
A European perspective

Quintin Oliver

Europe is poised at a great turning point in history. As the millennium approaches, the European Union – one of the world's greatest trading blocs – has enlarged to incorporate Austria, Finland and Sweden, and is now looking eastwards towards Central Europe for more possible member states with the Mediterranean coast of North Africa also being mentioned as a possible addition to the European family.

Meanwhile, the globalisation of the world economy and tele-communications means that there are fierce rivalries. The North American Free Trade Agreement has created an enormous trading bloc on the North American continent, covering the United States, Canada and Mexico, while China and the Pacific rim countries are growing economically, creating shock waves around the world.

The United Nations seems to be teetering on the edge of an abyss, caused by inertia and internal administrative, political and financial problems, while the World Trade Organisation only just made the leap from the protracted negotiations of the Uruguay Round of General Agreement on Tariffs and Trade.

Meanwhile, more than one-fifth of the world survives on less than the equivalent of US $1 per day, as famine, hunger and pestilence stalk many countries still, and 1,000 children die each day from preventable illnesses. More than half the world has never made a telephone call (there are more telephone lines on Manhattan Island than on the whole of sub-Saharan Africa). Disadvantage and division persist across the world.

These regional and global changes have, of course, made their impact on the voluntary sector, too. It is traditional and natural for those working within systems to try to mirror the structures of those systems. So, at local level many voluntary organisations organise around local authority or health board areas, at national level it is relatively obvious and straightforward to match governmental structures and in recent years more and more organisations have sought to work at European Union level or at least to organise in alliances and coalitions so that they can have their impact at the level where decisions are made. If former European Commission President Jacques Delors' controversial prophecy that 80 per cent of all social policy decisions will soon be made at European level is true, then it is natural that organisations will want to organise to influence them. This is similarly true at the global level, but the history of global voluntary organisations is one dogged by the eternal conflict between high aspirations and low resources. Thus, the International Council on Social Welfare is relatively ineffective and recent moves to establish CIVICUS, a world citizens' organisation, are finding it hard to move beyond the relatively wealthy and well-organised countries' voluntary sectors.

A key year for social policy activists was 1994, as the ten-year Delors presidency moved to a close. Within that time, he was keen to create a lasting testimony to his endeavours and many have spent much time debating and arguing about the two main white papers of his last year: *Growth, Competitiveness and Employment* and *Social Policy*. The tensions reflected within these two documents neatly encapsulate the tensions within the new Europe.

The debate goes to the very heart of the fundamental concept of what the European model is, how that can be sustained and how it has shifted in character since the 1980s. The key question is whether Europe can continue to strive to achieve an equitable balance between economic and social development, given the supposedly shared values upon which this model is based, such as democracy and individual rights, free collective bargaining, the market economy and opportunities for all. All of these are held together by the conviction that economic and social progress must go hand in hand and that competitiveness and solidarity have both to be taken into account in building a successful Europe of the future.

Delors' early project was the creation of the Single Market and the lifting of unnecessary trade and tariff barriers between the then twelve member states. This was to create a freer market, unleash economies of scale, and promote competitiveness through increases in productivity to place Europe at the centre of the growing world market. However, the single economic market brings with it political, social and cultural corollaries, with which Europe is still grappling. It is now more clearly recognised that, as we move towards increased convergence, as imposed by the strict economic criteria for the achievement of economic and monetary union by the turn of the century, there is a need to preserve the internal social cohesion of the union. While there must be a respect for diversity across member states, we also need to establish and enforce common minimum standards (as evidenced by the small increase in the structural funds and community initiatives to assist those areas deemed to be lagging behind and to create the fabled level playing field).

At the same time, the European Union is keen not to over-stretch the economically weaker member states, nor to prevent the more developed from implementing higher standards – perhaps an irreconcilable tension. Crucially, the richer member states are concerned that lower standards of social protection should not be used as an instrument of unfair economic competition, but the debate has a long way to go. The rather unseemly scramble by Ireland to be seen to be among the members of the so-called 'fast track' to economic and monetary union underlines the problems. If only Germany, Luxembourg and Ireland meet the Maastricht criteria for convergence, as they now do, then surely something must be wrong with the criteria. While Ireland has reduced its public spending and its public debt, it has notoriously high unemployment (currently 16 per cent) and much of its modest economic success has been known to have been based on substantial emigration from the island. The city state of Luxembourg is economically powerful for a number of peculiar reasons and Germany, despite the acquisition of the new *Länder* from the former East Germany, is an economic phenomenon unparalleled in Europe.

Meanwhile, the two-tier society of Europe is apparently unchecked: the dual society, *la société à deux vitesses*, the haves and the haves-not, the rich and the poor – the words may be different, but the meaning is the same. Wealth creation is concentrated in the hands of a highly qualified labour force, while income is transferred to a growing number of non-active people as the basis for a reasonable level of social justice. For some in

Europe, the lack of competitiveness is due to the high social costs of production, punitive taxation and inflexible labour markets. They argue that future job growth hinges on de-regulation and diminution of social spending – the 'trickle across', rather than the 'trickle down' effect, as in the United States, which has much lower levels of social protection and where low pay rather than unemployment is the biggest cause of poverty.

For others, such as Delors, the challenge is to put into effect a range of policies which integrate economic and social objectives and yet continue to promote international competitiveness to avoid the worst excesses of a dual society and the ravages of the global economy.

The white paper on *Growth, Competitiveness and Employment* does its best to formalise the social policy which was almost non-existent in the 1960s in Europe and which was certainly a very junior partner to economic policy in the following two decades. A testimony to Delors was that he was not only able to assert with some, albeit limited, success that a social and economic Europe had to march hand in hand, even if to slightly discordant tunes, but that certainly in the context of the United Kingdom and even Ireland over the last five years and longer, he was able to raise a number of fundamental issues and inject a new political, social and even intellectual rigour into the debate about the relationship between social and economic justice. While jobs remain the number one priority for Europe, some other useful approaches have been developed. The first of these is citizenship. In the United Kingdom and Ireland, citizenship, where it is talked about at all, is a one-dimensional concept, reducible to the act of voting every so often for a party political representative. The more important and interesting concept of 'active citizenship', seen as the opposite of exclusion and marginalisation, is rooted in the concept of social and economic, cultural and political rights across a broad range of areas which comprise the multi-faceted nature of what citizenship should be about. Linking it to the European principle of 'subsidiarity', if the lowest level of government is the individual citizen, and if decisions should be made at the lowest possible level, then the concept of citizenship should be pre-eminent.

Second is the concept of solidarity. The European model is also rooted in the concept of active solidarity, between those with jobs and the unemployed, between generations, between developed and underdeveloped regions, and between Europe's better-off population and its 55 million poorer citizens. This represents the polar opposite of the Reagan/Thatcher 'enterprise culture', at least as practised in Britain and the United States.

Third, we have the social economy. In the United Kingdom the social economy is not recognised. There are no shades of grey between the economic and the social, which results in a very polarised body politic and a polarised economic model. However, within the European model, the social economy is recognised and rated, where social objectives or outcomes and economic activity are encouraged to come together in a more productive fusion, especially in disadvantaged or poorer communities.

Fourth is social partnership. The model of partnership, enshrined in several European institutions, is born of the model of capital and labour meeting with government to reach consensus. It has already challenged traditional concepts of public or private corporations, or municipalities, acting on behalf of, rather than for or with, communities, by trying to engage those local communities as the authors of their own change, rather than the objects of actions by others.

Last, non-governmental organisations (NGOs) are seen as social partners. With the passage of time and other factors which have reduced the sharpness of the dialectic between capital and labour, some have recognised the role of 'civil society', as represented by NGOs, and have attempted to broaden the formal partnership to include them not simply as service providers, nor just as the promoters of solidarity, but as real and meaningful partners in giving a voice to the voiceless and a little power to the powerless, to combat poverty, marginalisation and the exclusion from society so endemic in the developed West.

So, the possibilities of a social union are still under debate. As the economic framework is set within the Single Market, so the debate about the political institutions required to control and fetter the market should run parallel with the social and cultural debate about the tensions between recognising the diversity of culture and language, and providing minimum standards for social provision, participation and pluralism.

There is a commonly stated view that the British voluntary sector is the best in Europe and we must preserve its special identity and culture. The vibrant, energetic and lively voluntary sector in this country has a lot to teach others (so runs the argument); and the voluntary sector here is unique, so we should not be absorbed into an inappropriate European model. Yet the foundation of the UK system of charity law (or, more accurately, that of England and Wales, since it does not cover Scotland or Northern Ireland) can be traced back to Tudor times and the rather archaic notion of 'heads of charity'. Similarly, the incremental development of our fiscal incentives for charities, based on the complicated covenanting arrangement, followed by an equally complicated payroll-giving incentive and most recently the allowance of one-off gifts for tax relief, can hardly be said to represent a coherent and simple framework for philanthropy. In most other European countries, one funding source – often the local authority or municipality – is sufficient for most non-governmental organisations to plan and implement their work programmes. The UK system, where the ingenuity of voluntary organisations patching together seven or eight different funding sources is heralded as a model of innovation, brings puzzlement to the continental European.

Even our knowledge about the voluntary and community sector leaves much to be desired. In France, for example, we know that 655,521 charities were formed between 1975 and 1991, that most were in the south and Alpine regions, that one quarter were in rural areas, and that the principal beneficiary group was older people. There, they have a complete register from which statistics can be drawn and policy analysis undertaken. And yet our Charity Commission only operates in England and Wales, and offers a statistical base which is inadequate for most European, far less international, comparisons. Even our terminology is difficult to transfer. We boast in this country about 'volunteering' and 'partnerships', for example, but in many continental countries volunteering carries a military connotation, pre-dating even the nation-state: witness the Garibaldi volunteers from Italy and, until the ceasefires of 1994, the 'volunteers' of the Irish Republican Army! 'Partnership' is used in the German language, but primarily in the context of joint employer–employee enterprise committees, while in the European Union's Poverty 3 Programme partnership was foreseen:

> as a means of mobilising into a new relationship a wider range of bodies, agencies and authorities in a concentrated and con-

certed action against poverty to the benefit of larger numbers
of people over greater geographical areas.

(Conroy 1994: 8)

Human rights gives us another example. In many countries it
is the voluntary sector which is the watchdog on human rights,
challenging and exposing government. But why is it that the
United Kingdom is second from the top (only Turkey is above)
of the league in European Court judgments against it for human
rights abuses? Why is it that within part of the United Kingdom
– Northern Ireland – over the past twenty-five years, basic rights
to freedom of association, freedom of speech and free movement
were all restricted, with limited voluntary sector interest or reaction? Contrarily, Northern Ireland also displays some examples
of extremely positive and rigorous anti-discrimination legislation,
stronger than that found elsewhere in the United Kingdom, and
including the obligation not to discriminate on grounds of perceived religion or political opinion. Indeed, here is an excellent
example of how effective voluntary sector lobbying has led to the
promise in the European white paper on social policy to create
an anti-discrimination framework, largely based and tested in
Northern Ireland!

Are we at all near the heart of Europe, as UK prime minister
John Major once promised? The United Kingdom has opted
out, vetoed and objected to many proposals. We have language
problems and we have an aversion to speaking other people's
languages. How often are we embarrassed by continental Euro-
peans speaking English as their third, fourth or sometimes fifth
language with greater precision and idiom than even we can
sometimes muster?

Too much red tape? Why is our system, which allows what is
not expressly forbidden, inherently better than most other European systems, which do not allow what is not explicitly permitted?
The Greeks have complicated rules and procedures, but think that
we operate with an arrogant anarchy. Opening a bank account in
Belgium is notoriously difficult, but they feel that our system
promotes a lack of accountability.

The then prime minister, Margaret Thatcher, speaking in 1981
at a meeting of the Women's Royal Voluntary Service, argued
that voluntary organisations were significant in the very maintenance of a free society:

They are not just a way of giving help and caring, vitally important though it is, and the wonderful work that you do; they are an example that we are a free people, and continue to be that and do things our own way. And when we are free, this is the important thing, we do rise to our responsibilities and carry them out far better than any Government. And so I could say that the great volunteer associations are really a vital part of the defence of our freedom.

(quoted in Loney 1986: 46)

And yet, what exactly is government policy on involving the voluntary sector in decision-making around the policy table? *Think Voluntary* (Voluntary Services Unit 1993), a leaflet reminding civil servants to remember the voluntary sector, comes to mind as one of the few serious contributions from what is now recognised as a classic own goal by Margaret Thatcher, when she unleashed the 'efficiency scrutiny' on government funding of the voluntary sector in 1989. It found that it was government which had no clothes – and no objectives for its £2.2 billion spend – rather than the efficient and strategic voluntary sector, operating on a shoe-string and yet still delivering significant 'added value'. Compare this with France, where the Conseil National pour la Vie Associative is a standing body charged with promotion of voluntary sector issues and questions. Non-governmental organisation nominees are full members of the Economic and Social Committee of France. In Ireland, NGOs and specific representatives of the disadvantaged are full members of the National Economic and Social Forum. In Germany, the state offers all services to the voluntary sector first, before considering undertaking them itself, as its interpretation of the controversial European term 'subsidiarity'.

There is a real dearth of such partnership bodies in the United Kingdom. Most are a direct result of European Commission pressure, as delivery mechanisms for the European Social Fund or, in Northern Ireland's case, as a mechanism to deliver the 1995–9 Special Support Programme for Peace and Reconciliation. And, in terms of formal links with government, apart from *Think Voluntary*, there is the new Government/Voluntary Sector Forum on Europe promoted by government as having two main objectives: 'to be aware of the implications of European developments, and to be valuable in sharing information' (Peter Lloyd MP, then

Home Office minister with responsibility for the voluntary sector, NCVO annual conference, 21 January 1994). Voluntary sector delegates attending the first meeting of the Government/Voluntary Sector Forum on Europe will remember that the very remit of the forum specifically excluded discussion of policy questions.

The explosive growth of European networks and interest in the European Union from the United Kingdom during the 1980s has been well documented (Davison 1993; Harvey 1995; Armitage and Macfarlane 1994; Macfarlane and Laville 1992). Many organisations, however, will confess that their entry into the European 'market' has not been strategic, rather, it has been based on opportunism or luck. It is well known that as the closing date for another transnational European programme draws near, European fax machines are red hot with requests for what often turn out to be the most inappropriate, but necessary 'paper partnerships'.

A step-by-step approach would include: setting strategic objectives; identifying the best methodology; and lobbying for change. In devising a strategy for transnational, European or other work outside the United Kingdom, one might come up with any one or combination of the following objectives:

- to promote European integration, in line with the objectives of the European Union
- to learn from the experience of other cultures and countries, and to exchange models of good practice
- to seek to influence and lobby decision-makers for an organisation's policy objectives, or to create a legal or fiscal framework in which one's objectives can be more easily achieved (especially when it is felt that little progress is possible at the UK level)
- to gain access to European funding programmes – or simply because there appears to be money for such transnational activities
- to generate and earn resources for one's organisation through selling services, consultancy or by winning contracts
- to promote staff development by exposing them to learning opportunities and offering them a break from the pressures of domestic activity.

The ways of achieving strategic European objectives should properly consider any or all of the following:

- Setting up a base in Brussels, Luxembourg or Strasbourg. The representative body of the 'big six' German social welfare organisations, the Bundesarbeitsgemeinschaft der Freien Wohlfahrtspflege, has for long operated from a central Brussels office, while some others have opted for Strasbourg (where the European Parliament sits in plenary session for one week each month), while others again have gone for propinquity to the legal and financial institutions of Luxembourg. The costs of a continental base can be prohibitive, but the rewards for a constant presence can pay dividends.
- Joining or setting up a European network to gather information and effect change: there are now more than 300 such outfits, ranging from the highly structured and well-resourced consumer and environmental lobbies to the 'two activists and a word-processor' model adopted by most penurious voluntary organisations. The European Anti-Poverty Network and the European Women's Lobby are two such examples, in both cases largely designed and led by Irish (north and south) activists seeking to create a vehicle at European level for their self-explanatory objectives. In both cases, again, commission funding has been secured to run modest secretariats in Brussels and fund the expensive consultative processes of the democratic expression of local and national networks' demands and aspirations.
- Engaging a consultant or consultancy, such as the highly respected European Citizens' Advice Service, which provides information, briefings and tailor-made guidance on points of contact and tactics through which to influence decision-makers.
- Attending conferences, seminars and events: this can be an expensive luxury, meeting many of the same people on the European circuit with limited or less tangible outcomes. Similarly, it can, if properly targeted, be a highly effective way of meeting the right people in semi-formal circumstances and making a name for one's organisation or one's demands.
- Direct lobbying of the institutions and decision-makers of Europe, many of whom are, of course, based in one's own country: members of the European Parliament, the Economic and Social Committee, the Committee of Regions, and of many other working groups and expert groups are appointed from the United Kingdom. Similarly, the European Commission and the European Parliament both have at least one UK

office and, therefore, much can be done at the European level without leaving the United Kingdom or even making an international phone call.

- Bidding for contracts: which can also be undertaken from a domestic base, through assiduous study of the *Official Journal* or other of the many and voluminous European information sources. Again, some of the biggest contracts have been won unexpectedly by organisations preparing competent tender documents, and scoring highly because of factors unknown to them, such as the requirement to balance a francophone contractor with an anglophone one, a southern European bidder against a northern, or an NGO against a statutory provider. Dansoc, a Danish social welfare provider, has become a multi-million, multi-national operation through careful targeting of social welfare contracts in other countries, just as Age Concern has successfully set up satellite operations including Age Concern Spain (Baleares).

The art of lobbying is much the same at European level as it is at any of the various local, regional or national, domestic levels. It is the context, the terminology, the culture and the language which differ. Three ways in which lobbying is similar are, first, in the fragmentation and departmentalism. Just as UK agricultural policies seem sometimes to work against the health strategy (e.g. by encouragement of the production of high-fat foods), so the strategies of different commission directorates-general seem sometimes to be either incompatible or directly opposed. One hand often does not know – nor seem to care! – what the other hand is doing. Second, the system is also run by civil servants and politicians who are prone, as elsewhere, to caution, conservatism and 'jobsworth' sensitivities. Third, European bureaucracy is as cumbersome and complex as any domestic system, with the European Commission initiating, the European Parliament advising and the Council of Ministers deciding, within an arcane framework with a constantly changing balance of power.

However, on the other hand there are many, often refreshing, differences at the European level, which have been identified as, first, a remarkable openness in Brussels, where officials are usually more than willing to open their doors to practitioners from the grass roots, who will give a different perspective from formal governmental and parliamentary representatives. Second, there is more often than not eagerness among officials to promote the European ideal and create something different and innovative from the information and within the margins available to them. Third, there exists a genuine fairness in wanting to ensure a fair crack of the whip to all parts of the union, reflected at its most negative in 'Buggins' turn' when contracts, resources or platform places are allocated by formula rather than on merit.

The good lobbyist will work to understand these problems and opportunities and will probably take extra care to:

- Identify the real target and the appropriate timing. Legislation often takes years to prepare and must go through many tiers of consultation, so finding the real pressure points at the key moment can be critical.
- Prepare the case well. It is not enough to argue a traditional UK position in the European context. Animal welfare is a good example, where activists in this field have had to learn how to excite French and Spanish interest in what was traditionally seen as a soft British issue. The answer, as it turned out, was an economic one.
- Make sure there is the support of activists in at least four other countries, preferably a mix of anglophone and francophone, large and small, northern and southern, and of organisations from different sectors and backgrounds – otherwise the case is seen not to be 'European', but merely sectional. Similarly, alliances need to be built with the other partners – the employers or trade unions – to show that each of the pillars of the European institutions are at least involved, if not actively backing the case.
- Translate documents and speeches (or just overheads) at least into French but also probably Spanish and German, if not as many of the other official languages as possible. The effort is worthwhile, since this is usually a British weakness and it shows respect for others. It is also important to check terminology and language, lest there be confusion over technical or conceptual terms.
- Make a distinction between the politicians, the civil servants and the 'political civil servants' in, for example, commissioners' cabinets, who operate on the French model (including obvi-

ously using the French term *cabinets*). This is different from the UK system and can take some getting used to.

For those who have made the jump into the European pond, and are *aficionados* of the jargon and modalities, working at the European level is just an extension to working at the local, regional or national tiers. The plane – or train – journey from London to Brussels is shorter and cheaper than that from London to Belfast and, indeed, many would argue that working in Europe is no more difficult than trying to bring together delegates from Sheffield, Stornoway, Strabane and Swansea!

Some have used Europe to leapfrog over what they saw as a recalcitrant or inhospitable UK political culture in recent decades and may shortly be caught out with a change of government in the United Kingdom on the one hand, and a retrenchment in European developments on the other, as the Franco-German right-wing alliance strengthens its grip and pushes through a strongly monetarist and deflationary agenda to achieve European monetary union and to reshape Europe at the 1996 inter-governmental conference which will revise the Maastricht Treaty. The tables may very well then be turned and current Europhiles may be forced to revise their positions. Alternatively, European federalism could bring significant advances in social policy through a stronger social partnership, a rebalancing of economic and social objectives and the creation of a more socially just and equitable society. Time will tell but, as the Chinese proverb has it, 'If we don't plan ahead, we'll end up where we're headed anyway.'

REFERENCES

Armitage, R. and Macfarlane, R. (1994) *Getting Going in Europe: A Guide to Developing Transnational Projects*, London: National Council for Voluntary Organisations.

Conroy, P. (1994) *Evaluation of the Achievements of Poverty 3*, Brussels: DGV/E/2 European Commission.

Davison, A. (1993) *Grants from Europe: How to Get Money and Influence Policy*, 7th edn, London: National Council for Voluntary Organisations.

Harvey, B. (1995) *Networking in Europe: A Guide to European Voluntary Organisations*, 2nd edn, London: National Council for Voluntary Organisations.

Loney, M. (1986) *The Politics of Greed: The New Right and the Welfare State*, London: Pluto Press.

Macfarlane, R. and Laville, J.-L. (1992) *Developing Community Partnerships in Europe: New Ways of Meeting Social Needs in Europe*, London: Directory of Social Change and the Calouste Gulbenkian Foundation.

Voluntary Services Unit (1993) *Think Voluntary*, London: Home Office.

Name Index

Aberdour, Lady 176
Andreasen, A. 196
Armitage, R. 215

Bar-Hillel, M. 137
Belcher, V. 113
Ben Ner, A. 26
Beresford, P. 70, 78
Bernstein, S. R. 59
Beveridge, W. 34
Billis, D. 25
Bishop, J. 24
Bitner, M. J. 194
Blois, K. J. 190
Booms, B. H. 194
Borden, N. H. 194
Bowis, J. 89, 90
Brooke, R. 51
Bruce, J. 170
Burnett, K. 178

Cadbury, Sir A. 94, 98, 159–60
Carnegie, A. 113
Carpenter, M. 40, 47
Carver, J. 158, 163–4
Chait, R. 97
Chamberlin, J. 76
Chanan, G. 24, 31
Common, R. 61
Conroy, P. 212–13
Cook, T. 113
Coram, T. 4

Davies, A. 47
Davison, A. 215

Dayton, K. N. 93
Delors, J. 208–9, 210
Denton, Baroness 105
Doven, R. 123
Drake, R. F. 80
Drucker, P. 189, 194

Edinburgh, Duke of 106–7
Edwards, K. 47
Elizabeth, S. 123
Ellis, F. 123
Evers, A. 28

Flynn, N. 41, 46, 51
Fox, K. 190–1

Griffiths, Sir R. 87
Gutch, R. 43, 44–5, 47, 55, 80;
    United States practice 59–60

Hancock, Sir D. 95
Harding, T. 70
Harris, M. 28
Harvey, B. 215
Harvey-Jones, J. 100
Hazell, R. 123
Hedley, R. 123
Hevey, D. 79
Hodgkin, C. 27
Hoggett, P. 22, 23, 29, 33; changes
    34; organisational forms 31;
    ownership of organisations 24;
    religion 27
Holman, B. 39
Houle, C. O. 109

Hudson, M. 200
Hughes, M. 71
Hunter, A. 26–7, 32–3, 35
Hurley, D. 66

Irving, K. 130

James, A. 39, 46, 50
James, E. 26
Jeavons, T. 27

Kendall, J. 23, 24
Kettner, P. M. 59
Knapp, M. 23, 24
Knight, B. 23, 24, 34
Kotler, P. 190–1, 196
Kramer, R. M. 163
Kunz, C. 43

Lacey, R. 29
Landry, C. 4
Lansley, J. 27
Laville, J.-L. 215
Leat, D. 50–1, 168, 194;
    organisational structure 160;
    responsive accountability 32;
    support agencies 53
Lewis, J. 1–2, 4
Lipskey, M. 59
Lloyd, P. 214–15
Loney, M. 214
Lovelock, C. H. 190–1, 196–7

McClure, R. 4
MacFarlane, R. 47, 215
McGowan, P. 137
Macnaghten, Lord 128
Major, J. 213
Marceau, J. 28
Martin, J. E. 2
Martin, L. L. 59
Milofsky, C. 26–7, 32–3, 35
Mocroft, I. 58
Morris, J. 74
Mulgan, G. 4

Nathan, Lord 93–4, 96, 99
Newton, A. 89
Norton, M. 119

Oliver, M. 80
Osborne, S. P. 62
Owens, D. J. 80

Paton, R. 24, 28
Philip, Duke of Edinburgh 106–7
Pilgrim, D. 29

Quint, F. 2

Reading, P. 75
Reagan, R. 211
Richardson, J. 62–3, 65
Rochester, C. 123
Rogers, A. 29
Rothschild-Whitt, J. 28, 31
Russell, L. 63, 64, 65

Sargant, N. 99, 103, 107
Scott, D. 63, 64, 65, 198–9
Shore, P. 23
Smith, H. 137
Smith, S. R. 59
Spencer, K. 43
Stewart, M. 35
Straw, E. 158, 165
Swinson, C. 94

Thatcher, M. 211, 213–14

van Hoomissen, T. 26

Warner, N. 88
Watson, C. M. 171
Weinberg, C. B. 190–1, 196–7
Weisbrod, B. A. 26
Whitelaw, Lord 175
Wicks, M. 89, 90
Wilding, P. 63, 64, 65
Winfield, M. 133
Wistow, G. 41

Zealley, C. 119

Subject Index

accountability 6, 49; managerial 51; performance 155–6; to funders 52–3; trustee boards 94, 95, 103, 105–7
Accounting Standards Board 146
ACENVO *see* Association for Chief Executives of National Voluntary Organisations
active citizenship 20, 210
advocacy 42, 48, 69, 78; community voluntary organisations 73–4; funding 112; service provision organisations 47
Aga Khan Foundation 120
Age Concern 217
Age Concern England 61
altruism 27
Amnesty International 2
animal welfare 17, 218
appeals 121–2
approving boards 100, 102
Arthritis Care 80
articles of association 134–5
arts: lottery funds 13, 17, 124; trusts 117, 118
Association of Charitable Foundations 111, 115, 124–5
Association of Charity Lawyers 142
Association for Chief Executives of National Voluntary Organisations 157; model job description 158–9; support 168, 170; training 169

Association of Directors of Social Services 66, 173–4
Australia 142

background communities 26–7, 32–3
Barnado's 61
Barrow Cadbury Fund 120
BBC Children in Need 119, 121
Belgium 213
beneficiaries 192, 193
benevolent funds 120
Birmingham University 169
blacks 10, 27, 33
boards of trustees *see* trustee boards
British Red Cross 161
broadcasting 11, 19; appeals 121–2
Brook Advisory Centres 139–40
Brussels 216
budgets 102–3
Bundesarbeitsgemeinschaft der Freien Wohlfahrtspflege 216
bureaucracy 213, 217
business rates 132

Cadbury Group 119, 120
campaigning 73–4, 82, 91–2, 112; Carers (Recognition and Services) Act 88–91; constituency 83–4; message 84–5; National Health Service and Community Care Act 1990

87–8; objectives 87; respect
85–6; success 86–7
campaigning organisations 73–4
Cancer Relief Macmillan 198–9
capital expenditure 148, 149
capital funds 150
Capital Radio 122
carers 44, 83, 90; and National
Health Service and Community
Care Act 1990 87–8
Carers Alliance 84
Carers National Association:
campaign message 84–5; Carers
(Recognition and Services) Act
88–91; constituency 83–4;
National Health Service and
Community Care Act 1990
87–8
Carers (Recognition and Services)
Act 88–91
Carnegie UK Trust 113
cashflow 64
central government funding 3,
9–10, 15, 40; grant-making
trusts 111–12, 114–15, 116
Centre for Inter-Firm
Comparisons 177
chairperson 103–4
change 34, 39, 50, 164–5; in public
services 40
charitable status 2, 128, 132–4
Charities Act 1960 128–9, 133
Charities Act 1992 129; charitable
status 133; dealing with land
137; limited companies 132;
trustees 5, 95
Charities Act 1993: accounting
requirements 18, 105–6, 144,
146, 148; charitable status 133;
dealing with land 137;
expenditure classification 155;
fundraising 176; gross income
153; limited companies 132;
personal and family trusts 121;
signing requirements 135;
trustees 5, 95
Charities Aid Foundation 13, 115,
174
Charity Commission 116, 212;
accounting requirements 105,
145; charitable status 133–4;
deregulation 129; fundraising
173; governing documents 130;
legal structure 131; *On Trust*
163, 164; political activities 82,
120; and Public Concern at
Work 131; trustee training 94;
trustees' role 96–7
charity law 18, 128–33, 212
Charity Organisation Society 1–2
Cheshire (Leonard) Foundation
61, 174, 183
chief executives 171; and external
environment 166–7; and
internal environment 167–8;
managing change 164–5;
managing development 165–6;
public relations 170–1;
recruitment 168; role 157–60;
skills 160; training 168, 169; and
trustees 157–8, 163–5, 169–70
childcare charities 17, 175
Children in Need 119, 121
Church of England 120
church organisations 25
Church Urban Fund 120
citizenship 20, 210
City Parochial Foundation 113,
119
CIVICNS 208
co-option 34–5
coalitions 26
collaborative entrepreneurs 122–3
collections 183
collective action 25
Comic Relief 121
Committee on the Financial
Aspects of Corporate
Governance 94, 98, 159–60
community care 15, 46, 58, 91
*Community Care: Just a Fairy
Tale?* (Carers National
Association) 88
Community Development
Foundation 23
community fundraising 181, 182–4
Community Integrated Care 60, 61

community-run organisations 24, 27, 28, 35
community trusts 119, 122
community voluntary organisations 73–4
Companies Act 1985 132, 135
Companies Act 1989 132
Companies House 135
company donations 16, 181, 186
company trusts 121
competition 34, 96
competitor analysis 166, 167, 200
compulsory competitive tendering 55
conditional donations 152–3
confidentiality 138–40
Conseil National pour la Vie Associative 214
Conservative Party 20
constituencies 28, 83–4, 194
consumer choice 41
consumer research 197–9
contract culture 34, 49, 55, 80, 92; and grant-making trusts 112
contracting 58–9, 65–8, 140–1; in Europe 217; negative effects 60–5; positive aspects 65; and trustees 95, 108–9; in United States 59–60
Coram (Thomas) Foundation 4
corporate giving 16, 181, 186
corporate governance 98, 109
Corporate Responsibility Group 115
costs 64, 155–6, 173
Council for Charitable Support 175
Cranfield Institute 169
cultural trends 11–12, 19
customers 191–4, 204

Dansoc 217
demography 9
Department of the Environment 55
dependency 60–2, 65
Deregulation and Contracting Out Act 1994 129

Deregulation Task Force on Charities 129
designated funds 152
desk marketing research 198
development agencies 71–2, 73, 75, 113
development work 77–8
Dimensions of the Voluntary Sector 59; expenditure 117; funding 116; fundraising 161; volunteers 3, 6
direct-mail 14, 178, 184–5
direct marketing 178, 181–2, 184–6
Directory of Grant-Making Trusts 117, 119, 174, 187
disabled people 46, 78–80, 84, 181
distortion 61–2
distribution 194, 203–4
donations 3–4, 12–13, 66–7
donor organisations 24, 25, 28
donor pyramid 179, 180, 184
donors 178–9
Draft Guidelines for Funders of Voluntary Organisations 115–16

Economic and Social Committee of France 214
economies of scale 67
economy 7–9, 12–13
education 114, 117, 118
effectiveness 49
employment 3, 8, 19
empowerment 41, 75
endowed trusts 120–1
entrepreneurs 25
environment: grant-making trusts 117, 118; lottery funds 13; voluntary activity 10, 17, 19
ethnic minorities 10, 27, 79
European Anti-Poverty Network 216
European Citizens' Advice Service 216
European Commission 214, 216–17
European Council for Voluntary Organisations 142
European Parliament 216–17
European Union 207; bureaucracy

217; contracts 55, 217; lobbying
215–19; partnership 212–13;
social policy 208–11
European Women's Lobby 216
expenditure 2–3; accounting
154–6; grant-making trusts 117,
118

fairness 123–4, 218
Family Service Units (FSU) 140–1
family trusts 121
Family Welfare Association 1–2
fees 54, 60
Financial Reporting Standards 146
fixed costs 64
flexibility 64, 66
Flora 186
foundations *see* grant-making
trusts
France 212, 214
fund accounting 150–2
funding 173–4, 212; European 215;
grant-making trusts 120–2,
150–3, *see also* central
government funding; grants;
local government funding
funding mechanisms 40
funding relationship 48–9, 51–6,
76–7
fundraisers 177–8, 187
fundraising 5, 173–5, 202;
competition 175; principles
178–9, 181; professional 177–8;
regulation 176; techniques
181–7, *see also* donations

Gatsby Charitable Foundation 187
GDP 7, 8, 12
Germany 209, 212, 214
Gift Aid 119
gift-givers 122
governance 97, 98, 105
government policy 9–10, 213–15
Government/Voluntary Sector on
Europe 214–15
grant-making trusts 101–2, 111,
125–6; age 119; categorisations
119–23; codes of practice
115–16; fairness 123–4; funding

120–2; fundraising by charities
16, 181, 186–7; giving styles
122–3; legal structure 131–2; and
National Lottery 124–5; pump-
priming role 111–15; risk 123;
size 117, 118; statistics 116–17;
subject interests 117, 118
grants 51–4, 70; percentage of
income 60, 61
Greece 213
Greenwich Association of
Disabled People 78–9
Griffiths report 87
Guardian 132
guardianship 108–9
Guide Dogs for the Blind 174
Guide to the Major Trusts, A 117,
186–7
Gulbenkian Foundation 114

Halsbury's Laws of England 135,
142
health 117, 118, *see also* medical
research
health care 11, 13
Heart of Variety Appeal 121
Help a London Child 122
Henderson Top 2000 Charities, The
59, 174
Henry Smith's Charity 137–8
heritage 19; lottery funds 13, 124,
177
Home Office 23, 144
Home Office Voluntary Services
Unit 115
honorary officers 103–4
house-to-house collections 183–4
housing associations 24–5; central
government funding 10, 116;
governance 94–5, 105
Housing Associations' Charitable
Trust 122
human rights 18, 213

ICA (Invalid Care Allowance) 86
ICFM 175, 176, 177–8
idea products 201–2
Imperial Cancer Research Fund
174

income 2–3, 60, 61, 116–17, *see also* funding; fundraising; investments
income and expenditure account 146–8, 149
Income Tax Special Purposes Comrs v *Pemsel* 128
incorporated structure 142
independent living 46, 78–9
individual giving 3–4, 12–13, 66–7
information: about charities 161; for service users 70–1, 72–3, 78, 79, *see also* marketing research
information technology 9, 19
innovation: and contracting 62–3, 66; and grant-making trusts 113, 123
Insolvency Act 1986 141
Institute of Charity Fundraising Managers 175, 176, 177–8
intermediary customers 193–4
intermediary trusts 122
International Council on Social Welfare 208
Invalid Care Allowance 86
investments 137–8, 173, 174
investors 122–3
involved boards 101
Ireland 209, 210, 214
Irish Republican Army 212
Islam 120
Italy 212

Jews 120
Joseph Rowntree Foundation 61
Joseph Rowntree Reform Trust 120

Kennet Rural Development Agency 71–2
King Edward's Hospital Fund for London 121

Labour Party 20, 88
land 135–8
Landlord and Tenant Act 1954 136
language 213, 218
leadership boards 100–1, 102, 103
leases 134–8

legacies 14, 185–6
legal structure 131–2, 142
Leonard Cheshire Foundation 61, 174, 183
Leverhulme Trust 187
life-cycle stages 165–6
limited companies 131, 132
Lions 182
livery companies 121
Living Options Partnership Project 79
lobbying 48, 58–9, 87, 216–19
local enterprise councils (LECs) 94
local government funding 3, 15–16, 41–2; Special Transitional Grant 58, 67, 129; and user-controlled organisations 80
London Business School 169
London Marathon 183, 186
London School of Economics 169
lottery *see* National Lottery
Luxembourg (city) 216
Luxembourg (country) 209

Maastricht Treaty 142
McGovern v *Att. Gen.* 2
Making Carers Count (Labour Party) 88
management by walking about 167–8
management committees 28, 72
market segmentation 199–200
market share 41
market structure 17
marketing 189–91, 205–6; customers 191–4; in fundraising 175–6; models 195–7; products 194; tools 197–200
marketing mix 194–5, 200–5
marketing research 197–9
MBA courses 169
media 86–7
medical research 13, 17, 114, 119
Members of Parliament (MPs) 83, 90
membership 25, 83
membership organisations 18, 101, 108

memorandum of association 134–5
Mental Health Foundation 122
Millennium Fund 124, 177
MIND 60, 61
motivators 27
Muscular Dystrophy Group 183

Nathan report 93–4, 96, 99
National AIDS Trust 122
National Council for Voluntary
    Organisations: contracting 60,
    66; future of the voluntary
    sector 164–5; legal structure
    142; National Lottery 176–7;
    trustees 94, 96, 99, 103, 107, 163,
    164
National Economic and Social
    Forum (Ireland) 214
National Federation of Housing
    Associations 95, 103
National Health Service and
    Community Care Act 1990 34,
    129; needs-led services 69–70;
    Special Transitional Grant 58,
    87–8
National Hospital 176
National Lottery 13–14, 16, 17,
    95–6, 122; and fundraising
    176–7; impact on trusts 124–5;
    pump-priming 112
National Lottery Charities Board
    5, 124–5, 176–7, 187
national organisations 26, 32
National Westminster Bank 186
NatWest Group 88–9, 90
NCH Action For Children 179,
    181
NCVO see National Council for
    Voluntary Organisations
networks 32–3, 216
New Right 39
New Zealand 142
NHS trusts 94, 105, 174
Nolan Committee 18
non-charitable trusts 120
non-governmental organisations
    (NGOs) 211, 214
North American Free Trade
    Agreement 207

Northern Ireland 212, 213, 214
not-for-profit organisations 24, 25,
    76
NSPCC 185–6
Nuffield Foundation 114, 133

Official Journal 217
Open University Business School
    169
opportunism 64–5
organisation risk 123
organisational development 165–6
organisational goals 47
organisational structure 29, 30–2,
    66, 71
other-player analysis 166, 167, 200
overheads 155–6
overseas aid 13, 17, 19
ownership 24
Oxfam 93, 184

Pampers 186
Parents for Children 130
participation 30, 44–6, 72–3
partnership 211, 212–13
partnership bodies 214–15
payroll giving 175
PCAW see Public Concern at
    Work
people 194, 204
performance 40–1, 49, 52, 155–6
person risk 123
personnel 71, 204, *see also*
    volunteers
philanthropy 115
philosophy 194, 200–1
physical evidence 194, 204–5
place 194, 203–4
political activities *see* campaigning
*Political Activities and
    Campaigning by Charities*
    (Charity Commissioners) 82
political neutrality 85
political risk 123
pressure group role 47, 48
pricing 194, 202
Prince's Trust 119
private sector 33, 58
process 194, 205

products 194, 201–2
professional values 27
project risk 123
promotion 194, 203
property 135–8
psychiatric survivor movement 78
Public Concern at Work 131, 132;
  charitable status 133–4;
  premises 135–6
public relations 170–1
public sector *see* statutory agencies
public services 40–1
public subscription 121
pump-priming 111–13

Quakers 120
qualitative marketing research 198
quality 18–19, 67, 71, 72
quangos 10, 18, 41, 94–5, 105
quantitative marketing research
  198–9

recruitment agencies 168
red tape 213
referrals 64
regionalisation 10
regulation 18, 34, 40
regulators 192–3
relationship fundraising 178, 184–5
relief in need charities 120
religion 27, 120
representational boards 101
research 112, 117, 118
reserves 174
Resourcing the Voluntary Sector
  115
respect 85–6
Responsibilities of Charity Trustees
  (Charity Commission) 96–7
restricted income funds 150
Rights Now campaign 84
risk 123
Road Traffic Act 83
Roof 25
Rotary 182
Round Table 182
Rowntree family 120
Rowntree (Joseph) Foundation 61

Rowntree (Joseph) Reform Trust
  120
Royal Jubilee Trusts 121
Royal National Institute for Deaf
  People 93

sales promotion 203
Save the Children Fund 93, 181
school governors 105
Scope 60, 61
Scotland 176, 212
*Scottish Guide to Fundraising
  Practice, The* (ICFM) 176
scratch-card games 177
secondments 3
self-help organisations 10, 18, 24,
  25, 27; and development
  agencies 73; funding 77, 80;
  governance 108; management
  committees 28; and service
  users 74
Sense 60
service agreements 53
service delivery 85, 94; user-
  controlled 78
service delivery organisations
  47–8, 70–3
service products 201
service users 80–1; and community
  voluntary organisations 73–4;
  definition 69; and development
  agencies 73; dilemmas 80;
  expectations 70–1; flow 63;
  involvement 29–30, 34, 35,
  44–6; and self-help groups 74;
  and service delivery
  organisations 70–3; as trustees
  108
short-term funding 111–13
signing requirements 135
single-issue campaigns 10
Single Market 208–9
Sir Halley Stewart Trust 120
social care 11, 13, 15–16, 17;
  contracting out 41, 55; grants
  117, 118
social care organisations 44–6
social economy 211
social justice 27

social partnership 211
solicitors 133–4, 140–1
solidarity 27, 28, 210–11
South Kensington Estate 137–8
Special Support Programme for
  Peace and Reconciliation 214
Special Transitional Grant 15, 58,
  67, 129
sponsored activities 183
sport 17, 19; lottery funds 13, 124,
  177
stability 64, 66
stakeholders 192, 193
stamp duty 132
state funding *see* central
  government funding; local
  government funding
Statement of Financial Activities
  (SOFA) 144, 148–9; cost
  headings 155; fund accounting
  150–1, 152
Statement of Recommended
  Practice (SORP) 144, 145–6, 176;
  accountability 105–6;
  expenditure 154–5; fund
  accounting 150, 151, 152–3
Statements of Standard
  Accounting Practice 146
Statute of Charitable Uses 2, 128,
  133
statutory agencies 2; changes
  39–41, 50, 55–6; and grant-
  making trusts 114; and voluntary
  sector 33, 41–3
statutory bodies 26
statutory income *see* funding
statutory sector professionals
  25–6, 33
Strasbourg 216
strategic management 160–1, 162
sub-committees 104
support costs 155
supporters 192, 193
supportive organisations 76

take-up behaviour 196–7
tax-efficient giving 12–13, 175
tax relief 132
Taylor v *Millington* 141

technology 9, 19
telecommunications 9, 19, 207
Tenovus 177
Think Voluntary (Voluntary
  Services Unit) 214
Thomas Coram Foundation 4
trade unions 11–12, 40
trading 16, 175
training: chief executives 168, 169;
  trustees 99
training and enterprise councils
  (TECs) 94
transnational activities 215–17
transparency 146, 156
trust 28–9
trust law 145, 149–50
trustee boards 93–4, 98–9, 109;
  budgeting 102–3; and chief
  executives 157–8, 163–5; grant-
  making 101–2; power balance
  103–4; size 103; typology 100–1
Trustee Investments Act 1961 137
trustees 5–6, 93–5; changing role
  99–100; Charities Acts 95; and
  chief executives 169–70;
  competence 107–8; guardianship
  model 108–9; liability 141–2;
  public unease 104–5;
  remuneration 18;
  responsibilities 98; role 96–8;
  selection 106–7; strategic
  leadership role 96
trusts *see* grant-making trusts
Turkey 213

unincorporated associations 131–2
Unison 40
United Nations 207
United States 106, 175, 210;
  contracting 59–60
University of Kent 23
University of Liverpool 142
unrestricted funds 150
user-run organisations *see* self-
  help organisations
users *see* service users

value for money 49
values 27–8

VAT 175
voluntary income *see* fundraising
Voluntary Services Unit 214
volunteers 3, 5–6, 212; active
    citizenship 19–20; vetting
    29

Warwick University 169
Wellcome Trust 16, 17, 119, 187;
    assets 117, 137–8

wills 14, 185–6
Wiltshire Community Care User
    Involvement Network 72, 75–9
Wiltshire Independent Living
    Fund 75–6, 79
Windsor Group 175
Women's Institute 182
World Trade Organisation 207
World Wide Fund for Nature 178,
    186